THE
FABER BOOK OF
APHORISMS

A Personal Selection

BY

W. H. AUDEN

AND

LOUIS KRONENBERGER

FABER AND FABER LIMITED
London & Boston

First published in USA by The Viking Press Inc
First published in England in 1964
by Faber and Faber Limited
3 Queen Square, London WC1
Reprinted 1965 (twice)
First published in this edition 1970
Reprinted 1974 and 1978
Printed in Great Britain
by Whitstable Litho, Whitstable, Kent
All rights reserved

ISBN 0 571 09519 4 (Faber Paperbacks)
ISBN 0 571 06013 7 (hard bound edition)

THE
FABER BOOK
OF APHORISMS

ACKNOWLEDGMENTS

The compilers and publishers would like to express their thanks for the co-operation of the owners and controllers of copyright listed below. If there are others whose names should have appeared, but whom the publishers have been unable to identify or trace, they would be grateful if the copyright owners would write to them so that the list in the next edition may be appropriately extended.

George Allen & Unwin, Ltd.: José Ortega y Gasset, Bertrand Russell, Tobias Dantzig, Oswald Spengler; Beacon Press: Georg Christoph Lichtenberg, Eugen Rosenstock-Huessy; Jonathan Cape, Ltd. Jane Jacobs; Chatto & Windus, Ltd.: Marcel Proust; Clarendon Press: Logan Pearsall Smith; T. & T. Clark: Martin Buber; Miss D. E. Collins, A. P. Watt & Son, Methuen & Co, Ltd., Cassell & Co., Ltd., Sheed & Ward, Ltd., Bodley Head, Ltd.: G. K. Chesterton; Constable & Co., Ltd.: Sir William Osler, George Santayana, Logan Pearsall Smith; Editions Gallimard: Paul Valéry; The Hon. Robert Gathorne Hardy: Logan Pearsall Smith; Harper & Row: Eric Hoffer; Houghton Mifflin Co.: John Jay Chapman; James Nisbet & Co., Ltd.: Logan Pearsall Smith; Oxford University Press: Logan Pearsall Smith, A. N. Whitehead, Charles Williams; Peter Owen, Ltd.: Cesare Pavese; Routledge & Kegan Paul, Ltd.: Martin Buber, Simone Weil, Paul Valéry; Martin Secker & Warburg, Ltd.: Franz Kafka; Society of Authors and the Public Trustee: George Bernard Shaw; St. Martin's Press, Inc.: Stanislaw Lec; Thames & Hudson Ltd.: Martin Buber; Karl Kraus: Dr. J. van Loeven Ltd.; Heinrich Fischer and Kösel Verlag, Munich.

Foreword

This anthology is devoted to aphoristic writing, not to epigrams. An epigram need only be true of a single case, for example, *Coolidge opened his mouth and a moth flew out*; or effective only in a particular polemical context, for example, *Foxhunting is the pursuit of the uneatable by the unspeakable*, which is an admirable remark when made in a country house in the Shires, but a cheap one if addressed to a society of intellectuals who have never known the pleasures of hunting. An aphorism, on the other hand, must convince every reader that it is either universally true or true of every member of the class to which it refers, irrespective of the reader's convictions. To a Christian, for example, *The knowledge of God is very far from the love of Him* is a true statement about a defect in the relation between himself and God; to the unbeliever, it is a true statement about the psychology of religious belief. An aphorism can be polemic in form but not in meaning. *Do not do unto others as you would they should do unto you—their tastes may not be the same*—is not a denial of the Gospel injunction but an explanation of what it really means. *The road of excess leads to the palace of wisdom* is a borderline case. It is a valid aphorism if one can safely assume that every reader knows the importance of self-control; one cannot help feeling that, were Blake our contemporary, he would have written *sometimes leads*.

Again, an epigram must be amusing and brief, but an aphorism, though it should not be boring and must be succinct in style, need not make the reader laugh and can extend itself to several sentences.

Aphorisms are essentially an aristocratic genre of writing. The aphorist does not argue or explain, he asserts; and implicit in his assertion is a conviction that he is wiser or more intelligent than his readers. For this reason the aphorist who adopts a folksy style with "democratic" diction and grammar is a cowardly and insufferable hypocrite.

No anthologist of aphorisms can be impartial, nor should he try to be. Two statements may be equally true, but, in any society at any given point in history, one of them is probably more important than the other; and, human nature being what it is, the most important truths are likely to be those which that society at that time least wants to hear. In making his selection, it is up to the anthologist to guess what bubbles, intellectual, moral, and political, are at the moment most in need of pricking.

Ignorance has imposed on us a further limitation, which we hope will not be mistaken for arrogance. We have limited our choice to writers belonging to what, for lack of a better term, is called Western civilization, not because we consider that civilization superior to any other, but because it would be folly and presumption on our part to claim that our knowledge of, say, Chinese, Japanese, Indian, or Islamic literature could possibly give an adequate representation of their aphorisms. At a time, however, when it seems as if it were precisely the worst aspects of our technological culture—our noise, our vulgarity, our insane waste of natural resources—which are the most exportable (European intellectuals who imagine these vices to be of American origin are willfully deceiving themselves), we are bold to think of this volume as evidence that there are others—such as humor and a capacity for self-criticism—which, though less intrusive than jukeboxes and bombs, are neither negligible nor unworthy of respect.

W. H. A.
L. K.

Contents

HUMANITY 1

The Human Creature 3
Human Suffering 16
Self-Knowledge 21
Sleep and Dreams 24
The Human Mind 26
Memory and Conscience 32
Self-Love 36
Human Vices 41
Human Virtues 49
Success and Failure 51
Habit 61
Humor 62
Human Types 63
The Talker 66
Human Folly 68

RELIGION AND GOD 71

NATURE 95

EDUCATION 107

SOCIETY 117

The Drawing Room 119
The Market Place 134
The Arena 157

[ix]

Contents

THE SEXES   165

LOVE, MARRIAGE, AND
  FRIENDSHIP   177

THE PROFESSIONS   205

HISTORY   225

ACTION   241

SCIENCE   257

THE ARTS   265

    Theory and Practice   267
    Writers and Readers   275
    Sights and Sounds   289

STATES AND GOVERNMENTS   295

    Politics and Power   297
    Liberty and Union   309
    People and Princes   314

THE LIFE OF THE MIND   319

    Truth and Error   321
    Opinions and Beliefs   327
    Reason and Thought   339
    Language and Ideas   356
    Memories and Dreams   360

LIFE'S MINOR PLEASURES AND
  TRIALS   363

AGES OF MAN   381

INDEX OF AUTHORS   397

HUMANITY

The Human Creature

Man is an exception, whatever else he is. If it is not true that a divine being fell, then we can only say that one of the animals went entirely off its head. CHESTERTON

From such crooked wood as that which man is made of, nothing straight can be fashioned. KANT

In nature a repulsive caterpillar turns into a lovely butterfly. But with human beings it is the other way round: a lovely butterfly turns into a repulsive caterpillar. CHEKHOV

The body is a thing, the soul is also a thing; man is not a thing, but a drama—his life. Man has to live with the body and soul which have fallen to him by chance. And the first thing he has to do is decide what he is going to do.

ORTEGA Y GASSET

      Bedizened or stark
   naked, man, the self, the being we call human, writing-
master to this world, griffons a dark
   "Like does not like like that is obnoxious"; and writes
                 error with four r's.
          MARIANNE MOORE

We're not at one. We've no instinctive knowledge
like migratory birds. Outstripped and late,

[3]

we force ourselves on winds and find no welcome
from ponds where we alight. We comprehend
flowering and fading simultaneously.
And somewhere lions still roam, all unaware
while yet their splendor lasts of any weakness.

RILKE

Natural man has only two primal passions: to get and to beget.

OSLER

It is chiefly through the instinct to kill that man achieves
intimacy with the life of nature.   CLARK

Man's chief difference from the brutes lies in the exuberant
excess of his subjective propensities. Prune his extravagance,
sober him, and you undo him.   WILLIAM JAMES

Shower upon him every blessing, drown him in a sea of
happiness, give him economic prosperity, such that he should
have nothing else to do but sleep, eat cakes, and busy himself with the continuation of his species, and even then, out
of sheer ingratitude, sheer spite, man would play you some
nasty trick. He would even risk his cakes and would deliberately desire the most fatal rubbish, the utmost economic
absurdity, simply to introduce into all this positive good
sense his fatal fantastic element.   DOSTOEVSKI

Man only plays when in the full meaning of the word he is
a man, and he is only completely a man when he plays.

SCHILLER

Man is a make-believe animal—he is never so truly himself
as when he is acting a part.   HAZLITT

Man is least himself when he talks in his own person. Give
him a *mask* and he will tell the truth.   WILDE

To breed an animal with the right to make promises—is not
this the paradoxical problem nature has set herself with regard to man?   NIETZSCHE

I believe the best definition of man is the ungrateful biped.
                                              DOSTOEVSKI

Man is the only animal that laughs and weeps; for he is the
only animal that is struck by the difference between what
things are and what they might have been.   HAZLITT

Man is only man at the surface. Remove his skin, dissect, and
immediately you come to machinery.   VALÉRY

BODY: O who shall me deliver whole
   From bonds of this Tyrannic Soul?
   Which, stretcht upright, impales me so,
   That mine own Precipice I go;
   And warms and moves this needless Frame:
   (A Fever could but do the same.)
   And, wanting where its spight to try,
   Has made me live to let me dye.
   A Body that could never rest,
   Since this ill Spirit it possest.

             MARVELL

No one hates his body.   SAINT AUGUSTINE

I am the owner of my shoulders, the tenant of my hips.
                                                CHAZAL

[5]

Animals, we have been told, are taught by their organs. Yes, I would add, and so are men, but men have this further advantage that they can also teach their organs in return.

GOETHE

All living beings have received their weapons through the same process of evolution that molded their impulses and inhibitions; for the structural plan of the body and the system of behavior of a species are parts of the same whole. There is only one being in possession of weapons which do not grow on his body and of whose working plan, therefore, the instincts of his species know nothing and in the usage of which he has no corresponding inhibition.   LORENZ

Imprisoned in every fat man, a thin one is wildly signaling to be let out.   CONNOLLY

The human face is really like one of those Oriental gods: a whole group of faces juxtaposed on different planes; it is impossible to see them all simultaneously.   PROUST

Excluding those faces which are beautiful, good-natured, or intellectual—and these are few and far between—I believe that a person of any sensibility hardly ever sees a new face without a sensation akin to shock at encountering a new and surprising combination of unedifying elements.

SCHOPENHAUER

When one shuts one eye, one does not hear everything.

SWISS PROVERB

The man who goes up in a balloon does not feel as if he were ascending; he only sees the earth sinking deeper below him.   SCHOPENHAUER

Eyes are compacted powers; they are an index of vision; they see and refer us to greater seeing. Nor has the stomach a less noble office. It digests food; that is, in its own particular method, it deals with the nourishment offered by the universe. It is the physical formula of that health which destroys certain elements—the bacteria which harmfully approach us. By it we learn to consume; by it therefore to be, in turn, consumed. So even with those poor despised things, the buttocks. There is no seated figure, no image of any seated figure, which does not rely on them for its strength and balance. They are at the bottom of the sober dignity of judges; the grace of a throned woman; the hierarchical session of the Pope himself reposes on them.   WILLIAMS

The head Sublime, the heart Pathos, the genitals Beauty, the hands and feet Proportion.   BLAKE

SOUL: O who shall, from this Dungeon, raise,
      A soul inslav'd so many wayes?
      With bolts of Bones, that fetter'd stands
      In Feet; and manacled in Hands.
      Here blinded with an Eye; and there
      Deaf with the drumming of an Ear.
      A Soul hung up, as 'twere, in Chains
      Of Nerves, and Arteries, and Veins.
      Tortured, besides each other part,
      In a vain Head, and double Heart.

                        MARVELL

The soul is the wife of the body. They do not have the same kind of pleasure or, at least, they seldom enjoy it at the same time.   VALÉRY

The body has its end which it does not know; the mind its means of which it is unaware.   VALÉRY

[7]

A brain weight of nine hundred grams is adequate as an optimum for human behavior. Anything more is employed in the commission of misdeeds. HOOTON

Man is a sun; and the senses are his planets. NOVALIS

Our body will become voluntary, our soul organic. NOVALIS

The various states of soul in a man must be like the letters in a dictionary, some of which are powerfully and voluminously developed, others having only a few words under them —but the soul must have a complete alphabet. KIERKEGAARD

Fine minds are seldom fine souls. RICHTER

It is usual enough with delicate beings to have a fine intelligence and a poor brain. JOUBERT

People are governed by the head; a kind heart is of little value in chess. CHAMFORT

Certainly there is a consent between the body and the mind; and where nature erreth in the one, she ventureth in the other. BACON

The mind, like the body, is subject to be hurt by everything it taketh for a remedy. HALIFAX

The mind cannot long act the role of the heart.
LA ROCHEFOUCAULD

The heart is either a *grand seigneur* or a nobody.   CHAZAL

There seems to be an unalterable contradiction between the
human mind and its employments. How can a *soul* be a
merchant? What relation to an immortal being have the price
of linseed, the tare on tallow, or the brokerage on hemp? Can
an undying creature debit *petty expenses* and charge for *car-
riage paid*? The soul ties its shoes; the mind washes its hands
in a basin. All is incongruous.   BAGEHOT

Every luxury must be paid for, and everything is a luxury,
starting with being in the world.   PAVESE

To live is like to love—all reason is against it, and all healthy
instinct is for it.   SAMUEL BUTLER (II)

Is life worth living? This is a question for an embryo, not for
a man.   SAMUEL BUTLER (II)

We both exist and know that we exist, and rejoice in this
existence and this knowledge.   SAINT AUGUSTINE

Life is not a spectacle or a feast; it is a predicament.
     SANTAYANA

Life is a maze in which we take the wrong turning before
we have learned to walk.   CONNOLLY

Life is like playing a violin solo in public and learning the
instrument as one goes on.   SAMUEL BUTLER (II)

Simply the thing I am shall make me live.   SHAKESPEARE

Life is too short to be small.   DISRAELI

Physiological life is of course not "Life." And neither is psychological life. Life is the world.   WITTGENSTEIN

Life is a language in which certain truths are conveyed to us; if we could learn them in some other way, we should not live.   SCHOPENHAUER

If one considered life as a simple loan, one would perhaps be less exacting.   DELACROIX

Love for life is still possible, only one loves differently: it is like love for a woman whom one does not trust.   NIETZSCHE

The three most important things a man has are, briefly, his private parts, his money, and his religious opinions.
   SAMUEL BUTLER (II)

I am and know and will; I am knowing and willing; I know myself to be and to will; I will to be and to know.
   SAINT AUGUSTINE

One can say: "I will, but my body does not obey me"; but not: "My will does not obey me."   SAINT AUGUSTINE

The will is the strong blind man who carries on his shoulders the lame man who can see.   SCHOPENHAUER

[10]

The human being is a blind man who dreams that he can see.
HEBBEL

The iron chain and the silken cord are both equally bonds.
SCHILLER

The basic test of freedom is perhaps less in what we are free to do than in what we are free not to do.   HOFFER

People hardly ever make use of the freedom they have, for example, freedom of thought; instead they demand freedom of speech as a compensation.   KIERKEGAARD

We feel free when we escape—even if it be but from the frying pan into the fire.   HOFFER

A man's worst difficulties begin when he is able to do as he likes.   T. H. HUXLEY

There is no freedom for the weak.   MEREDITH

No man is weak from choice.   VAUVENARGUES

When one has made a mistake, one says: "Next time I shall really know what to do." What one should say is: "I already know what I shall really do next time."   PAVESE

The faces of men tell us less than they should, because sleep as well as action traces lines upon them. The faces of the worst murderers can be paralleled in ugliness by the faces of the most blameless saints.   MUIR

There is no more miserable human being than one in whom nothing is habitual but indecision.　　WILLIAM JAMES

We are no more free agents than the queen of clubs when she takes the knave of hearts.　　LADY MARY MONTAGU

A man is always as good as the good which appears in his face, but he need not be as evil as the evil which appears in it, because evil does not always realize itself immediately; indeed, sometimes it never realizes itself at all.　　PICARD

Our notion of symmetry is derived from the human face. Hence, we demand symmetry horizontally and in breadth only, not vertically nor in depth.　　PASCAL

Who is unhappy at having only one mouth? And who is not unhappy at having only one eye?　　PASCAL

When two faces which resemble each other are brought together, they make us laugh because of the resemblance, though neither by itself would make us laugh.　　PASCAL

Chins are exclusively a human feature, not to be found among the beasts. If they had chins, most animals would look like each other. Man was given a chin to prevent the personality of his mouth and eyes from overwhelming the rest of his face, to prevent each individual from becoming a species unto himself.　　CHAZAL

The nose feels the cold, the chin feels the heat.　　CHAZAL

The eyes are more exact witnesses than the ears.   HERACLITUS

The eyes and ears are bad witnesses for men if they have barbarous souls.   HERACLITUS

The ears are the last feature to age.   CHAZAL

One's eyes are what one is; one's mouth, what one becomes.
GALSWORTHY

If the eyes are often the organ through which the intelligence shines, the nose is generally the organ which most readily publishes stupidity.   PROUST

Vice shows itself in the eyes; crime in the back of the neck.
KASSNER

The glance embroiders in joy, knits in pain, and sews in boredom.   CHAZAL

When indifferent, the eye takes still photographs; when interested, movies.   CHAZAL

The fingers must be educated, the thumb is born knowing.
CHAZAL

The thumb takes the responsibility, the index finger the initiative.   CHAZAL

The little finger looks through a magnifying glass, the index finger through a lorgnette.   CHAZAL

In the distance, the gestures of animals look human, the gestures of human beings bestial.   CHAZAL

Our expression and our words never coincide, which is why the animals don't understand us.   CHAZAL

There is an essential ambiguity in human gestures, and when someone raises the palms of his hands together, we do not know whether it is to bury himself in prayer or to throw himself into the sea.   ORTEGA Y GASSET

To walk behind anyone along a lane is a thing that, properly speaking, touches the oldest nerve of awe.   CHESTERTON

Extreme terror gives us back the gestures of our childhood.
CHAZAL

The animal has a serious expression, even in play, but laughs with his body. The more a man laughs, the more like an animal he looks.   CHAZAL

We sometimes laugh from ear to ear, but it would be impossible for a smile to be wider than the distance between our eyes.   CHAZAL

Laughter is regional: a smile extends over the whole face.
CHAZAL

Three smiles that are worse than griefs: the smile of snow melting, the smile of your wife when another man has been with her, the smile of a mastiff about to spring.
ANONYMOUS (tr. from Irish by T. Kinsella)

The wink was not our best invention.   HODGSON

The idealist walks on tiptoe, the materialist on his heels.
                                                        CHAZAL

Solemnity is a device of the body to hide the faults of the
mind.   LA ROCHEFOUCAULD

Ah is the shortest of human cries, *Oh* the longest. Man is
born in an *Ah* and dies in an *Oh*, for birth is immediate and
death is like an airplane taking off.   CHAZAL

The world of silence without speech is the world *before*
creation, the world of unfinished creation. In silence truth
is passive and slumbering, but in language it is wide-awake.
Silence is fulfilled only when speech comes forth from silence
and gives it meaning and honor.   PICARD

Singing is near miraculous because it is the mastering of what
is otherwise a pure instrument of egotism: the human voice.
                                                  HOFMANNSTHAL

We speak with our lips to explain, with our throats to convince.   CHAZAL

Grace is to the body what clear thinking is to the mind.
                                            LA ROCHEFOUCAULD

Half of us are blind, few of us feel, and we are all deaf.
                                                        OSLER

A deaf woman would be displeased at your shouting if she
were conscious of it.   STENDHAL

He whose vision is defective always sees less than those with good eyesight; but he who is hard of hearing always hears something extra.   NIETZSCHE

The same battle in the clouds will be known to the deaf only as lightning and to the blind only as thunder.   SANTAYANA

Men are very queer animals—a mixture of horse-nervousness, ass-stubbornness and camel-malice.   T. H. HUXLEY

In our corrupted state, common weaknesses and defects contribute more towards the reconciling us to one another than all the *precepts* of the *philosophers* and *divines*.   HALIFAX

Anger is never without an argument, but seldom with a good one.   HALIFAX

We care what happens to people only in proportion as we know what people are.   HENRY JAMES

Human Suffering

The human condition is such that pain and effort are not just symptoms which can be removed without changing life itself; they are rather the modes in which life itself, together with the necessity to which it is bound, makes itself felt. For mortals, the "easy life of the gods" would be a lifeless life.   HANNAH ARENDT

Woe is wondrously clinging: the clouds ride by.
                              ANONYMOUS (Anglo-Saxon)

Only one who is in pain really senses nothing but himself; pleasure does not enjoy itself but something beside itself. Pain is the only inner sense found by introspection which can rival in independence from experienced objects the self-evident certainty of logical and arithmetical reasoning.
                                            HANNAH ARENDT

The same suffering is much harder to bear for a high motive than for a base one. The people who stood motionless, from one to eight in the morning, for the sake of having an egg, would have found it very difficult to do in order to save a human life.   SIMONE WEIL

Those who do not feel pain seldom think that it is felt.
                                              DR. JOHNSON

The wretched have no compassion.   DR. JOHNSON

People in distress never think that you feel enough.
                                              DR. JOHNSON

Those who do not complain are never pitied.   JANE AUSTEN

Where there is leisure for fiction there is little grief.
                                              DR. JOHNSON

The only antidote to mental suffering is physical pain.

MARX

We often tremble at an empty terror; but the false fancy brings a real misery.　　SCHILLER

We have to endure the discordance between imagination and fact. It is better to say, "I am suffering," than to say, "This landscape is ugly."　　SIMONE WEIL

There are people who have an appetite for grief; pleasure is not strong enough and they crave pain.　　EMERSON

One can bear grief, but it takes two to be glad.　　E. HUBBARD

The tragedy of life is not so much what men suffer, but rather what they miss.　　CARLYLE

We are not miserable without feeling it. A ruined house is not miserable.　　PASCAL

Every man has a rainy corner of his life whence comes foul weather which follows him.　　RICHTER

A man must swallow a toad every morning if he wishes to be sure of finding nothing still more disgusting before the day is over.　　CHAMFORT

The world gets better every day—then worse again in the evening.　　KIN HUBBARD

The thought of suicide is a great consolation: with the help of it one has got through many a bad night. NIETZSCHE

He who makes a beast of himself gets rid of the pain of being a man. DR. JOHNSON

In the small hours when the acrid stench of existence rises like sewer gas from everything created, the emptiness of life seems more terrible than its misery. CONNOLLY

How like herrings and onions our vices are the morning after we have committed them, and even lawful pleasures are like the smell of a dinner room when you have gone out and entered it after dinner. COLERIDGE

It seems my soul is like a filthy pond, wherein fish die soon, and frogs live long. THOMAS FULLER

Melancholy, indeed, should be diverted by every means but drinking. DR. JOHNSON

When a man has reached a condition in which he believes that a thing must happen because he does not wish it, and that what he wishes to happen can never be, this is really the state called *desperation*. SCHOPENHAUER

Extremely happy and extremely unhappy men are alike prone to grow hardhearted. MONTESQUIEU

The more refined one is, the more unhappy. CHEKHOV

Men who are unhappy, like men who sleep badly, are always proud of the fact. RUSSELL

We are never so happy or so unhappy as we think.
LA ROCHEFOUCAULD

We must laugh before we are happy, for fear of dying without having laughed at all. LA BRUYÈRE

I sometimes try to be miserable that I may do more work.
BLAKE

If we only wanted to be happy it would be easy; but we want to be happier than other people, which is almost always difficult, since we think them happier than they are.
MONTESQUIEU

It is an aspect of all happiness to suppose that we deserve it.
JOUBERT

To describe happiness is to diminish it. STENDHAL

A peasant and a philosopher may be equally *satisfied*, but not equally *happy*. Happiness consists in the multiplicity of agreeable consciousness. DR. JOHNSON

Life does not agree with philosophy: there is no happiness that is not idleness, and only what is useless is pleasurable.
CHEKHOV

The only joy in the world is to begin. PAVESE

Not to call a thing good a day longer or a day earlier than it seems good to us is the only way to remain really happy.
NIETZSCHE

Self-Knowledge

"Know thyself?" If I knew myself, I'd run away.   GOETHE

It is as hard to see one's self as to look backwards without turning round.   THOREAU

One's own self is well hidden from one's own self: of all mines of treasure, one's own is the last to be dug up.

NIETZSCHE

We feel in one world, we think and name in another. Between the two we can set up a system of references, but we cannot fill the gap.   PROUST

One's real life is often the life that one does not lead.

WILDE

Where is your Self to be found? Always in the deepest enchantment that you have experienced.   HOFMANNSTHAL

Every enthusiast contains a false enthusiast, every lover a false lover, every man of genius a false man of genius, and, as a rule, every fault its counterfeit: this is necessary in order to assure the continuity of one's personality, not only in the eyes of others but in one's own—in order to understand oneself, count upon oneself, think of oneself; in order, in short, to *be* oneself.   VALÉRY

Long years must pass before the truths we have made for ourselves become our very flesh.   VALÉRY

"I remain true to myself." Exactly. That is your misfortune. Would that, just once, you could be untrue to yourself.

HEBBEL

It is impossible for a man to be cheated by anyone but himself.

EMERSON

We have to serve ourself many years before we gain our own confidence.

HASKINS

Our opinion of others is not so variable as our opinion of ourselves.

VAUVENARGUES

What others think of us would be of little moment did it not, when known, so deeply tinge what we think of ourselves.

SANTAYANA

Not all those who know their minds know their hearts as well.

LA ROCHEFOUCAULD

To know oneself is to foresee oneself; to foresee oneself amounts to playing a part.

VALÉRY

The greater part of those who have written their memoirs have only shown us their bad actions or their weaknesses when they happen to have mistaken them for deeds of prowess or fine instincts, a thing they often do.

TOCQUEVILLE

Our greatest pretenses are built up not to hide the evil and the ugly in us, but our emptiness. The hardest thing to hide is something that is not there.

HOFFER

Men often *mistake* themselves, but they never *forget* themselves.

HALIFAX

There is nothing, absolutely nothing, a man cannot forget except himself, his own character. SCHOPENHAUER

Nothing so much prevents our being natural as the desire to seem so. LA ROCHEFOUCAULD

To be sincere means to be the same person when one is with with oneself; that is to say, alone—but that is all it means. VALÉRY

Almost all absurdity of conduct arises from the imitation of those whom we cannot resemble. DR. JOHNSON

It is a law of nature that we defend ourselves from one affectation only by means of another. VALÉRY

There is nothing man cannot make natural; there is nothing natural which he cannot lose. PASCAL

Everyone is perfectly willing to learn from unpleasant experience—if only the damage of the first lesson could be repaired. LICHTENBERG

Sleep and Dreams

Animals awaken, first facially, then bodily. Men's bodies wake up before their faces do. The animal sleeps within its body; man sleeps with his body in his mind.   CHAZAL

In sleep, body and soul are chemically bound. The soul is divided into equal parts throughout the body; the personality is neutralized.   NOVALIS

Many a man's secret harm (to some favored beings secret even to themselves) may be discovered by observing where they place their hand or hands when lost in thought or vacant, and what is their commonest posture in sleep.
          COLERIDGE

Dreams and beasts are two keys by which we find out the secrets of our own nature. They are test objects.   EMERSON

We are near waking when we dream we are dreaming.
          NOVALIS

I could be bounded in a nutshell and count myself a king of infinite space, were it not that I have bad dreams.
          SHAKESPEARE

In dreams we see ourselves naked and acting out our real characters, even more clearly than we see others awake. But an unwavering and commanding virtue would compel even its most fantastic and faintest dreams to respect its ever-wakeful authority; as we are accustomed to say carelessly, we should never have *dreamed* of such a thing.   THOREAU

[24]

If a laborer were to dream for twelve hours every night that he was a king, I believe he would be almost as happy as a king who should dream for twelve hours every night that he was a laborer. PASCAL

We use up too much artistic effort in our dreams; in consequence our waking life is often poor. NIETZSCHE

Dreams have as much influence as actions. MALLARMÉ

I cannot say I was hostile to him, nor friendly either: I have never dreamed of him. LICHTENBERG

How many of our daydreams would darken into nightmares, were there any danger of their coming true. L. P. SMITH

Among all human constructions the only ones that avoid the dissolving hands of time are castles in the air.

DE ROBERTO

The Human Mind

Desire and force between them are responsible for all our actions; desire causes our voluntary acts, force our involuntary.   PASCAL

His passions make man live, his wisdom merely makes him last.   CHAMFORT

Wise people may say what they will, but one passion is never cured by another.   CHESTERFIELD

All passions exaggerate: it is because they do that they are passions.   CHAMFORT

We are sometimes moved by passion and suppose it zeal.
                                                                          THOMAS A KEMPIS

Fanaticism consists in redoubling your effort when you have forgotten your aim.   SANTAYANA

Every zeal or passion brings with it a superstitious conviction of having to face a day of reckoning: even the zeal of a disbeliever.   PAVESE

Nothing is more injurious to the character and to the intellect than the suppression of generous emotion.   CHAPMAN

Every extreme attitude is a flight from the self.   HOFFER

Terrible consequences there will always be when the mean vices attempt to mimic the grand passions. Great men will never do great mischief but for some great end.   E. BURKE

No indulgence of passion destroys the spiritual nature so much as respectable selfishness.   MACDONALD

Passion makes the best observations and draws the most wretched conclusions.   RICHTER

> To be in a Passion you Good may do,
> But no Good if a Passion is in you.
>
> BLAKE

The ardor chills us which we do not share.   PATMORE

Emotion has taught mankind to reason.   VAUVENARGUES

There is nothing that fear or hope does not make men believe.   VAUVENARGUES

Desire engenders belief: if we are not usually aware of this, it is because most belief-creating desires last as long as we do.   PROUST

Our actions are neither so good nor so evil as our impulses.   VAUVENARGUES

We are all capable of evil thoughts, but only very rarely of evil deeds: we can all do good deeds, but very few of us can think good thoughts.   PAVESE

He who desires but acts not, breeds pestilence.   BLAKE

Excesses are essentially gestures. It is easy to be extremely cruel, magnanimous, humble, or self-sacrificing when we see ourselves actors in a performance.   HOFFER

It is harder to hide feelings we have than to feign those we lack.   LA ROCHEFOUCAULD

Chemists at least can use analysis; patients suffering from a malady whose cause is unknown to them can call in a doctor; criminal cases are more or less cleared up by the examining magistrate. But for the disconcerting actions of our fellow men, we rarely discover the motive.   PROUST

The motive for a deed usually changes during its performance: at least, after the deed has been done, it seems quite different.   HEBBEL

Behind many acts that are thought ridiculous there lie wise and weighty motives.   LA ROCHEFOUCAULD

All our final resolutions are made in a state of mind which is not going to last.   PROUST

"Every man has his price." This is not true. But for every man there exists a bait which he cannot resist swallowing. To win over certain people to something, it is only necessary to give it a gloss of love of humanity, nobility, gentleness, self-sacrifice—and there is nothing you cannot get them to swallow. To their souls, these are the icing, the tidbit: other kinds of soul have others.   NIETZSCHE

The soul must have its chosen sewers to carry away its ordure. This function is performed by persons, relationships, professions, the fatherland, the world, or, finally, for the really arrogant—I mean our modern pessimists—by the Good God Himself. NIETZSCHE

Taken as a whole, men will only devote their enthusiasm, their time, and their energy to matters in which their passions have a personal interest. But their personal interests, however powerful they may be, will never carry them very far or very high unless they can be made to seem noble and legitimate in their own eyes by being allied to some great cause in which the whole human race can join.

TOCQUEVILLE

Imagination is nature's equal, sensuality her slave. GOETHE

A cathedral, a wave of a storm, a dancer's leap, never turn out to be as high as we had hoped. PROUST

To the eyes of a miser a guinea is far more beautiful than the sun, and a bag worn with the use of money has more beautiful proportions than a vine filled with grapes. The tree which moves some to tears of joy is in the eyes of others only a green thing which stands in the way. As a man is, so he sees.

BLAKE

The epithet *beautiful* is used by surgeons to describe operations which their patients describe as ghastly, by physicists to describe methods of measurement which leave sentimentalists cold, by lawyers to describe cases which ruin all the parties to them, and by lovers to describe the objects of their infatuation, however unattractive they may appear to the unaffected spectator. SHAW

Things don't change, but by and by our wishes change.

PROUST

How many people become abstract as a way of appearing profound!

JOUBERT

The map appears to us more real than the land.

LAWRENCE

We think in generalities, but we live in detail.

WHITEHEAD

Suspicion is rather a virtue than a fault, as long as it doth like a dog that watcheth, and doth not bite.

HALIFAX

There is no rule more invariable than that we are paid for our suspicions by finding what we suspected.

THOREAU

Nothing has an uglier look to us than reason, when it is not of our side.

HALIFAX

Our prejudices are our mistresses; reason is at best our wife, very often needed, but seldom minded.

CHESTERFIELD

With most men, unbelief in one thing springs from blind belief in another.

LICHTENBERG

The most positive men are the most credulous.

POPE

A very popular error—having the courage of one's convictions: rather it is a matter of having the courage for an attack upon one's convictions.

NIETZSCHE

I see men ordinarily more eager to discover a reason for things than to find out whether the things are so.

MONTAIGNE

Man is a reasonable animal who always loses his temper when he is called upon to act in accordance with the dictates of reason.

WILDE

Resort is had to ridicule only when reason is against us.

JEFFERSON

We are generally the better persuaded by the reasons we discover ourselves than by those given to us by others.

PASCAL

That Man, who flees from truth, should have invented the mirror is the greatest of historical miracles.

HEBBEL

Truth's a dog must to kennel; he must be whipt out when Lady the brach may stand by the fire and stink.

SHAKESPEARE

Man is ice to truth and fire to falsehood.

LA FONTAINE

I care about truth not for truth's sake but for my own.

SAMUEL BUTLER (II)

We are not satisfied to be right, unless we can prove others to be quite wrong.

HAZLITT

When a man say him do not mind, then him mind.

NEGRO PROVERB

No one lies so boldly as the man who is indignant.

NIETZSCHE

It's the deaf people that create the lies.   IRISH PROVERB

It is the unconscious liar that is the greatest liar.
                                        SAMUEL BUTLER (II)

Weak and impulsive people may be, and very often are, sincere, but they are seldom truthful.   COLLINS

It is hard to believe that a man is telling the truth when you know that you would lie if you were in his place.   MENCKEN

Honesty is often in the wrong.   LUCAN

The course of true anything never does run smooth.
                                        SAMUEL BUTLER (II)

Memory and Conscience

Could we know what men are most apt to remember, we might know what they are most apt to do.   HALIFAX

You can close your eyes to reality but not to memories.   LEC

What was hard to endure is sweet to recall.
                                        CONTINENTAL PROVERB

He who is not very strong in memory should not meddle with lying. MONTAIGNE

The memory will seldom be unmannerly but where it is unkind. HALIFAX

If mankind had wished for what is right, they might have had it long ago. HAZLITT

Conscience is a cur that will let you get past it but that you cannot keep from barking. ANONYMOUS

Conscience is thoroughly well bred and soon leaves off talking to those who do not wish to hear it. SAMUEL BUTLER (II)

Even the voice of conscience undergoes mutation. LEC

Conscience is, in most men, an anticipation of the opinion of others. SIR HENRY TAYLOR

Half-a-dozen superstitious terrors have saved many a cash drawer. HASKINS

He who has no conscience makes up for it by lacking it. LEC

Gentlemen, let us distrust our first reactions; they are invariably much too favorable. NIETZSCHE

The fox condemns the trap, not himself. BLAKE

Experience informs us that the first defense of weak minds is to recriminate.   COLERIDGE

One need not mind stealing, but one must cry out at people whose minds are so befuddled that they do not know theft when they see it.   CHAPMAN

The men who can be charged with fewest failings are generally most ready to allow them.   DR. JOHNSON

The greatest of faults, I should say, is to be conscious of none.
                                                        CARLYLE

A healthy appetite for righteousness, kept in due control by good manners, is an excellent thing; but to "hunger and thirst" after it is often merely a symptom of spiritual diabetes.
                                                          BROAD

No one knows what he is doing so long as he is acting rightly; but of what is wrong one is always conscious.   GOETHE

At times, although one is perfectly in the right, one's legs tremble; at other times, although one is completely in the wrong, birds sing in one's soul.   ROZINOV

Almost all our faults are more pardonable than the methods we resort to to hide them.   LA ROCHEFOUCAULD

> And ofttimes excusing of a fault
> Doth make the fault the worse by the excuse.
>   SHAKESPEARE

When someone behaves like a beast, he says: "After all, one is only human." But when he is treated like a beast, he says: "After all, one is human."   KRAUS

No man is rich enough to buy back his past.   WILDE

Our names are labels, plainly printed on the bottled essence of our past behavior.   L. P. SMITH

Where there is yet shame, there may in time be virtue.
                                        DR. JOHNSON

Remorse begets reform.   COWPER

There are some people who are very resourceful
At being remorseful,
And who apparently feel that the best way to make friends
Is to do something terrible and then make amends.
                                              NASH

True penitence condemns to silence. What a man is ready to recall, he would be willing to repeat.   BRADLEY

The memory and conscience never did, nor never will, agree about forgiving injuries.   HALIFAX

Many forgive injuries, but none ever forgave contempt.
                                         ANONYMOUS

We forgive others when it suits us.   PAVESE

Few heads are sensitive to coals of fire.   HASKINS

That which we call sin in others is experiment for us.

EMERSON

People who live in chateaux
Shouldn't throw tomateaux.

MORTON

Indulgence to oneself and severity toward others are at bottom
one and the same fault.   VAPEREAU

You cannot receive a shock unless you have an electric affinity
for that which shocks you.   THOREAU

Whatever you condemn, you have done yourself.

GRODDECK

Whoever supermoralizes unmoralizes.   COLERIDGE

Distaste which takes no credit to itself is best.

MARIANNE MOORE

Self-Love

If we were not all so excessively interested in ourselves, life
would be so uninteresting that none of us would be able to
endure it.   SCHOPENHAUER

Man would sooner have the void for his purpose than be
void of purpose. NIETZSCHE

How glorious it is—and also how painful—to be an exception.
MUSSET

Every man likes the smell of his own farts.
ICELANDIC PROVERB

Take egotism out, and you would castrate the benefactors.
EMERSON

The most vulnerable and at the same time the most un-
conquerable thing is human self-love; indeed, it is through
being wounded that its power grows and can, in the end, become tremendous. NIETZSCHE

When man, that master of destruction, of self-destruction,
wounds himself, it is that very wound which forces him to live.
NIETZSCHE

One never dives into the water to save a drowning man more
eagerly than when there are others present who dare not
take the risk. NIETZSCHE

He who despises himself nevertheless esteems himself as a
self-despiser. NIETZSCHE

We would rather run ourselves down than not speak of ourselves at all. LA ROCHEFOUCAULD

There is luxury in self-reproach. When we blame ourselves
we feel no one else has a right to blame us. WILDE

All censure of a man's self is oblique praise. It is in order to show how much he can spare. It has all the invidiousness of self-praise, and all the reproach of falsehood.

DR. JOHNSON

The most silent people are generally those who think most highly of themselves.　　HAZLITT

Never to talk about oneself is a very refined form of hypocrisy.

NIETZSCHE

Few men speak humbly of humility, chastely of chastity, skeptically of skepticism.　　PASCAL

The man who is ostentatious of his modesty is twin to the statue that wears a figleaf.　　MARK TWAIN

It is a form of coquetry to emphasize the fact that you do not indulge in it.　　LA ROCHEFOUCAULD

In disrespecting, we show that we still maintain a *sense* of respect.　　NIETZSCHE

Excessive scruple is only hidden pride.　　GOETHE

Intolerance itself is a form of egoism, and to condemn egoism intolerantly is to share it.　　SANTAYANA

Self-sacrifice enables us to sacrifice other people without blushing.　　SHAW

Pride will spit in pride's face.   THOMAS FULLER

Self-interest speaks all sorts of languages and plays all sorts of roles, even that of disinterestedness.   LA ROCHEFOUCAULD

There may be *Herostratoi* who set fire to the temples in which their image is worshiped.   NIETZSCHE

In *mere* solicitude man remains essentially with himself, even if he is moved with extreme pity.   BUBER

> To observations which ourselves we make
> We grow more fond for the observer's sake.
>
> POPE

He who is in love with himself has at least this advantage— he won't encounter many rivals in his love.   LICHTENBERG

The ring always believes that the finger lives for it.   CHAZAL

The golden fleece of self-love is proof against cudgel blows but not against pinpricks.   NIETZSCHE

Self-love is often rather arrogant than blind; it does not hide our faults from ourselves, but persuades us that they escape the notice of others.   DR. JOHNSON

Pride does not wish to owe and vanity does not wish to pay.
LA ROCHEFOUCAULD

Pride always recoups its losses and loses nothing even when it dispenses with vanity.   LA ROCHEFOUCAULD

Many men on the point of an edifying death would be furious if they were suddenly restored to health.   PAVESE

Self is the Gorgon. Vanity sees it in the mirror of other men and lives. Pride studies it for itself and is turned to stone.
    CHESTERTON

To be vain is rather a mark of humility than pride.   SWIFT

A man who is not a fool can rid himself of every folly but vanity.   ROUSSEAU

The vain man hates his like, the exceptional man seeks out his.   RICHTER

It is not to be imagined by how many different ways vanity defeats it own purposes.   CHESTERFIELD

Statesmen and beauties are very rarely sensible of the gradations of their decay.   CHESTERFIELD

Vanity plays lurid tricks with our memory.   CONRAD

Those who write against vanity want the glory of having written well, and their readers the glory of reading well, and I who write this have the same desire, as perhaps those who read this have also.   PASCAL

Vanity is the greatest of all flatterers.   LA ROCHEFOUCAULD

We sometimes imagine we hate flattery, but we only hate the way we are flattered.   LA ROCHEFOUCAULD

To ask for advice is in nine cases out of ten to tout for flattery.
COLLINS

We refuse praise from a desire to be praised twice.
LA ROCHEFOUCAULD

What really flatters a man is that you think him worth flattering.   SHAW

Undeserved praise causes more pangs of conscience later than undeserved blame, but probably only for this reason, that our powers of judgment are more completely exposed by being overpraised than by being unjustly underestimated.
NIETZSCHE

He who praises you for what you lack wishes to take from you what you have.   JUAN MANUEL

Human Vices

No man's vice is so much against nature that it destroys even the last traces of nature.   SAINT AUGUSTINE

Vice is a monster of so frightful mien,
As, to be hated, needs but to be seen;
Yet seen too oft, familiar with her face,
We first endure, then pity, then embrace.

POPE

More people are flattered into virtue than bullied out of vice.

SURTEES

To many people virtue consists chiefly in repenting faults, not in avoiding them.   LICHTENBERG

A man has virtues enough if, on account of them, he deserves forgiveness for his faults.   LICHTENBERG

The vices are never so well employed as in combating one another.   HAZLITT

There is a division of labor, even in vice. Some people addict themselves to the speculation only, others to the practice.

HAZLITT

The unfulfilled desires of the virtuous are evil; the unfulfilled desires of the vicious are good; and conduct is not, as Matthew Arnold said, three-fourths of life; it is not even three-fourths of conduct.   MUIR

There are bad people who would be less dangerous if they had no good in them.   LA ROCHEFOUCAULD

If virtue had everything her own way she would be as insufferable as dominant factions generally are.

SAMUEL BUTLER (II)

A few hours of mountain climbing turn a rascal and a saint into two pretty similar creatures. Fatigue is the shortest way to Equality and Fraternity—and, in the end, Liberty will surrender to Sleep.   NIETZSCHE

Hypocrisy is the homage that vice offers to virtue.
                                    LA ROCHEFOUCAULD

It is good to be without vices, but it is not good to be without temptations.   BAGEHOT

Men's virtues have their seasons even as fruits have.
                                    LA ROCHEFOUCAULD

The virtue which requires to be ever guarded is scarcely worth the sentinel.   GOLDSMITH

Virtue is too often merely local.   DR. JOHNSON

> Virtue she finds too painful an endeavor,
> Content to dwell in decencies forever.
>
>   POPE

Virtue knows to a farthing what it has lost by not having been vice.   WALPOLE

I am not mortified by our vice, but I own our virtue makes me ashamed.   EMERSON

Nothing is more unpleasant than a virtuous person with a mean mind.   BAGEHOT

Hate is always a clash between our spirit and someone else's body.   PAVESE

Impotent hatred is the most horrible of all emotions; one should hate nobody whom one cannot destroy.   GOETHE

He that fears you present will hate you absent.
                                            THOMAS FULLER

Like the greatest virtue and the worst dogs, the fiercest hatred is silent.   RICHTER

Revenge is barren: its delight is murder, and its satiety, despair.   SCHILLER

Weak men are apt to be cruel, because they stick at nothing that may repair the ill effect of their mistakes.   HALIFAX

Anger raiseth invention, but it overheateth the oven.
                                                 HALIFAX

The tigers of wrath are wiser than the horses of instruction.
                                                 BLAKE

To be angry is to revenge the fault of others upon ourselves.
                                                 POPE

How much more grievous are the consequences of anger than the causes of it.   MARCUS AURELIUS

Think, when you are enraged at anyone, what would probably become your sentiments should he die during the dispute.
                                              SHENSTONE

In all perplexity there is a portion of fear, which predisposes the mind to anger. COLERIDGE

Malice may be sometimes out of breath, envy never.

HALIFAX

Every scarecrow has a secret ambition to terrorize. LEC

A hurtful act is the transference to others of the degradation which we bear in ourselves. SIMONE WEIL

Malice is a greater magnifying glass than kindness.

HALIFAX

The malicious have a dark happiness. HUGO

Malice, like lust, when it is at the height, doth not know shame. HALIFAX

There is an accumulative cruelty in a number of men, though none in particular are ill-natured. HALIFAX

One does not hate so long as one despises. NIETZSCHE

The way we exclaim over certain people's good faith, disinterestedness, and honesty is not so much praise of them as disparagement of all mankind. LA BRUYÈRE

I love being superior to myself better than [to] my equals.
COLERIDGE

[45]

Arrogance in persons of merit affronts us more than arrogance in those without merit: merit itself is an affront.

NIETZSCHE

Love and envy make a man pine, which other affections do not, because they are not so continual.   BACON

Envy, among other ingredients, has a mixture of love of justice in it. We are more angry at undeserved than at deserved good fortune.   HAZLITT

The gilded sheath of pity conceals the dagger of envy.

NIETZSCHE

A man is very apt to complain of the ingratitude of those who have risen far above him.   DR. JOHNSON

Familiarity in one's superiors causes bitterness, for it may not be returned.   NIETZSCHE

There are minds so impatient of inferiority that their gratitude is a species of revenge, and they return benefits not because recompense is a pleasure but because obligation is a pain.

DR. JOHNSON

People hate those who make them feel their own inferiority.

CHESTERFIELD

Confronted by outstanding merit in another, there is no way of saving one's ego except by love.   GOETHE

His scorn of the great is repeated too often to be real; no man thinks much of that which he despises.   DR. JOHNSON

The girl who can't dance says the band can't play.

YIDDISH PROVERB

There are many things that we would throw away, if we were not afraid that others might pick them up.   WILDE

We grow tired of everything but turning others into ridicule, and congratulating ourselves on their defects.   HAZLITT

The dullard's envy of brilliant men is always assuaged by the suspicion that they will come to a bad end.   BEERBOHM

Cunning is the dark sanctuary of incapacity.

CHESTERFIELD

What's left over from the thief is spent on the fortune-teller.

YIDDISH PROVERB

I have always thought it rather interesting to follow the involuntary movements of fear in clever people. Fools coarsely display their cowardice in all its nakedness, but the others are able to cover it with a veil so delicate, so daintily woven with small plausible lies, that there is some pleasure to be found in contemplating this ingenious work of the human intelligence.   TOCQUEVILLE

Idleness and the incapacity for leisure correspond with one another; leisure is the contrary of both. Leisure is only possible to a man who is at one with himself and also at one with the world. These are the presuppositions of leisure, for leisure is an affirmation. Idleness, on the other hand, is rooted in the omission of these two affirmations.   PIEPER

Acedia: the malady of monks.   BAUDELAIRE

The essence of acedia is the refusal to acquiesce in one's own being. PIEPER

A loafer always has the correct time. KIN HUBBARD

To be idle and to be poor have always been reproaches, and therefore every man endeavors with his utmost care to hide his poverty from others, and his idleness from himself.
DR. JOHNSON

Ennui has made more gamblers than avarice, more drunkards than thirst, and perhaps as many suicides as despair.
COLTON

It is difficult to keep quiet if you have nothing to do.
SCHOPENHAUER

Work with some men is as besetting a sin as idleness with others. SAMUEL BUTLER (II)

Not everything that is more difficult is more meritorious.
SAINT THOMAS AQUINAS

As a rule, for no one does life drag more disagreeably than for him who tries to speed it up. RICHTER

It is better to do the most trifling thing in the world than to regard half an hour as a trifle. GOETHE

I have so much to do that I am going to bed.
SAVOYARD PROVERB

Only when vitality is low do people find material things oppressive and ideal things unsubstantial. SANTAYANA

Much benevolence of the passive order may be traced to a disinclination to inflict pain upon oneself.   MEREDITH

Those who are fond of setting things to rights have no great objection to seeing them wrong.   HAZLITT

The friend of all humanity is not to my taste.   MOLIÈRE

The most melancholy of human reflections, perhaps, is that on the whole it is a question whether the benevolence of mankind does most good or harm.   BAGEHOT

Human Virtues

We can do noble acts without ruling earth and sea.
ARISTOTLE

A good person can put himself in the place of a bad person more easily than a bad person can put himself in the place of a good person.   RICHTER

The good displeases us when we have not yet grown up to it.
NIETZSCHE

One good deed has many claimants.   YIDDISH PROVERB

We do not have to acquire humility. There is humility in us—only we humiliate ourselves before false gods.

SIMONE WEIL

It is always the secure who are humble.   CHESTERTON

I am not one of those who say, "It is nothing; it is a woman drowning."   ANONYMOUS

Real unselfishness consists in sharing the interests of others.

SANTAYANA

Kindness is in our power, but fondness is not.

DR. JOHNSON

When I am condemned, and condemn myself utterly, I think straightway, "But I rely on my love for some things."

THOREAU

Genuine responsibility exists only where there is real responding.   BUBER

Gratitude is one of those things that cannot be bought. It must be born with men, or else all the obligations in the world will not create it. A real sense of a kind thing is a gift of nature, and never was, nor can be acquired.   HALIFAX

I can promise to be sincere, but not to be impartial.

GOETHE

Whistling to keep up courage is good practice for whistling.

HASKINS

Perfect courage means doing unwitnessed what we would be capable of with the world looking on.

LA ROCHEFOUCAULD

Many would be cowards if they had courage enough.

THOMAS FULLER

He that can make a fire well can end a quarrel.

ENGLISH PROVERB

A wise man sees as much as he ought, not as much as he can.

MONTAIGNE

Tact consists in knowing how far to go in going too far.

COCTEAU

Tact is the intelligence of the heart.   ANONYMOUS

It is a great art to saunter.   THOREAU

Success and Failure

Passions tyrannize over mankind; but ambition keeps all the others in check.   LA BRUYÈRE

Ambition sufficiently plagues her proselytes by keeping them always in show and in public, like a statue in a street.

DR. FULLER

The slave has but one master; the ambitious man has as many as can help in making his fortune.   LA BRUYÈRE

Ambition is pitiless. Any merit that it cannot use it finds despicable.   JOUBERT

Nothing is enough to the man for whom enough is too little.   EPICURUS

There are three wants which can never be satisfied: that of the rich, who wants something more; that of the sick, who wants something different; and that of the traveler, who says, "Anywhere but here."   EMERSON

Everybody wants to *be* somebody: nobody wants to *grow*.   GOETHE

Men who pass most comfortably through the world are those who possess good digestions and hard hearts.   HARRIET MARTINEAU

Snobbery haunts those who are not reconciled with themselves; evolution is the hope of the immature.   SANTAYANA

Discontent is want of self-reliance; it is infirmity of will.   EMERSON

Only strong natures can really be sweet ones: those that seem sweet are in general only weak, and may easily turn sour.   LA ROCHEFOUCAULD

The web of this world is woven of Necessity and Chance. Woe to him who has accustomed himself from his youth up to find something capricious in what is necessary, and who would ascribe something like reason to Chance and make a religion of surrendering to it.   GOETHE

Every man who refuses to accept the conditions of life sells his soul.   BAUDELAIRE

Chance does nothing that has not been prepared beforehand.   TOCQUEVILLE

He that leaveth nothing to chance will do few things ill, but he will do very few things.   HALIFAX

Prudence is a rich, ugly old maid courted by incapacity.   BLAKE

Necessity poisons wounds which it cannot heal.   VAUVENARGUES

I must complain the cards are ill-shuffled, till I have a good hand.   SWIFT

A prudent man will think more important what fate has conceded to him than what it has denied.   GRACIAN

If a man look sharply and attentively, he shall see fortune; for though she be blind, yet she is not invisible.   BACON

A wise man will make more opportunities than he finds.   BACON

To maintain that our successes are due to Providence and not to our own cleverness is a cunning way of increasing in our own eyes the importance of our successes.   PAVESE

Fortune does not change men; it unmasks them.

MME. NECKER

Adversity introduces a man to himself.   ANONYMOUS

It has been said that misfortune sharpens our wits, but to the extent that it does so, it makes us worse; fortunately, it often simply dulls them.   NIETZSCHE

The greatest reverses of fortune are the most easily borne from a sort of dignity belonging to them.   HAZLITT

Characters that are depressed at a mere nothing are the kind best suited to endure heavy blows.   PAVESE

Experience is only half of experience.   GOETHE

Experience is not what happens to a man. It is what a man does with what happens to him.   ALDOUS HUXLEY

Few men are worthy of experience. The majority let it corrupt them.   JOUBERT

Experience is the name everyone gives to his mistakes.

WILDE

Our very life depends on everything's
Recurring till we answer from within.

FROST

If a man has character, he also has his typical experience, which always recurs.   NIETZSCHE

[54]

Late resounds what early sounded.   GOETHE

The search for a new personality is futile; what is fruitful is the human interest the old personality can take in new activities.   PAVESE

Better a monosyllabic life than a ragged and muttered one; let its report be short and round like a rifle, so that it may hear its own echo in the surrounding silence.   THOREAU

Many are stubborn in pursuit of the path they have chosen, few in pursuit of the goal.   NIETZSCHE

Not every end is a goal. The end of a melody is not its goal; however, if the melody has not reached its end, it would also not have reached its goal. A parable.   NIETZSCHE

Hope is generally a wrong guide, though it is very good company by the way.   HALIFAX

Men should do with their hopes as they do with tame fowl: cut their wings that they may not fly over the wall.

HALIFAX

Every year, if not every day, we have to wager our salvation upon some prophecy based upon imperfect knowledge.

O. W. HOLMES, JR.

Hope is a good breakfast, but it is a bad supper.   BACON

Hope has a good memory, gratitude a bad one.   GRACIAN

Hope . . . suggests that every conclusion unfavorable to oneself must be an error of the mind. VALÉRY

Every man expects some miracle—either from his mind or from his body or from someone else or from events.

VALÉRY

Vows begin when hope dies. LEONARDO DA VINCI

Optimism is a kind of heart stimulus—the digitalis of failure. E. HUBBARD

The basis of optimism is sheer terror. WILDE

A pessimist is a man who has been compelled to live with an optimist. E. HUBBARD

Humanity never produces optimists till it has ceased to produce happy men. CHESTERTON

A cripple in the right way may beat a racer in the wrong one. Nay, the fleeter and better the racer is, who hath once missed his way, the farther he leaveth it behind. BACON

We succeed in enterprises which demand the positive qualities we possess, but we excel in those which can also make use of our defects. TOCQUEVILLE

A man should not strive to eliminate his complexes but to get into accord with them: they are legitimately what directs his conduct in the world. FREUD

To do great work a man must be very idle as well as very industrious.　　　　　　　　　　　SAMUEL BUTLER (II)

Talent without genius isn't much, but genius without talent is nothing whatever.　　　　　　　　　　　VALÉRY

Make your cross your crutch; but, when you see another man do it, beware of him.　　　　　　　　　　　SHAW

We wholly conquer only what we assimilate.　　　　GIDE

A man must (as the books on success say) give "his best"; and what a small part of a man "his best" is! His second and third best are often much better.　　　　　　CHESTERTON

Talent is an adornment; an adornment is also a concealment.　　　　　　　　　　　NIETZSCHE

For precocity some great price is always demanded sooner or later in life.　　　　　　　　　　　MARGARET FULLER

To measure up to all that is demanded of him, a man must overestimate his capacities.　　　　　　　　　GOETHE

Consciousness of our powers augments them.　　　　　　　　　　　VAUVENARGUES

Nature reacts not only to physical disease, but also to moral weakness; when the danger increases, she gives us greater courage.　　　　　　　　　　　GOETHE

Sometimes a lack of tact—or what seems a mere lack of tact—comes between a character and its destiny; or a man dies from a cold in the head.   CHAPMAN

Fear gives sudden instincts of skill.   COLERIDGE

Of two things we cannot sufficiently beware: of obstinacy if we confine ourselves to our proper field, of inadequacy if we desert it.   GOETHE

Mistakes are always initial.   PAVESE

One seldom rushes into a single error. Rushing into the first one, one always does too much. Hence one usually commits another; and this time does too little.   NIETZSCHE

All men that are ruined are ruined on the side of their natural propensities.   E. BURKE

We run carelessly to the precipice, after we have put something before us to prevent us from seeing it.   PASCAL

As it will be in the future, it was at the birth of Man.
There are only four things certain since Social
                              Progress began:—
That the Dog returns to his Vomit and the Sow returns
                              to her Mire,
And the burnt Fool's bandaged finger goes wabbling
                              back to the Fire.
                              KIPLING

Man does not live long enough to profit from his faults.

LA BRUYÈRE

He that is used to go forward and findeth a stop, falleth out of his own favor, and is not the thing he was. · BACON

He that fails in his endeavors after wealth or power will not long retain either honesty or courage. DR. JOHNSON

More dangers have deceived men than forced them. BACON

There are people who so eagerly and insistently desire some one thing that, for fear of missing it, they omit doing nothing that will spoil their chances. LA BRUYÈRE

The greatest mistake you can make in life is to be continually fearing you will make one. E. HUBBARD

A man finds he has been wrong at every preceding stage of his career, only to deduce the astonishing conclusion that he is at last entirely right. STEVENSON

It is often the failure who is the pioneer in new lands, new undertakings, and new forms of expression. HOFFER

The secret of success in life is known only to those who have not succeeded. COLLINS

Perched on the loftiest throne in the world, we are still sitting on our own behind. MONTAIGNE

We can come to look upon the deaths of our enemies with as much regret as we feel for those of our friends, namely, when we miss their existence as witnesses to our success.

SCHOPENHAUER

There is but an inch of difference between the cushioned chamber and the padded cell.   CHESTERTON

Ease is seldom got without some pains, but it is yet seldomer kept without them.   HALIFAX

We combat obstacles in order to get repose and, when got, the repose is insupportable.   HENRY ADAMS

None think the great unhappy but the great.   YOUNG

Nothing makes a man so cross as success.   TROLLOPE

Every man has a right to be conceited until he is successful.

DISRAELI

When a man has been highly honored and has eaten a little he is most benevolent.   NIETZSCHE

The common idea that success spoils people by making them vain, egotistic, and self-complacent is erroneous; on the contrary, it makes them, for the most part, humble, tolerant, and kind. Failure makes people cruel and bitter.   MAUGHAM

All eminent sages are as despotic as generals, as discourteous and lacking in delicacy as generals, because they know they are safe from punishment.   CHEKHOV

Habit

Chaos often breeds life, when order breeds habit.

HENRY ADAMS

Charm of manner is a sex attribute which has become a habit.

E. HUBBARD

Habit may be second nature, but it prevents us from knowing the real nature whose cruelties and enchantments it lacks.

PROUST

Habit is . . . not to be flung out of the window by any man, but coaxed downstairs a step at a time.   MARK TWAIN

To change one's habits has a smell of death.

PORTUGUESE PROVERB

The fixity of a habit is generally in direct proportion to its absurdity.   PROUST

Men lose their tempers in defending their taste.   EMERSON

Vulgarity is the garlic in the salad of taste.   CONNOLLY

Between good sense and good taste is the difference between cause and effect.   LA BRUYÈRE

People care more about being thought to have taste than about being either good, clever, or amiable.

SAMUEL BUTLER (II)

It is as common for tastes to change as it is uncommon for traits of character.   LA ROCHEFOUCAULD

Humor

Only man has dignity; only man, therefore, can be funny.

FATHER KNOX

Every man is important if he loses his life; and every man is funny if he loses his hat and has to run after it.

CHESTERTON

If a man wants to set up as an innkeeper and he does not succeed, it is not comic. If, on the contrary, a girl asks to be allowed to set up as a prostitute and she fails, as sometimes happens, it is comic.

KIERKEGAARD

A joke is an epitaph on an emotion.

NIETZSCHE

If you want to be witty, work on your character and say what you think on every occasion.

STENDHAL

Fun I love, but too much fun is of all things the most loathsome. Mirth is better than fun, and happiness is better than mirth.

BLAKE

If you want to make people weep, you must weep yourself. If you want to make people laugh, your face must remain serious.

CASANOVA

When a man is not amused, he feels an involuntary contempt for those who are.

BULWER-LYTTON

Irony is an abnormal growth; like the abnormally enlarged liver of the Strasbourg goose, it ends by killing the individual.
KIERKEGAARD

Sentimental irony is a dog that bays at the moon while he pisses on a grave.
KRAUS

Human Types

The more intelligent a man is, the more originality he discovers in men. Ordinary people see no difference between men.
PASCAL

All men are ordinary men; the extraordinary men are those who know it.
CHESTERTON

There is as much difference between us and ourselves as between us and others.
MONTAIGNE

A man never reveals his character more vividly than when portraying the character of another.
RICHTER

There may be said to be two classes of people in the world: those who constantly divide the people of the world into two classes, and those who do not.
BENCHLEY

It is with trifles, and when he is off guard, that a man best reveals his character. SCHOPENHAUER

What divides men is less a difference in ideas than a likeness in pretensions. BÉRANGER

There are people who are followed all through their lives by a beggar to whom they have given nothing. KRAUS

There are people who so arrange their lives that they feed themselves only on side dishes. ORTEGA Y GASSET

One man is more concerned with the impression he makes on the rest of mankind, another with the impression the rest of mankind makes on him. The disposition of the first is subjective, of the second objective. The one is, in the whole of his existence, more in the nature of an idea which is merely presented, the other more of the being who presents it. SCHOPENHAUER

Two women. One when alone is exactly the same as she is in company, the other in company exactly what she is when she is alone. The latter holds herself badly in public, the former puts on evening dress when she dines by herself. One should marry neither. VALÉRY

There are no perfectly honorable men; but every true man has one main point of honor and a few minor ones. SHAW

There are persons who always find a hair in their plate of soup for the simple reason that, when they sit down before it, they shake their heads until one falls in. HEBBEL

We boil at different degrees.   EMERSON

On the heights it is warmer than those in the valley imagine.
                                                              NIETZSCHE

There are people who, like a little bridge, exist only that
others should run over them. And the little bridge serves
this, and the other, and the third generation.   ROZINOV

A man . . . so eager to be in advance of his age that he
pretended to be in advance of himself.   CHESTERTON

Many people wait throughout their whole lives for the chance
to be good in their own fashion.   NIETZSCHE

There are plenty of people to whom the crucial problems of
their lives never get presented in terms that they can understand.   CHAPMAN

With one man, resignation stores up treasure in heaven; with
another man, it does but store explosives in the heart.
                                                        BRADLEY

A man who lacks nobility cannot have kindliness, he can only
have good nature.   CHAMFORT

He who can take no interest in what is small will take false
interest in what is great.   RUSKIN

The dearer a thing is, the cheaper as a general rule we sell it.
                                          SAMUEL BUTLER (II)

Misers are very kind people: they amass wealth for those who wish their death.   STANISLAUS, KING OF POLAND

The idealist is incorrigible: if he is thrown out of his heaven he makes an ideal of his hell.   NIETZSCHE

He is a hard man who is only just, and a sad one who is only wise.   VOLTAIRE

The Talker

Men govern nothing with more difficulty than their tongues, and can moderate their desires more than their words.

SPINOZA

Most men cry better than they speak. You get more nature out of them by pinching than addressing them.   THOREAU

No man is exempt from saying silly things; the mischief is to say them deliberately.   MONTAIGNE

Watch your own speech, and notice how it is guided by your less conscious purposes.   GEORGE ELIOT

Our intonations contain our philosophy of life, what each of us is constantly telling himself about things.   PROUST

One often contradicts an opinion when what is uncongenial is really the tone in which it was conveyed. NIETZSCHE

The language of excitement is at best picturesque merely. You must be calm before you can utter oracles. THOREAU

Shy and unready men are great betrayers of secrets; for there are few wants more urgent for the moment than the want of something to say. SIR HENRY TAYLOR

The vanity of being known to be trusted with a secret is generally one of the chief motives to disclose it.

DR. JOHNSON

A person may be very secretive and yet have no secrets.

E. HUBBARD

A man wants to make an important confession; but the man to whom he wished to unbosom himself does not come at once, so he says something quite different. KIERKEGAARD

There is no refuge from confession but suicide; and suicide is confession. WEBSTER

A confidence always aims at glory, scandal, excuse, propaganda.

VALÉRY

What is said when drunk has been thought out beforehand.

FLEMISH PROVERB

He that talketh what he knoweth will also talk what he knoweth not. BACON

Three signs of a rogue: interrupting during a story, viciousness in play, telling nasty jokes. ANONYMOUS

It is the dread of something happening, something unknown and dreadful, that makes us do anything to keep the flicker of talk from dying out. L. P. SMITH

As he knew not what to say, he swore. BYRON

Abuse resembles a church procession; it always returns to the point from which it set out. MONTI

You have not converted a man because you have silenced him. MORLEY

Silence is the unbearable repartee. CHESTERTON

Human Folly

Neither man nor woman can be worth anything until they have discovered that they are fools. This is the first step toward becoming either estimable or agreeable; and until it is taken there is no hope. MELBOURNE

A fool is his own informer. YIDDISH PROVERB

Fortunately for themselves and the world, nearly all men are cowards and dare not act on what they believe. Nearly all our disasters come of a few fools having the "courage of their convictions." PATMORE

The hours of folly are measur'd by the clock; but of wisdom, no clock can measure. BLAKE

Folly is often more cruel in the consequence than malice can be in the intent. HALIFAX

The shlemiehl lands on his back and bruises his nose. YIDDISH PROVERB

Send a fool to close the shutters and he'll close them all over town. YIDDISH PROVERB

After taking ninety-nine years to climb a stairway, the tortoise falls and says there is a curse on haste. MALTESE PROVERB

When the ass was invited to the wedding feast he said, "They need more wood and water." BOSNIAN PROVERB

Nobody ever did anything very foolish except from some strong principle. MELBOURNE

Folly may often be only an abusive term of Envy signifying Courage. Hardihood and Foolhardiness are as disparate as green and yellow; but green and yellow will both appear yellow to the jaundiced eye. COLERIDGE

Nothing is more characteristic of a man than the manner in which he behaves toward fools.   AMIEL

He who has not lost his head over some things has no head to lose.   RICHTER

The man who lives free from folly is not so wise as he thinks.
                                        LA ROCHEFOUCAULD

Once upon a time there was a man who became wise. He learned not to make a single gesture which was not useful. Soon afterward he was shut up.   VALÉRY

His soul will never starve for exploits or excitements who is wise enough to be made a fool of. To be "taken in" every-where is to see the inside of everything.   CHESTERTON

RELIGION AND GOD

Religion and God

People who feel themselves to be exiles in this world are mightily inclined to believe themselves citizens of another.

SANTAYANA

Religion is a disease, but it is a noble disease.   HERACLITUS

The first ideas of religion arose, not from a contemplation of the works of nature, but from a concern with regard to the events of life.

HUME

Religion consists in believing that everything which happens is extraordinarily important. It can never disappear from the world, precisely for this reason.

PAVESE

Religion is the masterpiece of the art of animal training, for it trains people as to how they shall think.

SCHOPENHAUER

Apart from religion, expressed in ways generally intelligible, populations sink into the apathetic task of daily survival, with minor alleviations.

WHITEHEAD

Whatever the world thinks, he who hath not meditated much upon God, the human mind, and the *summum bonum*, may possibly make a thriving earthworm, but will most indubitably make a sorry patriot and a sorry statesman.

BERKELEY

To the symmetrical natures religion is indeed a crown of glory; nevertheless, so far as this world is concerned, they can grow and prosper without it. But to the unsymmetrical natures religion is a necessary condition of successful work even in this world.   ACTON

It is the test of a good religion whether you can make a joke about it.   CHESTERTON

Mysteries are not necessarily miracles.   GOETHE

A childish belief in the marvelous turns a grown man into a coward, and the same belief consoles him in his darkest hours.   HERZEN

We make trifles of terrors, ensconcing ourselves into seeming knowledge, when we should submit ourselves to an unknown fear.   SHAKESPEARE

Superstition is rooted in a much deeper and more sensitive layer of the psyche than skepticism.   GOETHE

The choice was put to them whether they would like to be kings or kings' couriers. Like children they all wanted to be couriers. So now there are a great many couriers; they post through the world and, as there are no kings left, shout to each other their meaningless and obsolete messages. They would gladly put an end to their wretched lives, but they dare not because of their oath of service.   KAFKA

To believe means to recognize that we must wait until the veil shall be removed. Unbelief prematurely unveils itself.
          ROSENSTOCK-HUESSY

[74]

Faith is illuminative, not operative; it does not force obedience, though it increases responsibility; it heightens guilt, it does not prevent sin.   NEWMAN

The crows maintain that a single crow could destroy the heavens. Doubtless that is so, but it proves nothing against the heavens, for the heavens signify simply: the impossibility of crows.   KAFKA

Faith is never identical with piety.   BARTH

Nothing fortifies skepticism more than that there are some who are not skeptics; if all were so, they would be wrong.
                                                       PASCAL

We are, I know not how, double in ourselves, so that what we believe we disbelieve, and cannot rid ourselves of what we condemn.   MONTAIGNE

There is a great deal of skepticism in believers; and a good deal of belief in non-believers; the only question is where we decide to give our better energy. "Lord, I believe; help thou mine unbelief" may, and should, be prayed two ways.
                                                     WILLIAMS

A man often preaches his beliefs precisely when he has lost them and is looking everywhere for them, and, on such occasions, his preaching is by no means at its worst.
                                                   MELANCTHON

He who believes in nothing still needs a girl to believe in him.
                                         ROSENSTOCK-HUESSY

The means that allow men, up to a certain point, to go without religion are perhaps, after all, the only means we still
possess for bringing mankind back, by a long and roundabout
path, to a state of faith.   TOCQUEVILLE

Anti-clericalism is part of the price the priesthood pay for
their vocation—just as, if ever poets were to become the
acknowledged legislators of the world, a strong anti-poetic
movement would have to be encouraged. But then also the
vocation of the poets as of the priesthood must be respected.
                                                        WILLIAMS

You can change your faith without changing gods, and vice
versa.   LEC

Oaths are the fossils of piety.   SANTAYANA

The superstition of science scoffs at the superstition of faith.
                                                         FROUDE

As students of nature we are pantheists, as poets polytheists,
as moral beings monotheists.   GOETHE

Truth rests with God alone, and a little bit with me.
                                                  YIDDISH PROVERB

It is easy to know God so long as you do not tax yourself
with defining Him.   JOUBERT

We dance around in a ring and suppose,
But the Secret sits in the middle and knows.
                                                         FROST

The task of theology is to show how the world is founded on something beyond transient fact, and how it issues in something beyond the perishing of occasions. The temporal world is the stage of finite accomplishment. We ask of theology to express that element in perishing lives which is undying by reason of its expression of perfection proper to our finite natures. In this way we shall understand how life includes a mode of satisfaction deeper than joy or sorrow.

WHITEHEAD

Among medieval and modern philosophers anxious to establish the religious significance of God, an unfortunate habit has prevailed of paying him metaphysical compliments.

WHITEHEAD

To stand on one leg and prove God's existence is a very different thing from going down on one's knees and thanking him.

KIERKEGAARD

The knowledge of God is very far from the love of Him.

PASCAL

From a Christian point of view the whole of learned theology is really a corollary; and is declined like *mensa*.

KIERKEGAARD

It is as difficult to be quite orthodox as to be quite healthy. Yet the need for orthodoxy, like the need for health, is imperative.

WILLIAMS

Orthodoxy is reticence.

ANONYMOUS

Speculations over God and the World are almost always idle, the thoughts of idlers, spectators of the theater of life.

"Is there a God?" "Has Man a soul?" "Why must we die?" "How many hairs has the Devil's Grandmother?" "When is the Day of Judgment?"—all these are idle questions, and one fool can ask more of them than a hundred wise men can answer. Nevertheless, teachers, parents, bishops, must give answers to such questions because, otherwise, the idlers will spread their corruption. Every idle question can ensnare at least one innocent heart. The Church Councils found themselves in the position of parents whose daughters are on the point of being seduced by young louts. The dogmas of the Church have to deal with blasphemous scoundrels, and therefore they have to speak their language, the language of shamelessness.   ROSENSTOCK-HUESSY

The idea of birth through a Holy Spirit, of the death of a Divine being, of the forgiveness of sins, or the fulfillment of prophecies, are ideas which, anyone can see, need but a touch to turn them into something blasphemous or ferocious. If some small mistake were made in doctrine, huge blunders might be made in human happiness. A sentence phrased wrong about the nature of symbolism might have broken all the best statues in Europe. A slip in the definitions might stop all the dances; might wither all the Christmas trees or break all the Easter eggs. Doctrines had to be defined within strict limits, even in order that man might enjoy general human liberties. The Church had to be careful; if only that the world might be careless.   CHESTERTON

The middle class in England did not wholly lose the habit of going to church until they acquired motor cars—so negligible in the end is intellect itself.   WILLIAMS

All the destruction in Christian Europe has arisen from deism, which is natural religion.   BLAKE

The various modes of worship which prevailed in the Roman world were all considered by the people as equally true; by the philosopher as equally false; and by the magistrate as equally useful.   GIBBON

Ethiopians have gods with snub noses and black hair; Thracians have gods with gray eyes and red hair.

XENOPHANES OF COLOPHON

The people would not believe in God at all if they were not permitted to believe wrong in Him.   HALIFAX

If God lived on earth, people would break his windows.

YIDDISH PROVERB

The world would use us just as it did the martyrs, if we loved God as they did.   BISHOP WILSON

A man who should act, for one day, on the supposition that all the people about him were influenced by the religion which they professed would find himself ruined by night.

MACAULAY

People will sacrifice themselves for the State, the Church, and even for God, so long as these remain their creation, their idea, and are not taken too personally.   NIETZSCHE

Men pretend to serve Almighty God who doth not need it, but make use of him because they need him.   HALIFAX

Alas, what should *we* do, said the girl, if there were no God.

LICHTENBERG

We have just enough religion to make us hate, but not enough to make us love one another.   SWIFT

Most people really believe that the Christian commandments (e.g., to love one's neighbor as oneself) are intentionally a little too severe—like putting the clock ahead half an hour to make sure of not being late in the morning.   KIERKEGAARD

The Christianity of the majority consists roughly of two notions: first of all the saying about the "little child," that one becomes a Christian as a little child, that of such is the Kingdom of Heaven; the second is the thief on the cross.

People live by virtue of the former—in death they reckon upon consoling themselves with the example of the thief. That is the sum of their Christianity; and correctly defined it is a mixture of childishness and crime.   KIERKEGAARD

A vision of truth which does not call upon us to get out of our armchair—why, this is the desideratum of mankind.

CHAPMAN

There are ladies who, finding by the too visible decay of their good looks that they can shine no more by that *light*, put on the *varnish* of an affected devotion to keep up some kind of figure in the world.   HALIFAX

When Lothario turns to God, the undertaker gets ready his bill.   TOLSTOI

Grigorovich has never been a caretaker at the docks; that is why he holds the Kingdom of Heaven so cheaply. He is fibbing.   CHEKHOV

There has never been a kingdom given to so many civil wars as that of Christ. MONTESQUIEU

Men never do evil so fully and so happily as when they do it for conscience's sake. PASCAL

Holy indignation is a proof that we should do the same thing ourselves, and easy tears are a certain sign of a hard heart. PATMORE

There is not even enough religion in the world to destroy the world's religions. NIETZSCHE

The Moral Christian is the Cause
Of the Unbeliever & his Laws.

BLAKE

He who begins by loving Christianity better than truth will proceed by loving his own sect or church better than Christianity and end in loving himself better than all. COLERIDGE

Most men's anger about religion is as if two men should quarrel for a lady they neither of them care for. HALIFAX

Defoe says that there were a hundred thousand country fellows in his time ready to fight to the death against popery, without knowing whether popery was a man or a horse.

HAZLITT

Every time a priest adds his *personal fervor* to the "canons," something terrible results (a hypocrite, a Torquemada); only when the priest is "slack" is it right. Why is this so? Why so *here*? ROZINOV

Fanaticism in religion is the alliance of the passions she condemns with the dogmas she professes.   ACTON

So long as there are earnest believers in the world, they will always wish to punish opinions, even if their judgment tells them it is unwise, and their conscience that it is wrong.

BAGEHOT

Where it is a duty to worship the sun it is pretty sure to be a crime to examine the laws of heat.   MORLEY

It is as absurd to argue men, as to torture them, into believing.

NEWMAN

Compulsion in religion is distinguished peculiarly from compulsion in every other thing. I may grow rich by an art I am compelled to follow; I may recover health by medicines I am compelled to take against my own judgment; but I cannot be saved by a worship I disbelieve and abhor.

JEFFERSON

Every sect is a moral check on its neighbor. Competition is as wholesome in religion as in commerce.   LANDOR

The Bible: a book which either reads us or is worthless.

CHAZAL

You cannot criticize the New Testament. It criticizes you.

CHAPMAN

He who created us without our help will not save us without our consent.   SAINT AUGUSTINE

My love is my weight.   SAINT AUGUSTINE

Nor creature nor creator was ever without love, natural or rational. The natural is always without error, but the other can err by having an evil object or through too little or too much vigor. Hence you may understand that love is the source of every virtue in you and of every deed which deserves punishment.   DANTE

Love is not consolation, it is light.   SIMONE WEIL

But humor is also the joy which has overcome the world.
                                                KIERKEGAARD

Ethics does not treat of the world. Ethics must be a condition of the world, like logic.   WITTGENSTEIN

What makes God happy? Seeing a poor devil find a treasure and give it back.   YIDDISH PROVERB

Men are not punished for their sins, but by them.
                                                E. HUBBARD

The alternative to being with Love at the center of the circle is to disorder the circumference for our own purposes.
                                                WILLIAMS

Perhaps there is only one cardinal sin: impatience. Because of impatience we were driven out of Paradise; because of impatience we cannot return.   KAFKA

To have sinned means that you are convinced that, *in some mysterious way*, what you have done will bring misfortune on you in the future; that it has broken some *mysterious* law of harmony, and is a link in a chain of past and future discords.   PAVESE

The difference between sin and tribulation is that the temptations of sin are with desire, and the temptations of tribulation against desire. The opposite tactics have therefore to be used. Those whom sin tempts with desire do well to avoid the danger, but in relation to tribulation that is precisely the danger, for each time one thinks one has saved oneself by avoiding the danger, the danger becomes greater next time.

KIERKEGAARD

Every contrition for sin is apt to encourage a not quite charitable wish that other people should exhibit a similar contrition.

WILLIAMS

It is much easier to repent of sins that we have committed than to repent of those we intend to commit.

BILLINGS

Certainly our sins and faults destroy the good. But our efforts after the good also destroy it. The very pursuit of goodness becomes a hunt; that which was to be our lord becomes our victim. It is necessary to behave well here? We do. What is the result? The destruction of some equal good.

WILLIAMS

When our first parents were driven out of Paradise, Adam is believed to have remarked to Eve: "My dear, we live in an age of transition."

DEAN INGE

The devil's boots don't creak.

SCOTTISH PROVERB

Leopards break into the temple and drink the sacrificial chalices dry; this occurs repeatedly, again and again: finally it can be reckoned upon beforehand and becomes part of the ceremony.

KAFKA

The devil never tempts us with more success than when he tempts us with a sight of our own good actions.

BISHOP WILSON

If evil did not make its dwelling in man, it would be much more evil than it is. Evil cannot be as evil as it wills to be because it is tied to man. Because it is in man, a watch is kept on evil. In man, the image of God, evil is constricted; it is there under custody as in a prison. The destructive power of evil would be unlimited if it were on earth alone, unsheltered by God's image. The earth is saved from destruction because, in God's image, a watch is kept upon evil.   PICARD

Many might go to Heaven with half the labor they go to Hell.

JONSON

The safest road to Hell is the gradual one—the gentle slope, soft underfoot, without sudden turnings, without milestones, without signposts.   C. S. LEWIS

When a man has gone astray to the point of perdition and is about to sink, his last speech, the sign, is: "And yet something better in me is being lost."   KIERKEGAARD

Only our concept of time makes it possible for us to speak of the Day of Judgment by that name; in reality it is a summary court in perpetual session.   KAFKA

It requires moral courage to grieve; it requires religious courage to rejoice.   KIERKEGAARD

In German the word *sein* signifies both things: to be, and to belong to Him.   KAFKA

[85]

Never let fear create the God of childhood; fear is the creation of a wicked spirit; shall the devil become the grandfather of God?   RICHTER

It always strikes me, and it is very peculiar, that, whenever we see the image of indescribable and unutterable desolation —of loneliness, poverty, and misery, the end and extreme of things—the thought of God comes into one's mind.

VAN GOGH

God offers to every mind its choice between truth and repose. Take which you please; you can never have both.   EMERSON

We have to believe in a God who is like the true God in everything, except that he does not exist, since we have not reached the point where God exists.   SIMONE WEIL

The more we understand individual things, the more we understand God.   SPINOZA

The finger of God never leaves identical fingerprints.   LEC

God gives Himself to men as powerful or as perfect—it is for them to choose.   SIMONE WEIL

The distance between the necessary and the good is the distance between the creature and the creator.

SIMONE WEIL

We always keep God waiting while we admit more importunate suitors.   CHAZAL

In a small house God has His corner, in a big house He has to stand in the hall.   SWEDISH PROVERB

There is not the least use preaching to anyone unless you chance to catch them ill.   SYDNEY SMITH

Prayer does not change God, but it changes him who prays.
                                        KIERKEGAARD

When the gods wish to punish us they answer our prayers.
                                        WILDE

What men usually ask of God when they pray is that two and two not make four.   ANONYMOUS

Oaths in anguish rank with prayers.   HODGSON

There are few men who dare publish to the world the prayers they make to Almighty God.   MONTAIGNE

If God bores you, tell Him that He bores you, that you prefer the vilest amusements to His presence, that you only feel at your ease when you are far from Him.   FÉNELON

My God, my God, though I be quite forgot,
Let me not love Thee if I love Thee not.
                                        HERBERT

O God, for as much as without Thee
We are not enabled to doubt Thee,
    Help us all by Thy grace
    To convince the whole race
It knows nothing whatever about Thee.

                                        ANONYMOUS

> That learning, thine Ambassador,
> From thine allegeance wee never tempt,
> That beauty, paradises flower
> For physicke made, from poyson be exempt,
> That wit, born apt high good to doe,
> By dwelling lazily
> On Natures nothing, be not nothing too,
> That our affections kill us not, nor dye,
> Heare us, weake ecchoes, O thou eare, and cry.
>
> DONNE

Make me chaste and continent, but not just yet.

SAINT AUGUSTINE

"Heaven help me," she prayed, "to be decorative and to do right." FIRBANK

God will provide—ah, if only He would till he does so!

YIDDISH PROVERB

Heaven is too much like Earth to be spoken of as it really is, lest the generality should think it like their Earth, which is Hell. PATMORE

The joys of this life are not its own, but our dread of ascending to a higher life; the torments of this life are not its own, but our self-torment because of that dread. KAFKA

The law imposed what it did not give. Grace gives what it imposes. PASCAL

All the passions produce prodigies. A gambler is capable of watching and fasting almost like a saint; he has his premonitions, etc. There is a great danger of loving God as the gambler loves his game. SIMONE WEIL

We should only do those righteous actions which we cannot stop ourselves from doing, which we are unable not to do, but, through well-directed attention, we should always keep on increasing the number of these actions which we are unable not to do.   SIMONE WEIL

Grace is indeed required to turn a man into a saint; and he who doubts this does not know what either a man or a saint is.
                                                                            PASCAL

Most saints in the past were created by the people in spite of the priests.   GOURMONT

Are you not scared by seeing that the gypsies are more attractive to us than the apostles?   EMERSON

There is a goal but no way; what we call the way is mere wavering.   KAFKA

The true way goes over a rope which is not stretched at any great height but just above the ground. It seems more designed to make people stumble than to be walked upon.
                                                                            KAFKA

There are countless places of refuge, there is only one place of salvation; but the possibilities of salvation, again, are as numerous as all the places of refuge.   KAFKA

Even the things you do after the flesh are spiritual.
                                                                    SAINT IGNATIUS

> Who sweeps a room as for Thy laws
> Makes that and the action fine.
>   HERBERT

While others talked about what they would do if they heard that they had to die within that very hour, Saint Charles Borromæus said he would continue his game of chess. For he had begun it only in honor of God, and he could wish for nothing better than to be called away in the midst of an action undertaken in the honor of God.　　FABER

If our worship is inward only, with our hearts and not our hats, something necessary is lacking.　　ANDREWES

Sunday should be different from another day. People may walk, but not throw stones at birds.　　DR. JOHNSON

The unproductive man is not a Christian, much less the Destroyer.　　BLAKE

Belief in the existence of other human beings as such is love.
　　SIMONE WEIL

Love makes everything lovely; hate concentrates itself on the one thing hated.　　MACDONALD

Love has but one word and it never repeats itself.
　　LACORDAIRE

Love does not make you weak, because it is the source of all strength, but it makes you see the nothingness of the illusory strength on which you depended before you knew it.
　　BLOY

You can hold back from the suffering of the world, you have free permission to do so, and it is in accordance with your nature, but perhaps this very holding back is the one suffering you could have avoided.　　KAFKA

The word of him who wishes to speak with men without speaking with God is not fulfilled; but the word of him who wishes to speak with God without speaking with men goes astray.   **BUBER**

We cannot know whether we love God, although there may be strong reasons for thinking so, but there can be no doubt about whether we love our neighbor or no.   **SAINT THERESA**

The majority of men are subjective toward themselves and objective toward all others, terribly objective sometimes, but the real task is in fact to be objective toward oneself and subjective toward all others.   **KIERKEGAARD**

Justice: to be ever ready to admit that another person is something quite different from what we read when he is there, or when we think about him. Or rather, to read in him that he is certainly something different, perhaps something completely different, from what we read in him.

Every being cries out to be read differently.   **SIMONE WEIL**

To be in a distressing and painful condition because of others is a thing we all naturally resent. Yet until we are willing to accept the mere fact without resentment we can hardly be said to admit that other people exist. We may reject, we may rebuke, we may contend against their action. But the very first condition of admitting that their existence is as real as our own is to allow that they have, as individuals, as much right to act in the way they decide as we have. They may be wicked and we good, or vice versa; that is a question of moral judgment, and therefore another question. The main fact is that we are compelled to admit their decision, and to admit that our lives, and often our deaths, depend on that.

WILLIAMS

To love our neighbor as ourselves does not mean that we should love all people equally, for I do not have an equal love for all the modes of existence of myself. Nor does it mean that we should never make them suffer, for I do not refuse to make myself suffer. But we should have with each person the relationship of one conception of the universe to another conception of the universe, and not to a part of it.

SIMONE WEIL

It is impossible to forgive whoever has done us harm if that harm has lowered us. We have to think that it has not lowered us but revealed our true level.   SIMONE WEIL

Whoever takes up the sword shall perish by the sword. And whoever does not take up the sword (or lets it go) shall perish on the cross.   SIMONE WEIL

One must not cheat anybody, not even the world of its triumph.   KAFKA

He eats the droppings from his own table; thus he manages to stuff himself fuller than the others for a little, but meanwhile he forgets how to eat from the table; thus in time even the droppings cease to fall.   KAFKA

> Each Man is in his Spectre's power
> Until the arrival of that hour,
> When his humanity awake
> And cast his own Spectre into the Lake.
>
> BLAKE

There is superstition in avoiding superstition: when men think to do best, if they go farthest from the superstition formerly received.   BACON

If the central cores of light, beauty, love, reason, power, and order could—as perhaps they can—be presented in form to the human faculties, man would discern in them mere blackness, monstrosity, fatuity, weakness, terror, and chaos. The hideousness of some of the images worshiped by those among the ancients who best understood the gods was not without its meaning.   PATMORE

Theory of the true civilization. It is not to be found in gas or steam or table turning. It consists in the diminution of the traces of original sin.   BAUDELAIRE

The preponderance of pain over pleasure is the cause of our fictitious morality and religion.   NIETZSCHE

NATURE

Nature

The creation was an act of mercy.   BLAKE

One real world is enough.   SANTAYANA

> The Atoms of Democritus
> And Newton's Particles of light
> Are sands upon the Red sea shore
> Where Israel's tents do shine so bright.
>
>   BLAKE

Things solely good can, in some circumstances, exist; things solely evil, never; for even those natures which are vitiated by an evil will, so far indeed as they are vitiated, are evil, but insofar as they are natures they are good.   SAINT AUGUSTINE

The world is the best of all possible worlds, and *everything* in it is a necessary evil.   BRADLEY

It can be shown that a mathematical web of some kind can be woven about any universe containing several objects. The fact that our universe lends itself to mathematical treatment is not a fact of any great philosophical significance.   RUSSELL

No region can include itself as well. WHITEHEAD

Time is a child playing a game of draughts; the kingship is in the hands of a child. HERACLITUS

There is no nature at an instant. WHITEHEAD

Nature uses as little as possible of anything. KEPLER

Nature has neither kernel nor shell; she is everything at once. GOETHE

There is nothing useless in nature; not even uselessness itself. MONTAIGNE

Inequality is the cause of all local movements. LEONARDO DA VINCI

Force is only a desire for flight: it lives by violence and dies from liberty. LEONARDO DA VINCI

Nature is full of infinite causes that have never occurred in experience. LEONARDO DA VINCI

In the physical world, one cannot increase the size or quantity of anything without changing its quality. Similar figures exist only in pure geometry. VALÉRY

There was no Omphalos, either in the center of the earth or of the sea. If any there be, it is visible to the gods, not visible to mortals. EPIMENIDES OF CRETE

In nature, a thing is often full of character because of the slightness of accentuation or even of character itself that, at the first glance, it appears to have. DELACROIX

Repetition is the only form of permanence that nature can achieve. SANTAYANA

The mere material world suggests to us no concepts of good or evil, because we can discern in it no system of grades of value. WHITEHEAD

How can we be so willfully blind as to look for causes in nature when nature herself is an effect? MAISTRE

Nature hath no goal though she hath law. DONNE

Nature never breaks her own laws. LEONARDO DA VINCI

What is a miracle? The natural law of a unique event. ROSENSTOCK-HUESSY

In nature there are neither rewards nor punishments; there are consequences. INGERSOLL

Nature is a hanging judge. ANONYMOUS

Men argue, nature acts. VOLTAIRE

Nature does not bestow virtue; to be good is an art. SENECA

If the Sun & Moon should doubt
They'd immediately Go out.

BLAKE

The sun and the moon and the stars would have disappeared
long ago . . . had they happened to be within the reach of
predatory human hands. ELLIS

If you go expressly to look at the moon, it becomes tinsel.

EMERSON

The ever-present phenomenon ceases to exist for our senses.
It was a city dweller, or a prisoner, or a blind man suddenly
given his sight, who first noted natural beauty. GOURMONT

If the stars should appear one night in a thousand years, how
would men believe and adore! EMERSON

The sky is the daily bread of the eyes. EMERSON

Noon: Light is taking its riding lesson. CHAZAL

Noon puts shadow to bed. CHAZAL

The night has no bedroom; it sleeps anywhere. CHAZAL

The afternoon knows what the morning never suspected.

SWEDISH PROVERB

Noon one may keep as one will, but evening sets in on its
own account. SWEDISH PROVERB

Light is half a companion.   GENOESE PROVERB

Colors are the deeds and sufferings of light.   GOETHE

Everything factual is, in a sense, theory. The blue of the sky exhibits the basic laws of chromatics. There is no sense in looking for something behind phenomena: they *are* theory.
    GOETHE

All colors are the friends of their neighbors and the lovers of their opposites.   CHAZAL

Water speaks in long syllables, air in short.   CHAZAL

The cistern contains: the fountain overflows.   BLAKE

Every mirror is false because it repeats something it has not witnessed.   CHAZAL

A mirror has no heart but plenty of ideas.   CHAZAL

No scent is a virgin.   CHAZAL

Every stink that fights the ventilator thinks it is Don Quixote.
    LEC

> Each mortal thing does one thing and the same:
> Deals out that being indoors each one dwells;
> Selves—goes itself; *myself* it speaks and spells,
> Crying *What I do is me: for that I came.*
    HOPKINS

[101]

How do we distinguish the oak from the beech, the horse from the ox, but by the bounding outline? How do we distinguish one face or countenance from another, but by the bounding line and its infinite inflections and movements? Leave out this line, and you leave out life itself; all is chaos again, and the line of the Almighty must be drawn out upon it before man or beast can exist.   BLAKE

Life is an offensive, directed against the repetitious mechanism of the universe.   WHITEHEAD

All that is alive tends toward color, individuality, specificity, effectiveness, and opacity: all that is done with life inclines toward knowledge, abstraction, generality, transfiguration, and transparency.   GOETHE

Life is the art of drawing sufficient conclusions from insufficient premises.   SAMUEL BUTLER (II)

All progress is based upon a universal, innate desire on the part of every organism to live beyond its income.
                    SAMUEL BUTLER (II)

Nature has wit, humor, fantasy, etc. Among animals and plants one finds natural caricatures. Nature is at her wittiest in the animal kingdom; there she is humorous throughout. The mineral and vegetable kingdoms bear more the stamp of fantasy: In the world of man, rational nature is bejeweled with fantasy and wit.   NOVALIS

It is remarkable, that in the circumscription and complication of many leaves, flowers, fruits, and seeds, nature affects a regular figure.   RAY

Heredity is nothing but stored environment.   BURBANK

As we manure the flowerbeds, for the plants, so they manure the air beds for us.   NOVALIS

Flowers have the glances of children and the mouths of old men.   CHAZAL

The flower in the vase still smiles, but no longer laughs.

CHAZAL

Flowers are tolerant and cosmopolitan. Animals strive for individual lordship.   NOVALIS

Are not plants, perhaps, the product of a feminine nature and a masculine spirit, animals the product of a masculine nature and a feminine spirit? Are not plants, as it were, the girls, animals the boys, of nature?   NOVALIS

We can divide animals into people with intelligence and people with talent. The dog and the elephant are people with intelligence; the nightingale and the silkworm, people of talent.   RIVAROL

The apple tree never asks the beech how he shall grow, nor the lion, the horse, how he shall take his prey.   BLAKE

No animal admires another animal.   PASCAL

Even a flea doesn't jump merely for joy.   LEC

One main factor in the upward trend of animal life has been the power of wandering. WHITEHEAD

Only the finest and most active animals are capable of boredom. A subject for a great poet—God's boredom on the seventh day of creation. NIETZSCHE

Eating is touch carried to the bitter end.

SAMUEL BUTLER (II)

All creatures obey the great game laws of nature and fish with nets of such meshes as permit many to escape and preclude the taking of many. COLERIDGE

Animal voices are only chinks in the silence. It is as though the animal were trying to tear open the silence with the force of its body. PICARD

No bird soars too high, if he soars with his own wings.

BLAKE

It is only cold-blooded animals whose bite is poisonous.

SCHOPENHAUER

A worm is as good a traveler as a grasshopper or a cricket, and a much wiser settler. THOREAU

The world was made to be inhabited by beasts, but studied and contemplated by man. BROWNE

Monkeys are superior to men in this: when a monkey looks into a mirror, he sees a monkey. CHAZAL

Monkeys . . . very sensibly refrain from speech, lest they should be set to earn their livings. GRAHAME

The polar bear and the tiger cannot fight.   FREUD

Swans have an air of being proud, stupid, and mischievous—three qualities that go well together.   DIDEROT

To be sure, the dog is loyal. But why, on that account, should we take him as an example? He is loyal to men, not to other dogs.   KRAUS

That man can interrogate as well as observe nature was a lesson slowly learned in his evolution.   OSLER

Nature is a labyrinth in which the very haste you move with will make you lose your way.   BACON

If nature be regarded as the teacher and we poor human beings as her pupils, the human race presents a very curious picture. We all sit together at a lecture and possess the necessary principles for understanding it, yet we always pay more attention to the chatter of our fellow students than to the lecturer's discourse. Or, if our neighbor copies something down, we sneak it from him, stealing what he may himself have heard imperfectly, and add to it our own errors of spelling and opinion.   LICHTENBERG

It is a false dichotomy to think of nature *and* man. Mankind is that factor *in* nature which exhibits in its most intense form the plasticity of nature.   WHITEHEAD

The reason why I prefer the society of nature to any other is that nature is always right and the error, if any, can only be on my side. But if I hold converse with men, they will err, then I will, and so on forever, and we never get to see matters clearly.   GOETHE

Without my work in natural science I should never have known human beings as they really are. In no other activity can one come so close to direct perception and clear thought, or realize so fully the errors of the senses, the mistakes of the intellect, the weaknesses and greatnesses of human character.

GOETHE

We don't see words in nature but always only the initial letters of words, and when we set out to spell, we find that the so-called new words are in their turn merely the initial letters of others.
LICHTENBERG

Only we who have erected the objectivity of a world of our own from what nature gives us, who have built it into the environment of nature so that we are protected from her, can look upon nature as something "objective." Without a world between man and nature, there is eternal movement, but no objectivity.
HANNAH ARENDT

Whatever the word "secular" is made to signify in current usage, historically it cannot be equated with worldliness. Modern man, when he lost the certainty of a world to come, was thrown back upon himself and not upon this world; far from believing that the world might be potentially immortal, he was not even sure that it was real.
HANNAH ARENDT

Once the concept of infinity has been taken seriously, a human dwelling can no longer be made of the universe. The universe can still be thought but it can no longer be imaged; the man who thinks it no longer really lives in it.
BUBER

The father of geology was he who, seeing fossil shells on a mountain, conceived the theory of the deluge.
SAMUEL BUTLER (II)

EDUCATION

Education

Education should be gentle and stern, not cold and lax.

JOUBERT

It is true that children pick up coarse expressions and bad manners in the company of servants; but in the drawing room they learn coarse ideas and bad feelings.   HERZEN

I am always . . . a great pedant with myself, and in the world as little a pedant as possible.   MAISTRE

What boy well raised can compare with your street gamin who has the knowledge and the shrewdness of a grown-up broker. But the Arab never becomes a man.   E. HUBBARD

Sexual enlightenment is justified insofar as girls cannot learn too soon how children do not come into the world.   KRAUS

Diogenes struck the father when the son swore.   BURTON

Most young men, when going through an "artistic" stage, find a guide and philosopher in some hoary sinner, an extinct celebrity who lives by sponging on his young friends—an actor who has lost his voice, or an artist whose hand is beginning to shake. Telemachus imitates his Mentor's pronunciation and his drinks, and especially his contempt for social problems and profound knowledge of gastronomy.　　HERZEN

The advice of their elders to young men is very apt to be as unreal as a list of the hundred best books.

O. W. HOLMES, JR.

The diploma gives society a phantom guarantee and its holders phantom rights. The holder of a diploma passes officially for possessing knowledge . . . comes to believe that society owes him something. Never has a convention been created which is more unfortunate for every one—the state, the individual (and, in particular, culture).　　VALÉRY

The surest way to corrupt a young man is to teach him to esteem more highly those who think alike than those who think differently.　　NIETZSCHE

You had better be a round peg in a square hole than a square peg in a square hole. The latter is in for life, while the first is only an indeterminate sentence.　　E. HUBBARD

The true teacher defends his pupils against his own personal influence.　　ALCOTT

A schoolmaster should have an atmosphere of awe, and walk wonderingly, as if he was amazed at being himself.

BAGEHOT

The gift of teaching is a peculiar talent, and implies a need and a craving in the teacher himself.　　CHAPMAN

The *Koran* is the educator's ideal: its pages simultaneously contain an example of writing, a model of style, a code of religion, and a handbook of morals.   GOURMONT

A true university can never rest upon the will of one man. A true university always rests upon the wills of many divergent-minded old gentlemen, who refuse to be disturbed, but who growl in their kennels.   CHAPMAN

The function of dons is to expound a few classic documents, and to hand down as large and pleasant a store as possible of academic habits, maxims, and anecdotes.   SANTAYANA

Nothing is so useless as a general maxim.   MACAULAY

Disciples do owe their masters only a temporary belief, and a suspension of their own judgment till they be fully instructed; and not an absolute resignation nor perpetual captivity.   BACON

The Socratic manner is not a game at which two can play.
          BEERBOHM

"For example" is not proof.   YIDDISH PROBERB

The eagle never lost so much time as when he submitted to learn of the crow.   BLAKE

Mediocre men often have the most acquired knowledge.
          BERNARD

Lessing's belief that he had read almost too much for his good sense shows how good his sense really was.   LICHTENBERG

We have rudiments of reverence for the human body, but we consider as nothing the rape of the human mind.

HOFFER

Ideals travel upward, manners downward.   BULWER-LYTTON

Reading means borrowing.   LICHTENBERG

The man of imagination and no culture has wings without feet.   JOUBERT

The cultivated often treat practical matters as the ignorant do books, quite without understanding.   JOUBERT

Knowledge without sense is double folly.   GRACIAN

One must learn to think well before learning to think; afterward it proves too difficult.   FRANCE

What does not destroy me, makes me stronger.   NIETZSCHE

The school of necessity is kept by a violent mistress.

MONTAIGNE

The more a work is admired, the more beautiful it grows for the multitude.   GOURMONT

We live less and less and learn more and more. I have seen a man laughed at for examining a dead leaf attentively and with pleasure. No one would have laughed to hear a string of botanical terms muttered over it. GOURMONT

Ignorance is not so damnable as humbug, but when it prescribes pills it may happen to do more harm.

GEORGE ELIOT

The stupider the peasant, the better the horse understands him. CHEKHOV

When I take up the end of the web, and find it pack-thread, I do not expect by looking further to find embroidery.

DR. JOHNSON

Some people will never learn anything, for this reason, because they understand everything too soon. POPE

How is it possible to expect that mankind will take advice, when they will not so much as take warning? SWIFT

Those who know the least obey the best. FARQUHAR

When a thing ceases to be a subject of controversy, it ceases to be a subject of interest. HAZLITT

Reformers are those who educate people to appreciate what they need. E. HUBBARD

Civilized man's brain is a museum of contradictory truths.

GOURMONT

Great men's errors are to be venerated as more fruitful than little men's truths. NIETZSCHE

It is as necessary, or rather more necessary, for most men to know how to take mice, than how to take elephants.
TOPSELL

Expect poison from the standing water. BLAKE

He who desires but acts not, breds pestilence. BLAKE

Sooner murder an infant in its cradle than nurse unacted desires. BLAKE

The soul lives by avoiding what it dies by affecting.
SAINT AUGUSTINE

There is more than one way of sacrificing to the fallen angels.
SAINT AUGUSTINE

Other sins find their vent in the accomplishment of evil deeds, whereas pride lies in wait for good deeds to destroy them.
SAINT AUGUSTINE

Love slays what we have been that we may be what we were not. SAINT AUGUSTINE

Where everything is bad it must be good to know the worst.
BRADLEY

He who knows how to be poor knows everything.
MICHELET

[114]

To most men, experience is like the stern lights of a ship, which illumine only the track it has passed.   COLERIDGE

Those who have endeavored to teach us to die well, have taught few to die willingly.   DR. JOHNSON

How people keep correcting us when we are young! There's always some bad habit or other they tell us we ought to get over. Yet most bad habits are tools to help us through life.
                                                           GOETHE

You teach your daughters the diameters of the planets, and wonder when you have done that they do not delight in your company.   DR. JOHNSON

In later life as in earlier, only a few persons influence the formation of our character; the multitude pass us by like a distant army. One friend, one teacher, one beloved, one club, one dining table, one work table, are the means by which his nation and the spirit of his nation affect the individual.

                                                           RICHTER

Our disciples never forgive us if we take sides against ourselves, for, in their eyes, this means not only that we have rejected their love but also exposed their judgment.

                                                           NIETZSCHE

Like Leporello, learned men keep a list, but the point is what they lack; while Don Juan seduces girls and enjoys himself, Leporello notes down the time, the place, and a description of the girl.   KIERKEGAARD

The first book of Moses cites as one of the distinctive marks of man: to give animals names. Now it is characteristic of the ordinary man, the man of the people, to have that gift. If the ordinary man sees a bird for some years, which is not normally seen, he immediately gives it a name, and a characteristic name. But take ten learned men and how incapable they are of finding a name. What a satire on them when one reads scientific works and sees the names which come from the people, and then the silly miserable names when once in a while a learned man has to think of a name. Usually they can think of nothing better than calling the animal or the plant after their own names.   KIERKEGAARD

SOCIETY

The Drawing Room

To establish oneself in the world, one does all one can to
seem established there already.   LA ROCHEFOUCAULD

I love good creditable acquaintance; I love to be the worst
of the company.   SWIFT

How convenient it would be to many of our great . . .
families of doubtful origin could they have the privilege of the
heroes of yore who, whenever their origin was involved in
obscurity, modestly announced themselves descended from a
god.   IRVING

Most noblemen call to mind their ancestors, the way a
cicerone in Italy recalls Cicero.   CHAMFORT

Good families are generally worse than any others.   HOPE

The virtues of society are vices of the saint.   EMERSON

The great with their long arms often do less damage than
their lackeys with short ones.   LICHTENBERG

There are two large sections to society: those with more dinners than appetite, those with more appetite than dinners.

CHAMFORT

The highest qualities often unfit a man for society. We don't take ingots with us to market, we take silver or small change.

CHAMFORT

He . . . met every kind of person except the ordinary person. He knew everybody, so to speak, except everybody.

CHESTERTON

The great, terrible, important powers of the world, like social caste and religious domination, always rest on secrets. A man is born on the wrong side of the street and can therefore never enter into certain drawing rooms, even though he be in every way superior to everyone in those drawing rooms. When you try to find out what the difference is between him and the rest, and why he is accursed, you find that the reason is a secret. It is a secret that a certain kind of straw hat is damnable. Little boys know these things about other little boys. The world is written over with mysterious tramp-languages and symbols of Masonic hieroglyphics.   CHAPMAN

Academic and aristocratic people live in such an uncommon atmosphere that common sense can rarely reach them.

SAMUEL BUTLER (II)

Lady Kent articled with Sir Edward Herbert that he should come to her when she sent for him; and stay with her as long as she would have him, to which he set his hand; then he articled with her that he should go away when he pleased, and stay away as long as he pleased, to which she set her hand. This is the epitome of all the contracts in the world.

SELDEN

'Tis from high life high characters are drawn;
A saint in crape is twice a saint in lawn.

POPE

Whatever people may say, the fastidious formal manner of the upper classes is preferable to the slovenly easygoing behavior of the common middle class. In moments of crisis, the former know how to act, the latter become uncouth brutes.

PAVESE

Society is like sex in that no one knows what perversions it can develop once aesthetic considerations are allowed to dictate its choices.

PROUST

Necessity is the constant scourge of the lower classes, ennui of the higher ones.

SCHOPENHAUER

Life at court does not satisfy a man, but it keeps him from being satisfied with anything else.

LA BRUYÈRE

People in high life are hardened to the wants and distresses of mankind as surgeons are to their bodily pains.

CHESTERFIELD

Men of letters are often criticized for not going out into society. . . . People expect them to be forever present at a lottery in which they hold no ticket.

CHAMFORT

Snobbery is a grave disease, but it is localized and so does not utterly destroy the soul.

PROUST

Without the aid of prejudice and custom, I should not be able to find my way across the room.

HAZLITT

There are no persons more solicitous about the preservation of rank than those who have no rank at all. . . . You will find no court in Christendom so ceremonious as the quality of Brentford.   SHENSTONE

An aristocrat among hounds will snarl at beggars,
                                                but then
Your true democratic lurcher snaps at
                                silk-stockinged men.
                                                    GOETHE

Ladies and gentlemen are permitted to have friends in the kennel, but not in the kitchen.   SHAW

Solitude is impracticable, and society fatal.   EMERSON

There are bad manners everywhere, but an aristocracy is bad manners organized.   HENRY JAMES

It seldom pays to be rude. It never pays to be only half rude.
                                                    DOUGLAS

Society is like the air, necessary to breathe, but insufficient to live on.   SANTAYANA

Fortune rarely accompanies any one to the door.   GRACIAN

Punctuality is the thief of time.   WILDE

You can force anything upon society in the way of entertainment except the consistent pursuit of a topic.   GOETHE

Without discussion, intellectual experience is only an exercise in a private gymnasium. BOURNE

Questioning is not the mode of conversation among gentlemen. DR. JOHNSON

Constant popping off of proverbs will make thee a byword thyself. DR. FULLER

Beware of telling an improbable truth. DR. FULLER

That we seldom repent of talking too little and very often of talking too much is a . . . maxim that everybody knows and nobody practices. LA BRUYÈRE

He who praises everybody praises nobody. DR. JOHNSON

Never trust a man who speaks well of everybody. COLLINS

A flatterer must not lose his temper. YIDDISH PROVERB

People not used to the world . . . are unskillful enough to show what they have sense enough not to tell.

CHESTERFIELD

It is only shallow people who do not judge by appearances.

WILDE

Were it not for bunglers in the manner of doing it, hardly any man would ever find out he was laughed at. HALIFAX

If I blunder, everyone can notice it; not so, if I lie.

GOETHE

Who lies for you will lie against you.   BOSNIAN PROVERB

The cruelest lies are often told in silence.   STEVENSON

There are no secrets better kept than the secrets that everybody guesses.   SHAW

A man who tells nothing, or who tells all, will equally have nothing told him.   CHESTERFIELD

The secret of being a bore is to tell everything.   VOLTAIRE

We are almost always bored by just those whom we must not find boring.   LA ROCHEFOUCAULD

There is no bore like a clever bore.   SAMUEL BUTLER (II)

There is a freemasonry among the dull by which they recognize and are sociable with the dull, as surely as a correspondent tact in men of genius.   EMERSON

The worst part of an eminent man's conversation is, nine times out of ten, to be found in that part which he means to be clever.   BULWER-LYTTON

The most intolerable people are provincial celebrities.

CHEKHOV

Those who are contemptuous of everyone are more than anyone terrified of contempt.   L. P. SMITH

The greatest mistake is the trying to be more agreeable than you can be.   BAGEHOT

A vain man can never be utterly ruthless: he wants to win applause and therefore he accommodates himself to others.
          GOETHE

Modesty is the only sure bait when you angle for praise.
          CHESTERFIELD

If you will please people, you must please them in their own way.   CHESTERFIELD

The excessive desire of pleasing goes along almost always with the apprehension of not being liked.   DR. FULLER

If a person has no delicacy, he has you in his power.
          HAZLITT

She was not quite what you would call refined. She was not quite what you would call unrefined. She was the kind of person that keeps a parrot.   MARK TWAIN

The more things a man is ashamed of, the more respectable he is.   SHAW

Where it is customary, the cow is put to bed.
          SWISS PROVERB

Men of genius are rarely much annoyed by the company of vulgar people. COLERIDGE

Barbarism and rusticity may perhaps be instructed, but false refinement is incorrigible. HAZLITT

A fashion is nothing but an induced epidemic. SHAW

Only God helps the badly dressed. SPANISH PROVERB

The fashion wears out more apparel than the man.
SHAKESPEARE

Fashion is gentility running away from vulgarity, and afraid of being overtaken. HAZLITT

Never whisper to the deaf or wink at the blind.
SLOVENIAN PROVERB

I always treat fools and coxcombs with great ceremony; true good breeding not being a sufficient barrier against them.
CHESTERFIELD

The three rudenesses of this world: youth mocking at age, health mocking at sickness, a wise man mocking a fool.
ANONYMOUS (tr. from Irish by T. Kinsella)

We are less hurt by the contempt of fools than by the luke-warm approval of men of intelligence. VAUVENARGUES

Savages are fops and fribbles more than any other men.
BLAKE

The greatest advantage I know of being thought a wit by the world is that it gives me the greater freedom of playing the fool.   POPE

A fool who has a brief flash of wit both shocks and amazes us, like a cab horse at a gallop.   CHAMFORT

Arguments are to be avoided: they are always vulgar and often convincing.   WILDE

There is no such test of a man's superiority of character as in the well-conducting of an unavoidable quarrel.
                                                        SIR HENRY TAYLOR

Many promising reconciliations have broken down because, while both parties came prepared to forgive, neither party came prepared to be forgiven.   WILLIAMS

Nothing is more common than mutual dislike, where mutual approbation is particularly expected.   DR. JOHNSON

A man who is sure to cause injuries to be done to him wherever he goes is almost as great an evil and inconvenience as if he were himself the wrongdoer.   SIR HENRY TAYLOR

Mrs. Montagu has dropped me. Now, sir, there are people whom one should like very well to drop, but would not wish to be dropped by.   DR. JOHNSON

People count up the faults of those who are keeping them waiting.   FRENCH PROVERB

If he really does think that there is no distinction between virtue and vice, why, sir, when he leaves our house, let us count our spoons. DR. JOHNSON

The louder he talked of his honor, the faster we counted our spoons. EMERSON

A guest sticks a nail in the wall even if he stays but one night. POLISH PROVERB

Learn how to refuse favors. This is a great and very useful art. DR. FULLER

Do not love your neighbor as yourself. If you are on good terms with yourself, it is an impertinence; if on bad, an injury. SHAW

Our life is based upon the mutual interpenetration of play and earnest. So long as this happens, we live in peace. In a catastrophe the mixture is lacking, just as it is in the play of children. Catastrophe and child's play are the two poles of all social life. ROSENSTOCK-HUESSY

Civilized people have more time than they have life: idle time gives birth to idle thoughts. ROSENSTOCK-HUESSY

Civilizations can only be understood by those who are civilized. WHITEHEAD

Civilization, properly so called, might well be termed the organization of all those faculties that resist the mere excitement of sport. WILLIAM JAMES

The people I respect must behave as if they were immortal and as if society were eternal. Both assumptions are false: both of them must be accepted as true if we are to go on working and eating and loving, and are to keep open a few breathing holes for the human spirit.   FORSTER

Between cultivated minds the first interview is the best.
                                             EMERSON

All culture and art, and the best social order, are fruits of unsocial impulses, which compel one another to discipline themselves.   KANT

Nine times out of ten, the coarse word is the word that condemns an evil and the refined word the word that excuses it.   CHESTERTON

On how many people's libraries, as on bottles from the drugstore, one might write: "For external use only."   DAUDET

How awful to reflect that what people say of us is true!
                                          L. P. SMITH

Scandal is gossip made tedious by morality.   WILDE

Gossip is none the less gossip because it comes from venerable antiquity.   BISHOP CREIGHTON

Among the smaller duties of life I hardly know any one more important than that of not praising where praise is not due.
                                        SYDNEY SMITH

No siren did ever so charm the ear of the listener as the listening ear has charmed the soul of the siren.

SIR HENRY TAYLOR

If the commending others well, did not recommend ourselves, there would be few panegyrics.   HALIFAX

He is not praised whose praiser deserveth not praise.

HARVEY

It is false praise of a man when we say of him, on his entry, that he is a very clever poet; and it is a bad sign when a man is not asked to give his judgment on some verses.   PASCAL

Either a good or a bad reputation outruns and gets before people wherever they go.   CHESTERFIELD

Who has once the fame to be an early riser may sleep till noon.   HOWELL

Fame is something which must be won; honor is something which must not be lost.   SCHOPENHAUER

Glory: to become a literary theme, or a common noun, or an epithet.   VALÉRY

The final test of fame is to have a crazy person imagine he is you.   ANONYMOUS

Popularity is a crime from the moment it is sought; it is only a virtue where men have it whether they will or no.

HALIFAX

The delicious mixture of grace and *gaucherie* that touches the heart and clings to the memory.   SICKERT

In nothing do we lay ourselves so open as in our manner of meeting and salutation.   LAVATER

I live in the crowd of jollity, not so much to enjoy company as to shun myself.   DR. JOHNSON

By that time men are fit for company, they see the objections to it.   HALIFAX

One learns taciturnity best among people without it, and loquacity among the taciturn.   RICHTER

You could read Kant by yourself, if you wanted to; but you must share a joke with someone else.   STEVENSON

When people talk to me about the weather, I always feel they mean something else.   WILDE

Nothing seems to me so inane as bookish language in conversation.   STENDHAL

When we talk in company we lose our unique tone of voice, and this leads us to make statements which in no way correspond to our real thoughts.   NIETZSCHE

A nice person sits bodkin, never stops the bottle, always knows the day of the month and the name of everybody at table.
                                                         SYDNEY SMITH

Scoundrels are always sociable.   SCHOPENHAUER

Watch the faces of those who bow low.   POLISH PROVERB

There is no feast without cruelty.   NIETZSCHE

There is no such thing as a feast "without gods"—whether
it be a carnival or a marriage.   PIEPER

A hotel isn't like home, but it's better than being a house
guest.   FEATHER

Everyone, even the richest and most munificent of men, pays
much by check more lightheartedly then he pays little in
specie.   BEERBOHM

There are occasions on which all apology is rudeness.
                                                DR. JOHNSON

If I have said something to hurt a man once, I shall not get
the better of this by saying many things to please him.
                                                DR. JOHNSON

To praise princes for virtues they are lacking in is a way
of insulting them with impunity.   LA ROCHEFOUCAULD

To address an abdicated monarch is a nice point of breeding.
To give him his lost titles is to mock him; to withhold 'em
is to wound him.   LAMB

To quicken the memory of past kindness thou hast done to
anyone is a very nice point to manage.   DR. FULLER

Good manners are made up of petty sacrifices.   EMERSON

Politeness . . . is fictitious benevolence.   DR. JOHNSON

What once were vices are now manners.   SENECA

He was so generally civil that nobody thanked him for it.
DR. JOHNSON

It is superstitious to put one's faith in conventions; but it is arrogant to be unwilling to submit to them.   PASCAL

The lines of humanity and urbanity never coincide.
LICHTENBERG

People who have given us their complete confidence believe that they have a right to ours. The inference is false: a gift confers no rights.   NIETZSCHE

Certainly it is untrue that three is no company. Three is splendid company. But if you reject the proverb altogether; if you say that two and three are the same sort of company, then you shall have no company either of two or three, but shall be alone in a howling desert till you die.
CHESTERTON

Many get the name for being witty, only to lose the credit of being sensible.   GRACIAN

A wise man will live as much within his wit as his income.
CHESTERFIELD

Going away, I can generally bear the separation, but I don't like the leave-taking.   SAMUEL BUTLER (II)

We're too unseparate. And going home
From company means coming to our senses.

FROST

He who does not enjoy solitude will not love freedom.

SCHOPENHAUER

There is hardly any man so strict as not to vary a little from
truth when he is to make an excuse.   HALIFAX

It is never any good dwelling on good-bys. It is not the being
together that it prolongs, it is the parting.

ELIZABETH BIBESCO

The falling of a teacup puts us out of temper for a day; and
a quarrel that commenced about the pattern of a gown may
end only with our lives.   HAZLITT

The Market Place

Everybody is a bit right; nobody is completely right or completely wrong. The prevalence of this point of view among
all decent people nearly always has the same dreadful result
for, according to their doctrine, every time a contemporary is
quite right, he must be crucified. They can never forgive him
because he denies their dogma; worse still, he reveals that
they hold another dogma which they conceal. The unavowed
dogma of these diffusionists runs as follows. The truth is

everywhere and nowhere; it evolves itself without anyone knowing it, as if, in the end, Judas is just as right as Jesus. One can read that Jesus incited Judas, according to the maxim: "It is not the murderer but his victim who is guilty." Judas and Jesus must be "synthesized"; both are "only" human: all men are swine. ROSENSTOCK-HUESSY

City air makes free. ANONYMOUS

In the city, time becomes visible. MUMFORD

We do not worry about being respected in the towns through which we pass. But if we are going to remain in one for a certain time, we do worry. How long does this time have to be? PASCAL

The little stations are very proud because the expresses have to pass them by. KRAUS

So much are the modes of excellence settled by time and place, that men may be heard boasting in one street of that which they would anxiously conceal in another. DR. JOHNSON

No place in England where everyone can go is considered respectable. GEORGE MOORE

As a rule, people who read much in the street don't read much at home. LICHTENBERG

Worldly faces never look so worldly as at a funeral. GEORGE ELIOT

There is something which has never been seen yet, and which, to all appearances, never will be, and that is a little town which isn't divided into cliques, where the families are united, and the cousins trust each other; where a marriage doesn't start a civil war, and where quarrels about precedence don't arise every time a service, a ceremony, a procession, or a funeral are held; where gossip and lying and malice have been outlawed; where the landlord and the corporation are on speaking terms, or the ratepayers and their assessors; where the dean is friendly with the canons, and the canons don't despise the chaplains, and the chaplains tolerate the men in the choir.　　　　　　　　　　　　　　　　　LA BRUYÈRE

A crowd is not company, and faces are but a gallery of pictures, and talk but a tinkling cymbal, where there is no love.

　　　　　　　　　　　　　　　　　　　　　　　　BACON

The tyrant and the mob, the grandfather and the grandchild, are natural allies.　　　　　　　　　SCHOPENHAUER

A university does great things, but there is one thing it does not do: it does not intellectualize its neighborhood.

　　　　　　　　　　　　　　　　　　　　　　　　NEWMAN

Reformers have long observed city people loitering on busy corners, hanging around in candy stores and bars and drinking soda pop on stoops, and have passed a judgment, the gist of which is: "This is deplorable! If these people had decent homes and a more private or bosky outdoor place, they wouldn't be on the street!"

This judgment represents a profound misunderstanding of cities. It makes no more sense than to drop in at a testimonial banquet in a hotel and conclude that if these people had wives who could cook, they would give their parties at home.

The point of both the testimonial banquet and the social life of city street walks is precisely that they are public. They bring together people who do not know each other in an intimate, private social fashion, and in most cases do not care to know each other in that fashion.

Nobody can keep open house in a great city. Nobody wants to. And yet if interesting, useful, and significant contacts among the people of cities are confined to acquaintanceships suitable for private life, the city becomes stultified. Cities are full of people with whom a certain degree of contact is useful and enjoyable, but you do not want them in your hair. And they do not want you in theirs either. JANE JACOBS

There exist labor songs, but no work songs. The songs of the craftsman are social; they are sung after work.

HANNAH ARENDT

The beginning of error may be, and mostly is, from private persons, but the maintainer and continuer of error is the multitude. HALES

When are men most useless, would you say?
When they can't command and can't obey.

GOETHE

Work is of two kinds: first, altering the position of matter at or near the earth's surface relatively to other such matter; second, telling other people to do so. The first kind is unpleasant and ill paid; the second is pleasant and highly paid.

RUSSELL

To get an idea of our fellow countrymen's miseries, we have only to take a look at their pleasures. GEORGE ELIOT

From someone else's cart you have to get off halfway.

POLISH PROVERB

[137]

The young can bear solitude better than the old, for their passions occupy their thoughts. LA BRUYÈRE

One can acquire everything in solitude except character. STENDHAL

Solitude is dangerous to reason, without being favorable to virtue. DR. JOHNSON

Men that cannot entertain themselves want somebody, though they care for nobody. HALIFAX

Man is a gregarious animal, and much more so in his mind than in his body. He may like to go alone for a walk, but he hates to stand alone in his opinions. SANTAYANA

All men's misfortunes spring from their hatred of being alone. LA BRUYÈRE

Better be quarreling than lonesome. IRISH PROVERB

Consolation, for the condemned, is to be one of many. ITALIAN PROVERB

Crowds are comforting to those who are physically dissatisfied with themselves. CHAZAL

There are people whose position in life is that of the interjection, without influence on the sentence—they are the hermits of life, and at the very most take a case, e.g., *O! me miserum.* KIERKEGAARD

Fresh air and innocence are good if you don't take too much of them—but I always remember that most of the achievements and pleasures of life are in bad air.   O. W. HOLMES, JR.

Men always talk about the most important things to perfect strangers. In the perfect stranger we perceive man himself; the image of God is not disguised by resemblances to an uncle or doubts of the wisdom of a mustache.   CHESTERTON

There are many who dare not kill themselves for fear of what the neighbors will say.   CONNOLLY

Each social class has its own pathology.   PROUST

Society is a sort of organism on the growth of which conscious efforts can exercise little effect.   MARX

The minority is sometimes right; the majority always wrong.
     SHAW

Man is constrained to be more or less social by his mode of propagation.   SANTAYANA

Man seeks to acquire a rank among his fellow men, whom he detests, but without whom he cannot live.   KANT

A man that should call everything by its right name would hardly pass the streets without being knocked down as a common enemy.   HALIFAX

The world is neither wise nor just, but it makes up for all its folly and injustice by being damnably sentimental.
     T. H. HUXLEY

In a tavern everybody puts on airs except the landlord.

EMERSON

When we cast off the yoke of public opinion, it is seldom to rise above it, but almost always to fall below.   CHAMFORT

Men carry their character not seldom in their pockets: you might decide on more than half of your acquaintance, had you will or right to turn their pockets inside out.   LAVATER

So long as there is any subject which men may not freely discuss, they are timid upon all subjects.   CHAPMAN

I have seen gross intolerance shown in support of tolerance.

COLERIDGE

Injustice is relatively easy to bear; it is justice that hurts.

MENCKEN

No one looks at the blazing sun; all do when it is eclipsed.

GRACIAN

Humanity is composed but of two categories, the invalids and the nurses.   SICKERT

Pity is for the living, envy is for the dead.   MARK TWAIN

It is a good thing Heaven has not given us the power to alter our bodies as much as we would like to and as much as our theories might happen to require. One man would cover himself with eyes, another with sexual organs, a third with ears, etc.   LICHTENBERG

Do not do unto others as you would that they should do unto you. Their tastes may not be the same.   SHAW

A sense of duty is useful in work but offensive in personal relations.   RUSSELL

Perhaps every man is at heart a log-roller.   SICKERT

People may come to do anything almost, by talking of it.
                                                                                        DR. JOHNSON

In quarreling, the truth is always lost.   PUBLILIUS SYRUS

Most people are good only so long as they believe others to be so.   HEBBEL

In relation to each other men are like irregular verbs in different languages; nearly all verbs are slightly irregular.
                                                                                        KIERKEGAARD

Cut off from the worship of the divine, leisure becomes laziness and work inhuman.   PIEPER

There can be no such thing in the world of total labor as space which is not used *on principle*, no such thing as a plot of ground or a period of time withdrawn from *use*.   PIEPER

I hold that there is every variety of natural capacity, from the idiot to Newton and Shakespeare; the mass of mankind, midway between these extremes, being blockheads of different degrees: education leaving them pretty nearly as it found them, with this single difference, that it gives a fixed direction to their stupidity, a sort of incurable wry-neck to the thing they call understanding. So one nose points always east, another always west, and each is ready to swear that it points due north.   PEACOCK

That which everybody guards will soon disappear.

POLISH PROVERB

Men do not change their characters by uniting with one another, nor does their patience in the presence of obstacles increase with their strength.   TOCQUEVILLE

Truly decent people only exist among men with definite convictions, whether conservative or radical; so-called moderates are much drawn to rewards, orders, commissions, promotions.

CHEKHOV

Nations are like men; they love that which flatters their passions even more than that which serves their interests.

TOCQUEVILLE

The principle of self-interest rightly understood produces no great acts of self-sacrifice, but it suggests daily small acts of self-denial. By itself it cannot suffice to make a man virtuous; but it disciplines a number of persons in habits of regularity, temperance, moderation, foresight, self-command; and, if it does not lead men straight to virtue by the will, it gradually draws them in that direction by their habits. Observe some few individuals, they are lowered by it; survey mankind, it is raised.   TOCQUEVILLE

All *essential* production is for the mouth; and is finally measured by the mouth. The want of any clear insight of this fact is the capital error, issuing in rich interest and revenue of error among the political economists. Their minds are continually set on money gain, not on mouth gain.

RUSKIN

Every society rests on the death of men.   O. W. HOLMES, JR.

Divided duties are seldom split in the middle.   HASKINS

Cases of injustice, and oppression, and tyranny, and the most extravagant bigotry are in constant occurrence among us every day. It is the custom to trumpet forth much wonder and astonishment at the chief actors, therein setting at defiance so completely the opinion of the world; but there is no greater fallacy; it is precisely because they do consult the opinion of their own little world that such things take place at all, and strike the great world dumb with astonishment.

DICKENS

The universal demand for happiness and the widespread unhappiness in our society (and these are but two sides of the same coin) are among the most persuasive signs that we have begun to live in a labor society which lacks enough laboring to keep it contented. For only the *animal laborans,* and neither the craftsman nor the man of action, has ever demanded to be "happy" or thought that mortal man could be happy.

HANNAH ARENDT

In the "social order" one is the worker, and nine are idlers.

ROZINOV

Seek to oppress [men] and it is sometimes a proof of regarding them with esteem; depreciate their customs, it is always a mark of contempt.

MONTESQUIEU

Not sixteen per cent of the human race is, or ever has been, engaged in any of the kinds of activity at which they excel.

MAIRET

The difference between a slave and a citizen is that a slave is subject to his master and a citizen to the laws. It may happen that the master is very gentle and the laws very harsh: that changes nothing. Everything lies in the distance between caprice and rule.

SIMONE WEIL

[143]

Servitude degrades men even to making them love it.

VAUVENARGUES

It has always been true that the men who were defending Western ideals were bound to be in alliance with men who intended to defend only Western interests.   BUTTERFIELD

The longing to be primitive is a disease of culture; it is archaism in morals. To be so preoccupied with vitality is a symptom of anemia.   SANTAYANA

With the peasant, general custom holds the place of individual feeling.   RIEHL

The temptations of the wilderness are those of the flesh; the temptations of civilization those of the mind.

ROSENSTOCK-HUESSY

What is culture? To know what concerns one, and to know what it concerns one to know.   HOFMANNSTHAL

When one despairs of any form of life, the first solution which always occurs, as though by a mechanically dialectic impulse of the human mind, the most obvious, the simplest, is to turn all values inside out. If wealth does not give happiness, poverty will; if learning does not solve everything, then true wisdom will lie in ignorance.   ORTEGA Y GASSET

Belief in progress is a doctrine of idlers and Belgians. It is the individual relying upon his neighbors to do his work.

BAUDELAIRE

A man should be just cultured enough to be able to look with suspicion upon culture at first, not second, hand.

SAMUEL BUTLER (II)

Rome owed much of her patriotism to her many festivals.
RICHTER

One got the impression that the intellectual life of the country [England] was "hobbyized," that ideas were taken as sports, just as sports were taken as serious issues. BOURNE

If we tried to say that what governs [the Englishman] is convention, we should have to ask . . . where else would a man inform you, with a sort of proud challenge, that he lived on nuts, or was in correspondence through a medium with Sir Joshua Reynolds, or had been disgustingly housed when last in prison. SANTAYANA

Civilization aims at making all good things . . . accessible even to cowards. NIETZSCHE

Perhaps, for worldly success, we need virtues that make us loved and faults that make us feared. JOUBERT

Men are more ready to offend one who desires to be beloved than one who wishes to be feared. MACHIAVELLI

Men are never attached to you by favors. NAPOLEON

"Forgive us our virtues." That is what we should ask of our neighbors. NIETZSCHE

It is on seldom frequented paths that one risks meeting ugly characters. The rule does not apply to the path of virtue.
ANONYMOUS

Virtue, as such, naturally procures considerable advantages to the virtuous.   JOSEPH BUTLER

Virtues, like essences, lose their fragrance when exposed.
                                                            SHENSTONE

Innocence itself sometimes hath need of a mask.
                                                      ENGLISH PROVERB

Integrity is praised and starves.   JUVENAL

I am not sure just what the unpardonable sin is, but I believe it is a disposition to evade the payment of small bills.
                                                            E. HUBBARD

I have found men more kind than I expected, and less just.
                                                          DR. JOHNSON

If you're naturally kind you attract a lot of people you don't like.   FEATHER

One can always be kind to people about whom one cares nothing.   WILDE

Such is a very good man's face that people think him a detective.   CHEKHOV

In the world a man will often be reputed to be a man of sense, only because he is not a man of talent.
                                                        SIR HENRY TAYLOR

There are people who think that everything one does with a serious face is sensible.   LICHTENBERG

Those who are fond of setting things to rights have no great objection to seeing them wrong.　　　HAZLITT

You will not become a saint through other people's sins.
　　　CHEKHOV

Some have been thought brave because they were afraid to run away.　　　THOMAS FULLER

Protest long enough that you are right, and you will be wrong.
　　　YIDDISH PROVERB

Every hero becomes a bore at last.　　　EMERSON

Nothing is truer in a sense than a funeral oration: it tells precisely what the dead man should have been.
　　　VAPEREAU

Nothing is more original, more *oneself* than to be nourished by others; only one must be able to digest them.　　　VALÉRY

It is very disagreeable to seem reserved, and very dangerous not to be.　　　CHESTERFIELD

One must judge men, not by their opinions, but by what their opinions have made of them.　　　LICHTENBERG

Those who come first are the heirs of Fame; the others get only a younger brother's allowance.　　　GRACIAN

Fame is the beginning of the *fall* of greatness.　　　ROZINOV

In this age, when it is said of a man, He knows how to live, it may be implied he is not very honest. HALIFAX

There is a cunning . . . which is, when that which a man says to another, he says it as if another had said it to him. BACON

The lie is a condition of life. NIETZSCHE

A liar begins with making falsehood appear like truth, and ends with making truth itself appear like falsehood. SHENSTONE

Clever liars give details, but the cleverest don't. ANONYMOUS

Gravity is of the very essence of imposture. SHAFTESBURY

A really accomplished impostor is the most wretched of geniuses: he is a Napoleon on a desert island. CHESTERTON

Knaves have always a certain need of their honor, somewhat as police spies are paid less when they move in less good company. CHAMFORT

In baiting a mouse trap with cheese, always leave room for the mouse. SAKI

Charlatans are generally sublime. ROZINOV

He who fondles you more than usual has either deceived you or wants to do so. FRENCH PROVERB

There are some occasions when a man must tell half his secret, in order to conceal the rest.   CHESTERFIELD

It is usually where but little is involved that we gamble on not trusting to appearances.   LA ROCHEFOUCAULD

Just as those who practice the same profession recognize each other instinctively, so do those who practice the same vice.
                                                    PROUST

He who cannot love must learn to flatter.   GOETHE

A flatterer doesn't sufficiently value either himself or others.
                                                    LA BRUYÈRE

He who greatly excels in beauty, strength, birth, or wealth, and he, on the other hand, who is very poor, or very weak, or very disgraced, find it difficult to follow rational principles. Of these two, the one sort grows into violent and great criminals, the other into rogues and petty rascals.
                                                    ARISTOTLE

When you find three young cads and idiots going about together and getting drunk together every day, you generally find that one of the three cads and idiots is (for some extraordinary reason) not a cad and not an idiot.   CHESTERTON

Always be ready to speak your mind, and a base man will avoid you.   BLAKE

Cursing, swearing, reviling, and the like do not signify as speech but as the actions of a tongue accustomed.   HOBBES

Take care how thou offendest men raised from low condition.
THOMAS FULLER

A man cannot be too careful in the choice of his enemies.
WILDE

Better make a weak man your enemy than your friend.
BILLINGS

To imitate one's enemy is to dishonor.   HOBBES

It is no tragedy to do ungrateful people favors, but it is unbearable to be indebted to a scoundrel.   LA ROCHEFOUCAULD

Nothing knits man to man like the frequent passage from
hand to hand of cash.   SICKERT

As a general rule, nobody has money who ought to have it.
DISRAELI

Algebra and money are essentially levelers; the first intel-
lectually, the second effectively.   SIMONE WEIL

If you want to know what a man is really like, take notice
how he acts when he loses money.   NEW ENGLAND PROVERB

The Lord forbid that I should be out of debt, as if indeed I
could not be trusted.   RABELAIS

Nobody was ever meant
To remember or invent
What he did with every cent.

FROST

What makes all doctrines plain and clear?
About two hundred pounds a year.
And that which was prov'd true before
Prov'd false again? Two hundred more.

SAMUEL BUTLER (I)

When a poor man eats a chicken, one or the other is sick.

YIDDISH PROVERB

An ox for a penny—and if you haven't a penny?

YIDDISH PROVERB

Selfishness is not living as one wishes to live. It is asking others to live as one wishes to live.

WILDE

There is an accumulative cruelty in a number of men, though none in particular are ill natured.

HALIFAX

A man that is busy and inquisitive is commonly envious. For envy is a gadding passion, and walketh the streets, and doth not keep at home.

BACON

Nobody ever forgets where he buried the hatchet.

KIN HUBBARD

Societies for the suppression of vice

Beginning with the best intentions in the world, such societies must in all probability degenerate into a receptacle for every species of tittle-tattle, impertinence and malice. Men whose trade is rat-catching love to catch rats; the bug-destroyer seizes on his bug with delight; and the suppressor is gratified by finding his vice. The last soon becomes a mere tradesman like the others; none of them moralize, or lament that their respective evils should exist in the world. The public feeling is swallowed up in the pursuit of a daily occupation, and in the display of a technical skill.

SYDNEY SMITH

All else failing, a man's character may be inferred from nothing so surely as the jest he takes in bad part.   LICHTENBERG

Thousands are hated, but none is ever loved without a real cause.   LAVATER

What encourages the mocker is that he starts off with success; the punishment comes later.   MARBEAU

When the world has once begun to use us ill, it afterward continues the same treatment with less scruple or ceremony, as men do to a whore.   SWIFT

So long as men praise you, you can only be sure that you are not yet on your own true path but on someone else's.   NIETZSCHE

Calumny is like counterfeit money: many people who would not coin it circulate it without qualms.   DIANE DE POITIERS

More men hurt others they do not know why than for any reason.   HALIFAX

There is no man so friendless but what he can find a friend sincere enough to tell him disagreeable truths.
    BULWER-LYTTON

Our enemies' opinion of us comes closer to the truth than our own.   LA ROCHEFOUCAULD

If you injure your neighbor, better not do it by halves.   SHAW

We are much harder on people who betray us in small ways than on people who betray others in great ones.

LA ROCHEFOUCAULD

Many a friend will tell us our faults without reserve, who will not so much as hint at our follies.   CHESTERFIELD

The ultimate result of shielding men from the effects of folly is to fill the world with fools.   SPENCER

Severities should be dealt out all at once, that by their suddenness they may give less offense; benefits should be handed out drop by drop, that they may be relished the more.

MACHIAVELLI

If others had not been foolish, we should be so.   BLAKE

The embarrassment we feel in the presence of a ridiculous man is due to the fact that we cannot imagine him on his death bed.   CIORAN

The faults that make a man absurd seldom make him hateful; he escapes loathing through ridicule.   JOUBERT

Two protecting deities, indeed, like two sober friends supporting a drunkard, flank human folly and keep it within bounds. One of these deities is Punishment and the other Agreement.   SANTAYANA

I can understand anyone's allowing himself to be bullied by the living, but not, if he can help it, by the dead.

SAMUEL BUTLER (II)

The secret of prosperity in common life is to be common-place on principle.   BAGEHOT

It is always safe to assume that people are more subtle and less sensitive than they seem.   HOFFER

He that is never suspected is either very much esteemed or very much despised.   HALIFAX

Could we know what men are most apt to remember, we might know what they are most apt to do.   HALIFAX

There are some splenetic gentlemen who confine their favorable opinion within so narrow a compass that they will not allow it to any man that was not hanged in the late reigns.
                    HALIFAX

Almost all absurdity of conduct arises from the imitation of those whom we cannot resemble.   DR. JOHNSON

To understand the world, and to like it, are two things not easily to be reconciled.   HALIFAX

Two quite opposite qualities equally bias our minds—habit and novelty.   LA BRUYÈRE

It is a luxury to be understood.   EMERSON

The world may not be particularly wise—still we know of nothing wiser.   SAMUEL BUTLER (II)

A wise man knows everything; a shrewd one, everybody.

ANONYMOUS

It is one thing to understand persons, and another thing to understand matters: for many are perfect in men's humors, that are not greatly capable of the real part of the business.

BACON

Most of the grounds of the world's troubles are matters of grammar.

MONTAIGNE

One must be a god to be able to tell successes from failures without making a mistake.

CHEKHOV

There is none can baffle men of sense but fools, on whom they can make no impression.

SHENSTONE

Distrust all those who love you extremely upon a very slight acquaintance and without any visible reason.

CHESTERFIELD

The most useful part of wisdom is for a man to give a good guess, what others think of him. It is a dangerous thing to guess partially, and a melancholy thing to guess right.

HALIFAX

The pleasantest condition of life is in incognito.

COWLEY

Love your neighbor, but don't pull down the hedge.

SWISS PROVERB

I prefer the sign "No Entry" to the one that says "No Exit."

LEC

[155]

He who deserts us may not be insulting us, but he is certainly insulting our disciples.　　　　NIETZSCHE

Three things we should keep in mind [in conversation]: first, that we speak in the presence of people as vain as ourselves, whose vanity suffers in proportion as ours is satisfied; second, that there are few truths important enough to justify paining and reproving others for not knowing them; finally, that any man who monopolizes the conversation is a fool or would be fortunate if he were one.　　　　MONTESQUIEU

Let us leave . . . labels to those who have little else wherewith to cover their nakedness.　　　　SICKERT

Lessons are not given, they are taken.　　　　PAVESE

For the world, I count it not an inn but an hospital, and a place not to live but to die in.　　　　BROWNE

We need to be just before we are generous, as we need shirts before ruffles.　　　　CHAMFORT

The fox knows many things, but the hedgehog knows one big thing.　　　　ARCHILOCHUS

From a worldly point of view there is no mistake so great as that of being always right.　　　　SAMUEL BUTLER (II)

He who has suffered you to impose on him, knows you.
　　　　BLAKE

To take upon oneself not punishment, but *guilt*—that alone would be godlike.　　　　NIETZSCHE

[156]

The Arena

All rising to great place is by a winding stair.   BACON

Ambition hath no mean, it is either upon all fours or upon tiptoes.   HALIFAX

Courtiers speak well of a man for two reasons: that he may learn they have spoken well of him, and that he may speak well of them.   LA BRUYÈRE

There are more fools than knaves in the world, else the knaves would not have enough to live upon.

SAMUEL BUTLER (I)

To make astute people believe one is what one is not is, in most cases, harder than actually to become what one wishes to appear.   LICHTENBERG

Truth is the safest lie.   YIDDISH PROVERB

In dealing with cunning persons, we must ever consider their ends to interpret their speeches; and it is good to say little to them, and that which they least look for.   BACON

There is little or nothing to be remembered written on the subject of getting an honest living. Neither the New Testament nor Poor Richard speaks to our condition. One would think, from looking at literature, that this question had never disturbed a solitary individual's musings.   THOREAU

You can discover what your enemy fears most by observing the means he uses to frighten you.　　HOFFER

Timing of the suit is the principal: timing, I say, not only in respect of the person that should grant it, but in respect of those which are likely to cross it.　　BACON

How rightly do we distinguish men by external differences rather than by internal qualities. Which of us two shall have precedence? Who will give place to the other? The least clever? But I am as clever as he. We should have to fight over this. He has four lackeys, and I have only one. This can be seen; we have only to count. It falls to me to yield, and I am a fool if I contest the matter.　　PASCAL

Thou shalt not kill; but need'st not strive
Officiously to keep alive.

　　CLOUGH

When you have found out the prevailing passion of any man, remember never to trust him where that passion is concerned.　　CHESTERFIELD

He that seeketh to be eminent amongst able men hath a great task; but that is ever good for the public. But he that plots to be the only figure amongst ciphers is the decay of a whole age.　　BACON

The sick in soul insist that it is humanity that is sick, and they are the surgeons to operate on it. They want to turn the world into a sickroom. And once they get humanity strapped to the operating table, they operate on it with an ax.

　　HOFFER

He who can lick can bite.   FRENCH PROVERB

It is a trick among the dishonest to offer sacrifices that are
not needed, or not possible, to avoid making those that are
required.   GONCHAROV

Disgrace kills hatred and jealousy. Once someone is no longer
a favorite and no longer envied . . . he might even be a
hero and not annoy us.   LA BRUYÈRE

Great evils befall the world when the powerful begin to
copy the weak. The desperate devices which enable the weak
to survive are unequaled instruments of oppression and ex-
termination in the hands of the strong.   HOFFER

With someone who holds nothing but trumps, it is impossible to play cards.   HEBBEL

Manifest merits procure reputation; occult ones, fortune.
                                                   BACON

There is a certain cowardice, a certain weakness, rather,
among respectable folk. Only brigands are convinced—of
what? That they must succeed. And so they do succeed.
                                                   BAUDELAIRE

The only infallible criterion of wisdom to vulgar judgments—
success.   E. BURKE

The art of controversy: if your opponent proposes an *altera-
tion*, you can call it an *innovation*. If you are making the
proposal, it will be the other way round.   SCHOPENHAUER

To take away all animosity from a rivalry is like playing whist for love.   SAMUEL BUTLER (II)

There is nothing so common as to imitate the practice of enemies and to use their weapons.   VOLTAIRE

The pain of a dispute greatly outweighs its uses.   JOUBERT

One has not the right to betray even a traitor. Traitors must be fought, not betrayed.   PÉGUY

Irrational creatures cannot distinguish between *injury* and *damage*, and therefore, as long as they be at ease, they are not offended with their fellows; whereas man is then most troublesome when he is most at ease, for then it is that he loves to show his wisdom and control the actions of them that govern the commonwealth.   HOBBES

The innocent victim who suffers knows the truth about his executioner; the executioner does not know it. The evil which the innocent victim feels in himself is in his executioner, but the latter is not sensible of the fact. The innocent victim can only know the evil in the form of suffering. That which is not felt by the criminal is his crime. That which is not felt by the innocent victim is his own innocence.

SIMONE WEIL

Calumnies are answered best with silence.   JONSON

Even in a declaration of war one observes the rules of politeness.   BISMARCK

Thou shalt not covet, but tradition
Approves all forms of competition.

CLOUGH

If a man would cross a business that he doubts some other
would handsomely and effectively move, let him pretend
to wish it well, and move it himself in such sort as may
foil it.

BACON

A long table and a square table, or seats about the walls,
seem things of form but are things of substance: for at a
long table, a few at the upper end in effect sway all the
business; but in the other form, there is more use of the
counselors' opinions that sit lower.

BACON

"This dog belongs to me," said these poor children; "that
is my place in the sun." There is the beginning and image
of the usurpation of all the earth.

PASCAL

Great riches have sold more men than they have bought.

BACON

To suppose, as we all suppose, that we could be rich and
not behave the way the rich behave, is like supposing that
we could drink all day and stay sober.

L. P. SMITH

The aristocracy created by business rarely settles in the midst
of the manufacturing population which it directs; the object
is not to govern that population, but to use it.

TOCQUEVILLE

For the merchant, even honesty is a financial speculation.

BAUDELAIRE

Money swore an oath that nobody that did not love it should ever have it.   IRISH PROVERB

The best condition in life is not to be so rich as to be envied nor so poor as to be damned.   BILLINGS

We do not learn to know men through their coming to us. To find out what sort of persons they are, we must go to them.   GOETHE

It's always been and always will be the same in the world: the horse does the work and the coachman is tipped.
                                                     ANONYMOUS

If the rich could hire other people to die for them, the poor could make a wonderful living.   YIDDISH PROVERB

The bourgeoisie began to treat the work of man as a security on the stock exchange; so, in his turn, the worker began to treat his own work as a security on the stock exchange. The *political* socialist party is entirely composed of intellectual bourgeois. It is they who invented the double desertion, desertion from work and desertion from tools.   PÉGUY

It is seldom that the miserable can help regarding their misery as a wrong inflicted by those who are less miserable.
                                                   GEORGE ELIOT

Rich man down and poor man up—they are still not even.
                                                 YIDDISH PROVERB

Beggars should be abolished. It annoys one to give to them, and it annoys one not to give to them.   NIETZSCHE

To have a grievance is to have a purpose in life. A grievance can almost serve as a substitute for hope; and it not infrequently happens that those who hunger for hope give their allegiance to him who offers them a grievance.   HOFFER

Poverty is to be pitied, but impoverishment is a hundred times more pitiable.   RICHTER

Poverty is an anomaly to rich people. It is very difficult to make out why people who want dinner do not ring the bell.   BAGEHOT

The poor are the Negroes of Europe.   CHAMFORT

Those who escape from destitution do not escape from the memory of their destitution. Either by dwelling upon it or by reacting against it, all their future life is affected by it. The majority of the once destitute take refuge in voluntary amnesia.   PÉGUY

Men feel that cruelty to the poor is a kind of cruelty to animals. They never feel that it is injustice to equals; nay, it is treachery to comrades.   CHESTERTON

Short of genius, a rich man cannot imagine poverty.   PÉGUY

Thousands upon thousands are yearly brought into a state of real poverty by their great anxiety not to be thought poor.   COBBETT

To ruin those who possess something is not to come to the aid of those who possess nothing; it is merely to render misery general.   METTERNICH

THE SEXES

The Sexes

Women prefer to talk in two's; while men prefer to talk in three's.　　　　　　　　　　　　　　　CHESTERTON

Men's vows are women's traitors.　　　　SHAKESPEARE

Women eat while they talk, men talk while they eat. At table, men talk for a long time between mouthfuls, women while eating. At breakfast, when the courses are light and hurried, women preside; at banquets and formal dinners when the intervals between courses are long, the voices of the men are predominant.　　　　　　　　CHAZAL

Men who do not make advances to women are apt to become victims to women who make advances to them.　　BAGEHOT

In mixed company, women practice a sort of visual shorthand, which, later, they will laboriously and at great length decode in the company of other women.　　　　　　CHAZAL

A woman knows how to keep quiet when she is in the right, whereas a man, when he is in the right, will keep on talking
　　　　　　　　　　　　　　　　CHAZAI

The great question that has never been answered, and which I have not yet been able to answer despite my thirty years of research into the feminine soul, is: What does a woman want? FREUD

If a man hears much that a woman says, she is not beautiful. HASKINS

Most men who rail against women are railing at one woman only. GOURMONT

There is one phase of life that I have never heard
discussed in any seminar
And that is that all women think men are funny and
all men think that weminar. NASH

'Tis strange what a man may do, and a woman yet think him an angel. THACKERAY

Women do not properly understand that when an idea fills and elevates a man's mind it shuts out love and crowds out people. RICHTER

A woman may very well form a friendship with a man, but for this to endure, it must be assisted by a little physical antipathy. NIETZSCHE

One can, to an almost laughable degree, infer what a man's wife is like from his opinions about women in general. MILL

A woman is more responsive to a man's forgetfulness than to his attentions. JANIN

Feminine passion is to masculine as an epic to an epigram.
KRAUS

Men who cherish for women the highest respect are seldom popular with [them].
ADDISON

A man would create another man if one did not already exist, but a woman might live an eternity without even thinking of reproducing her own sex.
GOETHE

The woman possesses a theatrical exterior and a circumspect interior, while in the man it is the interior which is theatrical. The woman goes to the theater; the man carries it inside himself and is the impresario of his own life.
ORETGA Y GASSET

The best man for a man and the best man for a woman are not the same.
ORTEGA Y GASSET

Men are men, but Man is a woman.
CHESTERTON

Men are so made that they can resist sound argument, and yet yield to a glance.
BALZAC

Men who make money rarely saunter; men who save money rarely swagger.
BULWER-LYTTON

All the books extolling the simple life are written by men.
FEATHER

Chaste men engender obscene literatures.
AUSONIUS

Female murderers get sheaves of offers of marriage.   SHAW

The years that a woman subtracts from her age are not lost. They are added to other women's.   DIANE DE POITIERS

The fundamental fault of the female character is that it has no sense of justice.   SCHOPENHAUER

Even when they meet in the street, women look at one another like Guelphs and Ghibellines.   SCHOPENHAUER

Woman gives herself as a prize to the weak and as a prop to the strong, and no man ever has what he should.

PAVESE

Next to the wound, what women make best is the bandage.

BARBEY D'AUREVILLY

Women are the wild life of a country: morality corresponds to game laws.   ANONYMOUS

Women are always afraid of things which have to be divided.

BALZAC

Most women are not so young as they are painted.

BEERBOHM

A beautiful and sparkling, but superficial woman rules a wide circle; a woman of real culture a small one.   GOETHE

Can you recall a woman who ever showed you with pride her library?   DE CASSERES

Woman inspires us to great things, and prevents us from achieving them.   DUMAS

What is truly indispensable for the conduct of life has been taught us by women—the small rules of courtesy, the actions that win us the warmth or deference of others; the words that assure us a welcome; the attitudes that must be varied to mesh with character or situation; all social strategy. It is listening to women that teaches us to speak to men.

GOURMONT

A woman who cannot be ugly is not beautiful.   KRAUS

Women always show more taste in their choice of under-clothing than in their choice of jewelry.   CHAZAL

I have heard with admiring submission the experience of the lady who declared that the sense of being well-dressed gives a feeling of inward tranquillity, which religion is power-less to bestow.   EMERSON

Women who are either indisputably beautiful or indisputably ugly are best flattered upon the score of their understandings.

CHESTERFIELD

A beautiful woman should break her mirror early.   GRACIAN

The marvelous instinct with which women are usually credited seems too often to desert them on the only occasions when it would be of any real use. One would say that it was there for trivialities only, since in a crisis they are usually dense, fatally doing the wrong thing. It is hardly too much to say that most domestic tragedies are caused by the feminine intui-tion of men and the want of it in women.   ADA LEVERSON

You don't know a woman until you have had a letter from her. ADA LEVERSON

A woman, the more curious she is about her face, is commonly the more careless about her house. JONSON

Nature has given women so much power that the law has very wisely given them little. DR. JOHNSON

The woman whose behavior indicates that she will make a scene if she is told the truth asks to be deceived.
ELIZABETH JENKINS

I have met with women whom I really think would like to be married to a poem, and to be given away by a novel.
KEATS

The females of all species are most dangerous when they appear to retreat. MARQUIS

Woman learns how to hate in the degree that she forgets how to charm. NIETZSCHE

When women kiss it always reminds one of prizefighters shaking hands. MENCKEN

With women all ideas easily become human beings.
RICHTER

To tell a woman what she may not do is to tell her what she can. SPANISH PROVERB

A small woman always seems newly married.

GENOESE PROVERB

There is but an hour a day between a good housewife and a bad one. ENGLISH PROVERB

For women, history does not exist. Murasaki, Sappho, and Madame Lafayette might be their own contemporaries. Yet *fashion* exists for them. Is it a trick they have, or some great talent, that enables them to appear at any moment exactly as fashion decrees? PAVESE

Variability is one of the virtues of a woman. It obviates the crude requirements of polygamy. If you have one good wife you are sure to have a spiritual harem. CHESTERTON

A man keeps another's secret better than he does his own. A woman, on the other hand, keeps her own better than another's. LA BRUYÈRE

The two things that a healthy person hates most between heaven and hell are a woman who is not dignified and a man who is. CHESTERTON

Men are cleverer than women at reasoning, women are cleverer than men at drawing conclusions. A parliament in which the members were predominantly women would get through its legislation much faster. CHAZAL

It is a mistake for a taciturn, serious-minded woman to marry a jovial man, but not for a serious-minded man to marry a lighthearted woman. GOETHE

In contrast to the concentric structure of the feminine mind, there are always epicenters in that of the man. The more masculine, in a spiritual sense, a man is, the more his mind is disjointed in separate compartments.　ORTEGA Y GASSET

The man's desire is for the woman; but the woman's desire is rarely other than for the desire of the man.　COLERIDGE

I should like to know what is the proper function of women, if it is not to make reasons for husbands to stay at home, and still stronger reasons for bachelors to go out.
　GEORGE ELIOT

In Paris, when God provides a beautiful woman, the devil at once retorts with a fool to keep her.　BARBEY D'AUREVILLY

As the faculty of writing has been chiefly a masculine endowment, the reproach of making the world miserable has been always thrown upon the women.　DR. JOHNSON

When the husband drinks to the wife, all would be well; when the wife drinks to the husband, all is.　ENGLISH PROVERB

When men watch them, nursemaids kiss and rock children with vigor; when only women are looking on, they handle them very quietly.　LICHTENBERG

In woman the seat of the *point d'honneur* coincides with the center of gravity; in man it is located higher, in the chest near the diaphragm. Hence, in man, the buoyant fullness in that region when he embarks on splendid deeds, and the flabby emptiness when he embarks on petty ones.
　LICHTENBERG

The wife carries the husband on her face; the husband carries the wife on his linen.　　　　BULGARIAN PROVERB

Women are infinitely fonder of clinging to and beating about, hanging upon and keeping up and reluctantly letting fall, any doleful or painful or unpleasant subject, than men of the same class and rank.　　　　COLERIDGE

Woman's vanity demands that a man be more than a happy husband.　　　　NIETZSCHE

Women have served all these centuries as looking glasses possessing the . . . power of reflecting the figure of man at twice its natural size.　　　　VIRGINIA WOOLF

Men always want to be a woman's first love, women like to be a man's last romance.　　　　WILDE

It is because of men that women dislike one another.
　　　　LA BRUYÈRE

All women become like their mothers. That is their tragedy. No man does. That is his.　　　　WILDE

Love, Marriage, and Friendsh

The lover thinks oftener of reaching his mistre
the husband of guarding his wife; the prisoner tl
of escaping than does the jailer of shutting the

Love is immanent in nature, but not incarnate.

> Hail Sovereign Queen of secrets, that hast powe
> To call the fiercest Tyrant from his rage;
> And weep unto a girl; that hast the might
> Even with an eye-glance, to cloak Mars's Drum
> And turn th'allarm to whispers, that canst n
> A Cripple flourish with his Crutch, and cure
> Before Apollo; that may'st force the King
> To be his subjects' vassal, and induce
> Stale gravity to daunce.

SHA

EROS: As his parentage is, so also are his fortunes. In
place he is always poor, and anything but tender
as the many imagine him; and he is rough and squ₂
has no shoes, nor a house to dwell in; on the b₂
exposed he lies under the open heaven, in the stree
the doors of houses, taking his rest; and like his
(*Poverty*) he is always in distress. Like his father (

too, whom he also partly resembles, he is always plotting against the fair and good; he is bold, enterprising, strong, a mighty hunter, always weaving some intrigue or other, keen in the pursuit of wisdom, fertile in resources; a philosopher at all times, terrible as an enchanter, sorcerer, sophist. He is by nature neither mortal nor immortal, but alive and flourishing at one moment when he is in plenty, and dead at another moment, and again alive by reason of his father's nature.

PLATO

Cupid: his disgrace is to be called boy; but his glory is to subdue men.   SHAKESPEARE

For the butterfly, mating and propagation involve the sacrifice of life; for the human being, the sacrifice of beauty.

GOETHE

Love is either the shrinking remnant of something which was once enormous; or else it is part of something which will grow in the future into something enormous. But in the present it does not satisfy. It gives much less than one expects.

CHEKHOV

LOVE: A word properly applied to our delight in particular kinds of food; sometimes metaphorically spoken of the favorite objects of all our appetites.   FIELDING

Love is merely a madness; and, I tell you, deserves a dark house and a whip as madmen do: and the reason why they are not so punished and cured is that the lunacy is so ordinary that the whippers are in love too.   SHAKESPEARE

Love between the sexes is a sin in theology, a forbidden intercourse in jurisprudence, a mechanical insult in medicine, and a subject philosophy has no time for.   KRAUS

LOVE, MARRIAGE, AND FRIENDSHIP

Love: that self-love *à deux*.   MME. DE STAËL

Coition is a slight attack of apoplexy.
                                    DEMOCRITUS OF ABDERA

What they call "heart" is located far lower than the fourth
waistcoat button.   LICHTENBERG

You can construct a totalitarian goodness. But don't play
the fool: keep sex out of it.   PAVESE

Sexuality throws no light upon love, but only through love
can we learn to understand sexuality.   ROSENSTOCK-HUESSY

A taste for dirty stories may be said to be inherent in the
human animal.   GEORGE MOORE

When the representatives of the Church have talked about
such things as sexual love (to take one example) they may
have said the right things, but they said very few of them and
they have generally said them in the wrong style. The great
world and energy of the body have been either deprecated
or devotionalized; and by devotionalized I mean turned into
a pale imitation of "substance," of spirit; thus losing their
own powers and privileges without, in general, gaining any
others. There has been a wide feeling that the more like an
indeterminate soul the body can be, the better. But the
body is not "like" the soul; it is like nothing but itself.

                                    WILLIAMS

Nine-tenths of that which is attributed to sexuality is the
work of our magnificent ability to imagine, which is no longer
an instinct, but exactly the opposite: a creation.

                                    ORTEGA Y GASSET

Were it not for imagination, sir, a man would be as happy in the arms of a chambermaid as of a duchess.

DR. JOHNSON

The credulity of love is the most fundamental source of authority.

FREUD

There is nothing like desire for preventing the things we say from having any resemblance to the things in our minds.

PROUST

Passion often turns the cleverest men into idiots and makes the greatest blockheads clever.

LA ROCHEFOUCAULD

When we are in love, we often doubt what we most believe.

LA ROCHEFOUCAULD

Love, in distinction from friendship, is killed, or rather extinguished, the moment it is displayed in public.

HANNAH ARENDT

No disguise can long conceal love where it exists, or long feign it where it is lacking.

LA ROCHEFOUCAULD

Only with those we love do we speak of those we love.

RICHTER

Love does not dominate; it cultivates.

GOETHE

Love lessens woman's delicacy and increases man's.

RICHTER

A gentleman in love may behave like a madman but not like a dunce.

LA ROCHEFOUCAULD

The impassioned man hasn't time to be witty.   STENDHAL

Love is a talkative passion.   BISHOP WILSON

The speaking in a perpetual hyperbole is comely in nothing but in love.   BACON

Habit is everything—even in love.   VAUVENARGUES

When love is concerned, it is easier to renounce a feeling than to give up a habit.   PROUST

"His love is violent but base": a possible sentence. "His love is deep but base": an impossible one.   SIMONE WEIL

True love is like seeing ghosts: we all talk about it, but few of us have ever seen one.   LA ROCHEFOUCAULD

A lover who is absolutely in love does not know whether he is more or less in love than others, for anyone who knows this is, just on that account, not absolutely in love.

KIERKEGAARD

Perfect love means to love the one through whom one became unhappy.   KIERKEGAARD

The maxim for any love affair is: "Play and pray; but on the whole do not pray when you are playing and do not play when you are praying." We cannot yet manage such simultaneities.

WILLIAMS

There are two kinds of faithfulness in love: one is based on forever finding new things to love in the loved one; the other is based on our pride in being faithful.   LA ROCHEFOUCAULD

It is as absurd to say that a man can't love one woman all the time as it is to say that a violinist needs several violins to play the same piece of music.   BALZAC

The most exclusive love for someone is always a love for something else as well.   PROUST

It's not impossible to become bored in the presence of a mistress.   STENDHAL

In love, there is always one who kisses and one who offers the cheek.   FRENCH PROVERB

The discovery that one cannot well give back or be given back what one has given or been given in the same place is sometimes as painful as the discovery that one is being loved on principle and not from preference.   WILLIAMS

Love is ever rewarded either with the reciprocal, or with an inward and secret contempt.   BACON

We are nearer loving those who hate us than those who love us more than we wish.   LA ROCHEFOUCAULD

Mourning the loss of someone we love is happiness compared with having to live with someone we hate.   LA BRUYÈRE

Once love is purged of vanity, it resembles a feeble convalescent, hardly able to drag itself about. CHAMFORT

If you think you love your mistress for her own sake, you are quite mistaken. LA ROCHEFOUCAULD

The first spat in love, as the first misstep in friendship, is the only one we can turn to good use. LA BRUYÈRE

Aversion gives love its death wound, and forgetfulness buries it. LA BRUYÈRE

The magic of first love is our ignorance that it can ever end. DISRAELI

Love is space and time made directly perceptible to the heart. PROUST

We do not live in accordance with our mode of thinking, but we think in accordance with our mode of loving. ROZINOV

Love is too young to know what conscience is;
But who knows not conscience is born of love?
SHAKESPEARE

Time and love are both wasted so long as time remains working hours and love without song. ROSENSTOCK-HUESSY

Love decentralizes, truth universalizes: he who speaks addresses all mankind, he who loves incarnates all mankind in himself. ROSENSTOCK-HUESSY

Love does not consist in gazing at each other but in looking together in the same direction.   SAINT-EXUPÉRY

Love begins with love; friendship, however warm, cannot change to love, however mild.   LA BRUYÈRE

There is nothing that is so profoundly false as rationalist flirtation. Each sex is trying to be both sexes at once; and the result is a confusion more untruthful than any conventions.   CHESTERTON

At the beginning of love and at its end the lovers are embarrassed to be left alone.   LA BRUYÈRE

The only thing which is not purely mechanical about falling in love is its beginning. Although all those who fall in love do so in the same way, not all fall in love for the same reason. There is no single quality which is universally loved.

ORTEGA Y GASSET

Like everybody who is not in love, he imagined that one chose the person whom one loved after endless deliberations and on the strength of various qualities and advantages.

PROUST

It is a mistake to speak of a bad choice in love, since, as soon as a choice exists, it can only be bad.   PROUST

With the generosity of a great lord the happy lover smiles upon everything about him. But the great lord's generosity is always in moderation and involves no effort. It is not a very expansive sort of generosity; actually it originates in disdain.   ORTEGA Y GASSET

Love is a spaniel that prefers even punishment from one hand to caresses from another.　　　　　COLTON

There is not a woman in the world the possession of whom is as precious as that of the truth which she reveals to us by causing us to suffer.　　　　　PROUST

An absence, the decline of a dinner invitation, an unintentional coldness, can accomplish more than all the cosmetics and beautiful dresses in the world.　　　　　PROUST

No one was ever made wretched in a brothel.　　　　　CONNOLLY

Love is a sport in which the hunter must contrive to have the quarry in pursuit.　　　　　KERR

It is a common enough case, that of a man being suddenly captivated by a woman nearly the opposite of his ideal.
　　　　　GEORGE ELIOT

What attracts us in a woman rarely binds us to her.
　　　　　COLLINS

Women grow attached to men through the favors they grant them; but men, through the same favors, are cured of their love.　　　　　LA BRUYÈRE

The duration of passion is proportionate with the original resistance of the woman.　　　　　BALZAC

Women are won when they begin to threaten.
　　　　　AUTHOR OF *Nero*

No woman ever hates a man for being in love with her; but many a woman hates a man for being a friend to her.

POPE

Such is the rule of modesty, a woman of feeling betrays her sentiments for her lover sooner by deed than by word.

STENDHAL

Prudery is a form of avarice. STENDHAL

A wise women never yields by appointment. STENDHAL

A woman with eyes only for one person, or with eyes always averted from him, creates exactly the same impression.

LA BRUYÈRE

There is no fury like a woman searching for a new lover.

CONNOLLY

The man cries: Oh, my angel! The woman coos: Mama! Mama! And these two imbeciles are persuaded that they think alike. BAUDELAIRE

The Art of Love: knowing how to combine the temperament of a vampire with the discretion of an anemone. CIORAN

What is irritating about love is that it is a crime that requires an accomplice. BAUDELAIRE

A woman we love rarely satisfies all our needs, and we deceive her with a woman whom we do not love. PROUST

Jealousy is the great exaggerator. SCHILLER

A man does not look behind the door unless he has stood there himself.   DU BOIS

We are ashamed to admit that we are jealous, but proud that we were and that we can be.   LA ROCHEFOUCAULD

Jealousy is always born with love, but does not always die with it.   LA ROCHEFOUCAULD

Every attack of jealousy is unique and bears the stamp of the one who occasioned it.   PROUST

There is sanctuary in reading, sanctuary in formal society, in the company of old friends, and in the giving of officious help to strangers, but there is no sanctuary in one bed from the memory of another.   CONNOLLY

> Let the love-lorn lover cure insomnia
> By murmuring AMOR VINCIT OMNIA.
>
>   NASH

Love, as it is practiced in society, is merely the exchange of two momentary desires and the contact of two skins.

                                   CHAMFORT

How many girls are there for whom great beauty has been of no use but to make them hope for a great fortune?

                                   LA BRUYÈRE

Women's favors, M. de —— used to say, are auction-room transactions, where neither feeling nor merit ever bid successfully.   CHAMFORT

A lover . . . tries to stand in well with the pet dog of the house.   MOLIÈRE

A beautiful woman once told her sullen, much-married-looking lover: "When you are seen, monsieur, in society with my husband, you are expected to look more cheerful than he does."
                                                                    CHAMFORT

There are few men who do not place the felicity more in the opinion of the world, of their being prosperous lovers, than in the blessing itself.   HALIFAX

Don't give to lovers you will replace irreplaceable presents.
                                                              L. P. SMITH

She gave herself, he took her: the third party was time, who made cuckolds of them both.   CHAZAL

> Then talk not of Inconstancy,
>   False Hearts and broken Vows;
> If I, by Miracle, can be
> This live-long minute true to thee,
>   'Tis all that Heav'n allows.
>
>   ROCHESTER

Better to sit up all night, than to go to bed with a dragon.
                                                          JEREMY TAYLOR

That sudden and ill-timed love affair may be compared to this: you take boys somewhere for a walk; the walk is jolly and interesting—and suddenly one of them gorges himself with oil paint.   CHEKHOV

Man is lyrical, woman epic, marriage dramatic.   NOVALIS

One may be a blameless
bachelor, and it is but a
step to Congreve.

MARIANNE MOORE

Love-making is radical, while marriage is conservative.

HOFFER

Romantic love can very well be represented in the moment,
but conjugal love cannot, because an ideal husband is not
one who is such once in his life, but one who every day is
such.   KIERKEGAARD

It takes patience to appreciate domestic bliss; volatile spirits
prefer unhappiness.   SANTAYANA

Unmarried men very rarely speak the truth about the things
that most nearly concern them; married men, never.

SAMUEL BUTLER (II)

If it were not for the presents, an elopement would be preferable.   ADE

Love is an ideal thing, marriage a real thing; a confusion of
the real with the ideal never goes unpunished.   GOETHE

Love matches, as they are called, have illusion for their
father and need for their mother.   NIETZSCHE

One should only celebrate a happy *ending*; celebrations at
the outset exhaust the joy and energy needed to urge us forward and sustain us in the long struggle. And of all celebrations a wedding is the worst; no day should be kept more
quietly and humbly.   GOETHE

The music at a wedding procession always reminds me of the music of soldiers going into battle.   HEINE

Marriage, in life, is like a duel in the midst of a battle.
                                                    ABOUT

It doesn't much signify whom one marries, for one is sure to find out next morning that it was someone else.   ROGERS

Marriage is a covered dish.   SWISS PROVERB

To live with someone and to live in someone are two fundamentally different matters. There are people in whom one can live without living with them, and vice versa. To combine both requires the purest degree of love and friendship.
                                                    GOETHE

Marriage has many pains, but celibacy has no pleasures.
                                                DR. JOHNSON

Marriage is the only adventure open to the cowardly.
                                                    VOLTAIRE

Marriage is the only legal contract which abrogates as between the parties all the laws that safeguard the particular relation to which it refers.   SHAW

How I do hate those words "an excellent marriage." In them is contained more of wicked worldliness than any other words one ever hears spoken.   TROLLOPE

Be not hasty to marry; it's better to have one plow going than two cradles, and more profit to have a barn filled than a bed.   DR. FULLER

If you are afraid of loneliness, don't marry. CHEKHOV

A man who marries a woman to educate her falls into the same fallacy as the woman who marries a man to reform him. E. HUBBARD

Some cunning men choose fools for their wives, thinking to manage them, but they always fail. DR. JOHNSON

A naturally ironical man would always be henpecked if he married. KIERKEGAARD

A man too good for the world is no good for his wife. YIDDISH PROVERB

When I hear that "Possession is the grave of love," I remember that a religion may begin with the Resurrection. BRADLEY

When a man has married a wife he finds out whether Her knees and elbows are only glued together. BLAKE

"Adam knew Eve his wife and she conceived." It is a pity that this is still the only knowledge of their wives at which some men seem to arrive. BRADLEY

The majority of husbands remind me of an orangutan trying to play the violin. BALZAC

The man who enters his wife's dressing room is either a philosopher or a fool. BALZAC

[193]

It is often seen that bad husbands have very good wives: whether it be, that it raiseth the price of their husbands' kindness, when it comes, or that the wives take a pride in their patience. BACON

In marriage the husband should have two eyes and the wife but one. LYLY

The most happy marriage I can picture . . . would be the union of a deaf man to a blind woman. COLERIDGE

The true index of a man's character is the health of his wife. CONNOLLY

A wife is to thank God her husband hath faults. . . . A husband without faults is a dangerous observer. HALIFAX

Passionate men generally make amends at the foot of the account. Such a man, if he is angry one day without any sense, will the next day be as kind without any reason. HALIFAX

Forty years of romance make a woman look like a ruin and forty years of marriage make her look like a public building. WILDE

So heavy is the chain of wedlock that it needs two to carry it, and sometimes three. DUMAS

War is no strife
To the dark house and the detested wife.
SHAKESPEARE

A man may pass through a barrage with less damage to his character than through a squabble with a nagging wife. Many domestic and commercial experiences leave blacker and more permanent marks on the soul than thrusting a bayonet through an enemy in a trench fight.   SHAW

To marry a second time represents the triumph of hope over experience.   DR. JOHNSON

With all her experience, every woman expects to do better when she marries a second time, and some do.   FEATHER

Remarried widowers, it has been observed, tend to confound the persons of their wives. The reason, I suppose, is that they identify the substance.   BRADLEY

Marriage is to politics what the lever is to engineering. The state is not founded upon single individuals but upon couples and groups.   NOVALIS

The family is a good institution because it is uncongenial. The men and women who, for good reasons and bad, revolt against the family, are, for good reasons and bad, revolting against mankind. Aunt Elizabeth is unreasonable, like mankind. Papa is excitable, like mankind. Our younger brother is mischievous, like mankind. Grandpapa is stupid, like the world; he is old, like the world.   CHESTERTON

For millions of men and women the family is the one and only setting in which human relationships are not governed predominantly by considerations of bargaining.   MASCALL

[195]

Home life as we understand it is no more natural to us than a cage is natural to a cockatoo.   SHAW

A fool knows more in his own house than a wise body in another man's.   CERVANTES

When family pride ceases to act, individual selfishness comes into play.   TOCQUEVILLE

Murder, like talent, seems occasionally to run in families.   LEWES

The regal and parental tyrant differ only in the extent of their dominions and the number of their slaves.
                    DR. JOHNSON

When one has not had a good father, one must create one.
                    NIETZSCHE

Whenever there is a group of young people, there is a republic. With marriage the system changes. Married couples want order, safety, peace, and quiet; they wish to live as a family in a family, as an orderly household; they seek for a genuine monarchy.   NOVALIS

Children are aliens, and we treat them as such.   EMERSON

Children are horribly insecure; the life of a parent is the life of a gambler.   SYDNEY SMITH

A spoiled child never loves its mother.   SIR HENRY TAYLOR

A child tells in the street what its father and mother say at home.   THE TALMUD

The best brought-up children are those who have seen their parents as they are. Hypocrisy is not the parents' first duty.

SHAW

Children begin by loving their parents. After a time they judge them. Rarely, if ever, do they forgive them.   WILDE

When one makes children unhappy, one is a criminal and runs the risk of killing them. When one makes them happy, one does right, but one runs the risk of making them silly, presumptuous, and insolent.   PÉGUY

The words a father speaks to his children in the privacy of the home are not overheard at the time, but, as in whispering galleries, they will be clearly heard at the end and by posterity.

RICHTER

When a father gives to his son, both laugh; when a son gives to his father, both cry.   YIDDISH PROVERB

Pastors come for your wine and officers for your daughters.

DUTCH PROVERB

I cannot bear the crying of children, but when my child cries, I don't hear.   CHEKHOV

A man can deceive his fiancée or his mistress as much as he likes, and, in the eyes of a woman he loves, an ass may pass for a philosopher; but a daughter is a different matter.

CHEKHOV

When children appear, we justify all our weaknesses, compromises, snobberies, by saying: "It's for the children's sake."

CHEKHOV

Nobody can misunderstand a boy like his own mother.

DOUGLAS

One must have the courage to give children up; their wisdom is not ours.　　CHARDONNE

Men love their children, not because they are promising plants, but because they are theirs.　　HALIFAX

Love is presently out of breath when it is to go uphill, from the children to the parents.　　HALIFAX

Father's birthday. He would have been 96, 96, yes, today; and could have been 96, like other people one has known: but mercifully was not. His life would have utterly ended mine.　　VIRGINIA WOOLF

Come for your inheritance and you may have to pay for the funeral.　　YIDDISH PROVERB

We were already twenty in family, so my grandmother had a baby.　　SPANISH PROVERB

It is not easy to find the relatives of a poor man.

MENANDER

One would be in less danger
From the wiles of the stranger
If one's own kin and kith
Were more fun to be with.

NASH

The innkeeper loves the drunkard, but not for a son-in-law.

YIDDISH PROVERB

Simple people suffer from mothers-in-law; intellectuals from daughters-in-law.

CHEKHOV

The awe and dread with which the untutored savage contemplates his mother-in-law are amongst the most familiar facts of anthropology.

FRASER

A man is reputed to have thought and eloquence; he cannot, for all that, say a word to his cousin or his uncle.

EMERSON

Great geniuses have the shortest biographies. Their cousins can tell you nothing about them.

EMERSON

Unmarried men are best friends, best masters, best servants, but not always best subjects.

BACON

Friendship is almost always the union of a part of one mind with a part of another; people are friends in spots.

SANTAYANA

Shared joys make a friend, not shared sufferings.

NIETZSCHE

Man is full of desires: he loves only those who can satisfy them all. "This man is a good mathematician," someone will say. But I have no concern for mathematics; he would take me for a proposition. "That one is a good soldier." He would take me for a besieged town. I need, that is to say, a decent man who can accommodate himself to all my desires in a general sort of way.

PASCAL

Thus I was wretched and my wretched life was dearer to me than my friend had been. Gladly as I would have changed it, I would rather have been deprived of my friend than of my grief. SAINT AUGUSTINE

One must not become attached to animals: they do not last long enough. Or to men: they last too long. ANONYMOUS

If anyone is to remain pleased with you, he should be pleased with himself whenever he thinks of you. BRADLEY

In friendship nobody has a double. SCHILLER

The friend does not count his friends on his fingers; they are not numerable. THOREAU

The language of friendship is not words but meanings. THOREAU

What friends really mean to each other can be demonstrated better by the exchange of a magic ring or a horn than by psychology. HOFMANNSTHAL

Most men's friendships are too inarticulate. WILLIAM JAMES

Friendship cannot live with ceremony, nor without civility. HALIFAX

A man knows his companion in a long journey and a little inn. THOMAS FULLER

We have fewer friends than we imagine, but more than we know.   HOFMANNSTHAL

Sometimes we owe a friend to the lucky circumstance that we give him no cause for envy.   NIETZSCHE

A man who hides tyranny, patronage, or even charity behind the name and appearance of friendship suggests that infamous priest who poisoned people with holy wafers.

CHAMFORT

To have a good enemy, choose a friend: he knows where to strike.   DIANE DE POITIERS

Everybody's friend is nobody's.   SCHOPENHAUER

Who boasts to have won a multitude of friends has ne'er had *one*.   COLERIDGE

Somebody said: "There are two persons whom I have not thought deeply about. That is the proof of my love for them."

NIETZSCHE

The more we love our friends, the less we flatter them.

MOLIÈRE

Friendship is like money, easier made than kept.

SAMUEL BUTLER (II)

Few friendships would endure if each party knew what his friend said about him in his absence, even when speaking sincerely and dispassionately.   PASCAL

Whoever has flattered his friend successfully, must at once think himself a knave, and his friend a fool.　　POPE

To get to know a friend, you must share an inheritance with him.　　GERMAN PROVERB

The most fatal disease of friendship is gradual decay, or dislike hourly increased by causes too slender for complaint, and too numerous for removal.　　DR. JOHNSON

However fastidious we may be in love, we forgive more faults in love than in friendship.　　LA BRUYÈRE

There is not so good an understanding between any two, but the exposure by the one of a serious fault in the other will produce a misunderstanding in proportion to its heinousness.
　　THOREAU

Don't tell your friends their social faults; they will cure the fault and never forgive you.　　L. P. SMITH

No man regards himself as in all ways inferior to the man he most admires.　　LA ROCHEFOUCAULD

We are easily consoled for the misfortunes of our friends if they give us the chance to prove our devotion.
　　LA ROCHEFOUCAULD

She is such a good friend that she would throw all her acquaintances into the water for the pleasure of fishing them out.　　TALLEYRAND (of Mme. de Staël)

Most people enjoy the inferiority of their best friends.
　　CHESTERFIELD

Those friends who are above interest are seldom above jealousy.   HALIFAX

As in political, so in literary action, a man wins friends for himself mostly by the passion of his prejudices.   CONRAD

A wit remarked of an old companion who came back to him in his prosperity: "He not only wants his friends to be well off; he insists upon it."   CHAMFORT

If a friend tell thee a fault, imagine always that he telleth thee not the whole.   DR. FULLER

How few of his friends' houses would a man choose to be at when sick.   DR. JOHNSON

I might give my life for my friend, but he had better not ask me to do up a parcel.   L. P. SMITH

If you want a person's faults, go to those who love him. They will not tell you, but they know.   STEVENSON

Our friends show us what we can do, our enemies teach us what we must do.   GOETHE

Street angel, house devil.   GERMAN PROVERB

No one has ever loved anyone the way everyone wants to be loved.   MIGNON MCLAUGHLIN

THE PROFESSIONS

The Professions

Lawyers, I suppose, were children once.   LAMB

A lawyer's dream of heaven—every man reclaimed his property at the resurrection, and each tried to recover it from all his forefathers.   SAMUEL BUTLER (II)

It is easier to make certain things legal than to make them legitimate.   CHAMFORT

Poverty sets a reduced price on crime.   CHAMFORT

Said a man ingenuously to one of his friends: "This morning we condemned three men to death. Two of them definitely deserved it."   CHAMFORT

Such professions [as] the soldier and the lawyer . . . give ample opportunity for crimes but not much for mere illusions. If you have composed a bad opera you may persuade yourself that it is a good one; if you have carved a bad statue you can think yourself better than Michelangelo. But if you have lost a battle you cannot believe you have won it; if your client is hanged you cannot pretend that you have got him off.

CHESTERTON

Law is born from despair of human nature.

ORTEGA Y GASSET

I hear much of people's calling out to punish the guilty, but very few are concerned to clear the innocent. DEFOE

The more featureless and commonplace a crime is, the more difficult is it to bring it home. CONAN DOYLE

The sacredness of human life is a formula that is good only inside a system of law. O. W. HOLMES, JR.

The law, in its majestic equality, forbids the rich as well as the poor to sleep under bridges. FRANCE

It is questionable whether, when we break a murderer on the wheel, we aren't lapsing into precisely the mistake of the child who hits the chair he bumps into. LICHTENBERG

The law of diminishing returns holds good in almost every part of our human universe. ALDOUS HUXLEY

If the laws could speak for themselves, they would complain of the lawyers in the first place. HALIFAX

Laws are generally not understood by three sorts of persons, viz. by those that make them, by those that execute them, and by those that suffer if they break them. HALIFAX

A popular judge is a deformed thing, and plaudits are fitter for players than for magistrates. BACON

All those who have written of laws have written either as philosophers or as lawyers, and none as statesmen. As for the philosophers, they make imaginary commonwealths, and their discourses are as the stars, which give little light because they are so high. For the lawyers, they write according to the states in which they live, what is received law, and not what ought to be law; for the wisdom of a lawmaker is one, that of a lawyer is another. There are in nature certain fountains of justice, whence all civil laws are derived but as streams: and like as waters do take tinctures and tastes from the soils through which they run, so do civil laws vary according to the regions and governments where they are planted, though they proceed from the same fountains. Again, the wisdom of a lawmaker consisteth not only in a platform of justice, but in the wise application thereof. BACON

If human society cannot be carried on without lawsuits, it cannot be carried on without penalties. ARISTOTLE

The greatest crimes are caused by surfeit, not by want. Men do not become tyrants so as not to suffer cold. ARISTOTLE

The worse our habits, the more we have what is called good legislation. Æ.

Criminals do not die by the hands of the law. They die by the hands of other men. SHAW

A revolt of the judiciary is more dangerous to a government than any other, even a military revolt. Now and then it uses the military to suppress disorder, but it defends itself every day by means of the courts. TOCQUEVILLE

To render a people obedient and keep them so, savage laws inefficiently enforced are less effective than mild laws enforced by an efficient administration regularly, automatically, as it were, every day and on all alike.   TOCQUEVILLE

Civilization is nothing else but the attempt to reduce force to being the last resort.   ORTEGA Y GASSET

One law for the ox and the ass is oppression.   BLAKE

Whilst we have prisons, it matters little which of us occupy the cells.   SHAW

Every kind of government seems to be afflicted by some evil inherent in its nature, and the genius of the legislator consists in his having a clear idea of this evil. A state may survive the influence of a host of bad laws, and the mischief they cause is frequently exaggerated; but a law which encourages the growth of the canker within must prove fatal in the end, although its evil consequences may not be immediately apparent.   TOCQUEVILLE

A community is infinitely more brutalized by the habitual employment of punishment than . . . by the occasional occurrence of crime.   WILDE

It is criminal to steal a purse, daring to steal a fortune, a mark of greatness to steal a crown. The blame diminishes as the guilt increases.   SCHILLER

May you have a lawsuit in which you know you are in the right.   GYPSY CURSE

It is by its promise of an occult sense of power that evil often attracts the weak.　　　　　HOFFER

The criminal is prevented, by the very witnessing of the legal process, from regarding his deed as intrinsically evil.

NIETZSCHE

Some circumstantial evidence is very strong, as when you find a trout in the milk.　　　　　THOREAU

There are certain characters who, unable to read a writ from the court of conscience and reason, must be served with one from a court—even though it be inferior—whose language they understand.　　　　　A. B. SMITH

The people should fight for the law as for their city wall.

HERACLITUS

If there were no bad people there would be no good lawyers.

DICKENS

Men would be great criminals did they need as many laws as they make.　　　　　DARLING

At the beginning of a violent revolution, the laws, made in normal times, are milder than public opinion, suddenly made savage by new passions. But, as the revolution continues, this changes and, in the end, the laws become harsher than public opinion and the latter, by its mildness, paralyzes them. .

TOCQUEVILLE

Law cannot persuade where it cannot punish.

THOMAS FULLER

When a man wants to murder a tiger, he calls it sport: when the tiger wants to murder him, he calls it ferocity. The distinction between crime and justice is no greater.   SHAW

In the United States we easily perceive how the legal profession is qualified by its attributes, and even by its faults, to neutralize the vices inherent in popular government. They secretly oppose their aristocratic propensities to the nation's democratic instincts, their superstitious attachment to what is old to its love of novelty, their narrow views to its immense designs, and their habitual procrastination to its ardent impatience.   TOCQUEVILLE

Prisons are built with stones of law, brothels with bricks of religion.   BLAKE

The doctor sees all the weakness of mankind, the lawyer all the wickedness, the theologian all the stupidity.   SCHOPENHAUER

'Tis healthy to be sick sometimes.   THOREAU

Physicians who cut, burn, stab, and rack the sick demand a fee for it which they do not deserve to get.   HERACLITUS

He cures most in whom most have faith.   GALEN

One finger in the throat and one in the rectum make a good diagnostician.   OSLER

Every invalid is a physician.   IRISH PROVERB

Despise no new accident in your body, but ask opinion of it.
BACON

Keep up the spirits of your patient with the music of the
viol and the psaltery, or by forging letters telling of the death
of his enemies, or (if he be a cleric) by informing him that
he has been made a bishop.   MONDEVILLE

Health of body and mind is a great blessing, if we can bear
it.   NEWMAN

Wherever a doctor cannot do good, he must be kept from
doing harm.   HIPPOCRATES

Stay till I am well, and *then* you shall tell me how to cure
myself.   DR. JOHNSON

Fashions in therapy may have some justification; fashions in
diagnosis have none.   HERRICK AND TYSON

A soul which is truly in earnest is not above disabling the body
to discourage dangerous competition.   HASKINS

It is the manner of hypochondriacs to change often their
physician . . . for a physician who does not admit the
reality of the disease cannot be supposed to take much pains
to cure it.   CULLEN

The soul's maladies have their relapses like the body's. What
we take for a cure is often just a momentary rally or a new
form of the disease.   LA ROCHEFOUCAULD

When a man dies, he does not just die of the disease he has: he dies of his whole life.   PÉGUY

The physics of a man's circulation are the physics of the waterworks of the town in which he lives, but once out of gear you cannot apply the same rules for the repair of the one as of the other.   OSLER

Did you ever observe that there are two classes of patients in states, slaves and freemen; and the slave doctors run about and cure the slaves, or wait for them in dispensaries—practitioners of this sort never talk to their patients individually or let them talk about their own individual complaints. The slave doctor prescribes what mere experience suggests, as if he had exact knowledge, and when he has given his orders, like a tyrant, he rushes off with equal assurance to some other servant who is ill. But the other doctor, who is a freeman, attends and practices on freemen; and he carries his inquiries far back, and goes into the nature of the disorder; he enters into discourse with the patient and with his friends, and is at once getting information from the sick man and also instructing him as far as he is able, and he will not prescribe until he has at first convinced him. If one of those empirical physicians, who practice medicine without science, were to come upon the gentleman physician talking to his gentleman patient and using the language almost of philosophy, beginning at the beginning of the disease and discoursing about the whole nature of the body, he would burst into a hearty laugh—he would say what most of those who are called doctors always have at their tongues' end: Foolish fellow, he would say, you are not healing the sick man but educating him; and he does not want to be made a doctor but to get well.   PLATO

Don't ask the doctor; ask the patient.   YIDDISH PROVERB

It is astonishing with how little reading a doctor can practice medicine, but it is not astonishing how badly he may do it.

OSLER

Care more for the individual patient than for the special features of the disease.

OSLER

Don't touch the patient—state first what you see.

OSLER

The desire to take medicine is perhaps the greatest feature which distinguishes man from animals.

OSLER

One of the first duties of the physician is to educate the masses not to take medicine.

OSLER

Illnesses must be regarded as a madness of the body, indeed as *idées fixes*.

NOVALIS

The sick man lets the doctor call out because he cannot help him.

NOVALIS

Jaundice is the disease that your friends diagnose.

OSLER

Every sickness is a musical problem; every cure a musical solution.

NOVALIS

The relation between psychiatrists and other kinds of lunatic is more or less the relation of a convex folly to a concave one.

KRAUS

What fast friends picturesqueness and typhus often are!

DICKENS

A good deal of superciliousness
Is based on biliousness.
People seem as proud as peacocks
Of any infirmity, be it hives or dementia praecox.

NASH

Syphilis simulates every other disease. It is the only disease necessary to know. Know syphilis in all its manifestations and relations, and all other things clinical will be added to you.

OSLER

Medicine is the only profession that labors incessantly to destroy the reason for its existence.

BRYCE

Illness is the most heeded of doctors: to goodness and wisdom we only make promises; pain we obey.

PROUST

It often happens that the sicker man is the nurse to the sounder.

THOREAU

It is not the number of nervous diseases and patients that has grown, but the number of doctors able to study the diseases.

CHEKHOV

Neurosis does not deny the existence of reality, it merely tries to ignore it: psychosis denies it and tries to substitute something else for it. A reaction which combines features of both these is the one we call normal or "healthy"; it denies reality as little as neurosis, but then, like a psychosis, is concerned with effecting a change in it.

FREUD

A doctor used to say: "Only heirs really pay well."

CHAMFORT

No doubt fate would find it easier than I do to relieve you of your illness. But you will be able to convince yourself that much will be gained if we succeed in transforming your hysterical misery into common unhappiness. FREUD

It is not the business of the doctor to say that we must go to a watering place; it is his affair to say that certain results to health will follow if we do go to a watering place.

CHESTERTON

To talk of diseases is a sort of Arabian Nights entertainment.

OSLER

Medicine is a science, acquiring a practice an art.

ANONYMOUS

The priest's friend loses his faith, the doctor's his health, the lawyer's his fortune. VENETIAN PROVERB

A man who preaches in the stocks will always have hearers enough. DR. JOHNSON

Everything suffers by translation except a bishop.

CHESTERFIELD

Cardinal de Retz very sagaciously marked out Cardinal Chigi for a little mind, from the moment that he told him he had wrote three years with the same pen, and that it was an excellent good one still. CHESTERFIELD

The dreary thing about most new causes is that they are praised in such very old terms. Every new religion bores us with the same stale rhetoric about closer fellowship and the higher life. CHESTERTON

I am much tempted to say of metaphysicians what Scaliger said of the Basques: "They are said to understand one another, but I don't believe a word of it."   CHAMFORT

Always mistrust a subordinate who never finds fault with his superior.   COLLINS

I am unable to understand how a man of honor could take a newspaper in his hands without a shudder of disgust.

BAUDELAIRE

If one wishes to know the real power of the press, one should pay attention, not to what it says, but to the way in which it is listened to. There are times when its very heat is a symptom of weakness and prophesies its end. Its clamors and its fears often speak in the same voice. It only cries so loud because its audience is becoming deaf.

TOCQUEVILLE

The immense nausea of advertisements.   BAUDELAIRE

Advertising has annihilated the power of the most powerful adjectives.   VALÉRY

Advertising is the modern substitute for argument; its function is to make the worse appear the better.   SANTAYANA

Even were a cook to cook a fly, he would keep the breast for himself.   POLISH PROVERB

Modesty is ruin to a harlot.   THE HITOPADESA

Thieves hunt in couples but a liar alone.

AMERICAN PROVERB

Servants sometimes don't see what we show them, but they always see what we hide from them.   DÉPRET

The highest panegyric . . . that private virtue can receive is the praise of servants.   DR. JOHNSON

If I accustom a servant to tell a lie for *me*, have I not reason to apprehend that he will tell many lies for *himself*?   DR. JOHNSON

Anyone who is practically acquainted with scientific work is aware that those who refuse to go beyond fact rarely get as far as fact.   T. H. HUXLEY

Astronomy was the daughter of idleness.   FONTENELLE

An officer is always much more respected than any other man who has as little money.   DR. JOHNSON

Those who counsel do not pay.   FLEMISH PROVERB

The worst cliques are those which consist of one man.   SHAW

Those who cannot miss an opportunity of saying a good thing . . . are not to be trusted with the management of any great question.   HAZLITT

Some, for fear their orations should giggle, will not let them smile.   THOMAS FULLER

Critics are like brushers of noblemen's clothes.   HERBERT

A writer with real taste trying to attract our surfeited public is like a young woman set inside a circle of old libertines.

CHAMFORT

How these authors magnify their office! One dishonest plumber does more harm than a hundred poetasters.

BIRRELL

No man but a blockhead ever wrote, except for money.

DR. JOHNSON

No man forgets his original trade: the rights of nations, and of kings, sink into questions of grammar, if grammarians discuss them.

DR. JOHNSON

There is often found in commentators a spontaneous strain of invective and contempt more eager and venomous than is vented by the most furious controvertist in politics against those whom he is hired to defame.

DR. JOHNSON

I confess to some pleasure from . . . a rattling oath in the mouth of truckmen and teamsters. How laconic and brisk it is by the side of a page of the *North American Review*.

EMERSON

A professor's opinion: not Shakespeare is the thing, but the commentaries on him.

CHEKHOV

Devotees of grammatical studies have not been distinguished for any very remarkable felicities of expression.

ALCOTT

No place affords a more striking conviction of the vanity of human hopes than a public library.

DR. JOHNSON

There be some men are born only to suck out the poison of books. JONSON

A scholar reads the books of other scholars, lest he shall say something that shows ignorance. . . . He dare not miss a trick; just as the social climber dare not miss a party.

CHAPMAN

It is better to speak wisdom foolishly, like the saints, rather than to speak folly wisely, like the dons. CHESTERTON

One chops the wood, the other does the grunting.

YIDDISH PROVERB

If I dealt in candles, the sun would never set.

YIDDISH PROVERB

Patience is a most necessary quality for business: many a man would rather you heard his story than granted his request.

CHESTERFIELD

When a merchant speaks of sheep he means the hide.

SWISS PROVERB

The by-product is sometimes more valuable than the product.

ELLIS

A corporation cannot blush. ASCRIBED TO HOWEL WALSH

It is unquestionably possible for an incorruptible man to succeed in business. But his scruples are an embarrassment. He must make up in ability for what he lacks in moral obliquity. CHAPMAN

Men of business must not break their word twice.

THOMAS FULLER

Whatever is not nailed down is mine. Whatever I can pry loose is not nailed down.

ASCRIBED TO COLLIS P. HUNTINGTON

My business is to teach my aspirations to confirm themselves to fact, not to try and make facts harmonize with my aspirations.

T. H. HUXLEY

The investigator should have a robust faith—and yet not believe.

BERNARD

Basic research is when I'm doing what I don't know I'm doing.

BRAUN

Tolerably early in life I discovered that one of the unpardonable sins, in the eyes of most people, is for a man to go about unlabeled. The world regards such a person as the police do an unmuzzled dog.

T. H. HUXLEY

To make a trade of laughing at a fool is the highway to become one.

THOMAS FULLER

The best qualification of a prophet is to have a good memory.

HALIFAX

He who is not in some measure a pedant, though he may be a wise, cannot be a very happy man.

HAZLITT

The cleverly expressed opposite of any generally accepted idea is worth a fortune to somebody.

FITZGERALD

The humorist runs with the hare; the satirist hunts with the hounds.

FATHER KNOX

The test of a vocation is the love of the drudgery it involves.

L. P. SMITH

On the day when a young writer corrects his first proof sheets, he is as proud as a schoolboy who has just got his first dose of pox.

BAUDELAIRE

Journalists write because they have nothing to say, and have something to say because they write.

KRAUS

As a rule, hatred of strangers and love of his native soil comprise the whole of a soldier's feeling for the public good, even in free societies.

TOCQUEVILLE

That in the captain's but a choleric word
Which in the soldier is rank blasphemy.

SHAKESPEARE

Every man is a revolutionist concerning the thing he understands. For example, every person who has mustered a profession is a skeptic concerning it and, consequently, a revolutionist.

SHAW

You can tell the ideals of a nation by its advertisements.

DOUGLAS

A wit has said that one might divide mankind into officers, serving maids, and chimney sweeps. To my mind this remark is not only witty but profound, and it would require a great speculative talent to devise a better classification. When a classification does not ideally exhaust its object, a haphazard classification is altogether preferable, because it sets imagination in motion.

KIERKEGAARD

HISTORY

History

The essential matter of history is not what happened but what people thought or said about it.   MAITLAND

The tapestry of history has no point at which you can cut it and leave the design intelligible.   DIX

History is on every occasion the record of that which one age finds worthy of note in another.   BURCKHARDT

History is the science of what never happens twice.   VALÉRY

The handwriting on the wall may be a forgery.   HODGSON

Tales of noble self-sacrifice never remain mere adjuncts to a creed, or portions of a partisan tradition. They contain in themselves the whole of salvation. Here are the gems in the treasury of a nation's life; and it matters not to later ages whether the geological strata in which they lie embedded be Catholic or Protestant, Christian or pagan, political or religious.   CHAPMAN

There is properly no history, only biography.   EMERSON

The historians of antiquity taught how to command, those of our time only how to obey; in their writings, the author often appears great, but humanity is always diminutive.

TOCQUEVILLE

Every beginning is a consequence—every beginning *ends* something.

VALÉRY

What a vast difference there is between the barbarism that precedes culture and the barbarism that follows it.   HEBBEL

It is just possible to imagine what past epochs included in their thinking, but not what they excluded.

HOFMANNSTHAL

Doctrines must take their beginning from the beginning of the matters of which they treat.

VICO

Perhaps in time the so-called Dark Ages will be thought of as including our own.   LICHTENBERG

Just as the children's crusade may be said to typify the Middle Ages, precocious children are typical of the present age.

KIERKEGAARD

The Middle Ages may have been a time of salutary delay. If it had exploited the earth's surface as we are doing, we would perhaps not be around at all.   BURCKHARDT

The greatest inventions were produced in the times of ignorance, as the use of the compass, gunpowder, and printing.

SWIFT

To medieval man the world was itself the ultramundane and the supernatural. ORTEGA Y GASSET

It would be a good thing if man concerned himself more with the history of his nature than with the history of his deeds. HEBBEL

When gossip grows old it becomes myth. LEC

During a golden age, almost everything that glitters is real gold. ORTEGA Y GASSET

Histories of the downfall of kingdoms, and revolutions of empires, are read with great tranquillity. DR. JOHNSON

If all the dreams which men had dreamed during a particular period were written down, they would give an accurate notion of the spirit which prevailed at the time. HEGEL

History cannot be more certain than when he who creates the things also narrates them. VICO

Temporal things will have their weight in the world, and tho zeal may prevail for a time, and get the better in a skirmish, yet the war endeth generally on the side of flesh and blood, and will do so till mankind is another thing than it is at present. HALIFAX

The thought of the Middle Ages was not limited, but perhaps its vocabulary was. WILLIAMS

Is it progress if a cannibal uses knife and fork?   LEC

The great achievements of the past were the adventures of the past. Only the adventurous can understand the greatness of the past.   WHITEHEAD

It is not St. Augustine's nor St. Ambrose's works that will make so wise a divine as ecclesiastical history thoroughly read and observed.   BACON

In history, as soon as the man of action puts in an appearance and is discussed and pampered, it means that a period of rebarbarization looms.   ORTEGA Y GASSET

Real stories, in distinction from those we invent, have no author. Although history owes its existence to men, it is not "made" by them.   HANNAH ARENDT

The hour of their crime does not strike simultaneously for all nations: this explains the permanence of history.   CIORAN

The annals of all nations bear witness that an enslaved people always suffers more deeply from those of its own blood who take service under the conquerors than it suffers from the conquerors themselves.   FREEMAN

Two things we ought to learn from history: one, that we are not in ourselves superior to our fathers; another, that we are shamefully and monstrously inferior to them, if we do not advance beyond them.   T. ARNOLD

Someone said: "The dead writers are remote from us because we *know* so much more than they did." Precisely, and they are that which we know.   T. S. ELIOT

Tradition means giving votes to the most obscure of all classes—our ancestors. It is the democracy of the dead. Tradition refuses to submit to the small and arrogant oligarchy of those who merely happen to be walking around.

CHESTERTON

By no means every destruction has been followed by rejuvenation, and the great destroyers of life remain an enigma to us.   BURCKHARDT

Historic continuity with the past is not a duty, it is only a necessity.   O. W. HOLMES, JR.

One age cannot be completely understood if all the others are not understood. The song of history can only be sung as a whole.   ORTEGA Y GASSET

What forests of laurel we bring, and the tears of mankind, to those who stood firm against the opinion of their contemporaries.   EMERSON

History is the sole consolation left to the people, for it shows them that their ancestors were as unhappy as they are, or even more so.   CHAMFORT

In analyzing history, do not be too profound, for often the causes are quite superficial.   EMERSON

Civilized ages inherit the human nature which was victorious in barbarous ages, and that nature is, in many respects, not at all suited to civilized circumstances. BAGEHOT

"This or that hallway would have to be the most beautiful if only because it leads to our room." What coldness and heartlessness there is in this attitude: the ignoring of the silenced moans of all the vanquished who, as a rule, had wanted nothing else but to preserve what had come into being. How *much* must perish so that *something* new may arise! BURCKHARDT

The major fact about history is that in large part it appears criminal. W. E. ARNOLD, JR.

In history the way of annihilation is invariably prepared by inward degeneration, by decrease of life. Only then can a shock from outside put an end to the whole. BURCKHARDT

Every successful wickedness is, to say the least, a scandal. . . . The only lesson to be derived from the successful misdeeds of the strong is to hold life here and now in no higher esteem than it deserves. BURCKHARDT

All genuine records are at first tedious, because and insofar as they are alien. They set forth the views and interests of their time *for their time* and come no step to meet us. But the shams of today are addressed to us and are therefore made amusing and intelligible, as fake antiques generally are. BURCKHARDT

History is all improvisation, all will, all enterprise. There are no frontiers, there are no timetables, no itineraries. HERZEN

There are two camps which, under different disguises, remain the same throughout all history, and may be distinguished either in a great political party or in a group of a dozen young men. One represents logic; the other history: one stands for dialectics; the other for evolution. Truth is the main object of the former, and feasibility of the latter. There is no question of choice between them; thought is harder to tame than the passions and pulls with irresistible strength.

HERZEN

The word *urbanity* had gained circulation and become part of the language at the beginning of the seventeenth century; it was fair that the word *vulgarity* should become part of it at the end of the eighteenth.   **MME. DE STAËL**

I have come across men of letters who have written history without taking part in public affairs, and politicians who have concerned themselves with producing events without thinking about them. I have observed that the first are always inclined to find general causes, whereas the second, living in the midst of disconnected daily facts, are prone to imagine that everything is attributable to particular incidents, and that the wires they pull are the same as those that move the world. It is to be presumed that both are equally deceived.

TOCQUEVILLE

When government policies or historical accidents make the attainment of individual self-respect difficult, the nationalist spirit of the people becomes more ardent and extreme.

HOFFER

The French Revolution first introduced into Europe the notion of the tissue-paper frontier. Hitherto, all boundaries had been marches, forests, mountains, dikes; that is to say, significant boundaries. But when boundaries can be drawn on paper, they need have no more significance than the stroke of a pen or a piece of chalk.   **ROSENSTOCK-HUESSY**

In 1799 General Tamax received a proposal from Napoleon, who wished to enter the Russian service, but they were unable to agree, as Napoleon demanded the rank of major.

TOLSTOI

Great historical transformations are always bought dearly, often after one has already thought that one got them at a bargain price.   BURCKHARDT

During periods of crisis, positions which are false or feigned are very common. Entire generations falsify themselves to themselves; that is to say, they wrap themselves up in artistic styles, in doctrines, in political movements which are insincere and which fill the lack of genuine convictions. When they get to be about forty years old, those generations become null and void, because at that age one can no longer live on fictions.   ORTEGA Y GASSET

A historical judgment should always be such that it can be endorsed at least by all nations if not by all factions.

BURCKHARDT

Systems die; instincts remain.   O. W. HOLMES, JR.

After a lost war one should only write comedies.   NOVALIS

When the *canaille roturière* took the liberty of beheading the high *noblesse*, it was done less, perhaps, to inherit their goods than to inherit their ancestors.   HEINE

The future smells of Russian leather, blood, godlessness, and many whippings. I should advise our grandchildren to be born with very thick skins on their backs.   HEINE

So long as we read about revolutions in books, they all look very nice—like those landscapes which, as artistic engravings on white vellum, look so pure and friendly: dung heaps engraved on copper do not smell, and the eye can easily wade through an engraved morass.   HEINE

[The Victorians] were lame giants; the strongest of them walked on one leg a little shorter than the other. . . . There is a moment when Carlyle turns suddenly from a high creative mystic to a common Calvinist. There are moments when George Eliot turns from a prophetess into a governess. There are also moments when Ruskin turns into a governess, without even the excuse of sex.   CHESTERTON

The great mistake of the Marxists and of the whole of the nineteenth century was to think that by walking straight on one mounted upward into the air.   SIMONE WEIL

Men after death . . . are understood worse than men of the moment, but *heard* better.   NIETZSCHE

I have read . . . in Dionysius of Halicarnassus, I think, that history is philosophy teaching by examples.   BOLINGBROKE

Respect for the past must be pious, but not mad.   ROZINOV

The object of a New Year is not that we should have a new year. It is that we should have a new soul and a new nose, new feet, a new backbone, new ears, and new eyes. Unless a man starts on the strange assumption that he has never existed before, it is quite certain that he will never exist afterward.   CHESTERTON

Not only progress but mere change, mere movement, has had its countless martyrs. NIETZSCHE

Progress celebrates Pyrrhic victories over nature. KRAUS

Progress is the mother of problems. CHESTERTON

Persistent prophecy is a familiar way of assuring the event. GISSING

The newspaper is the second hand in the clock of history; and it is not only made of baser metal than those which point to the minute and the hour, but it seldom goes right. SCHOPENHAUER

Quite often in history action has been the echo of words. An era of talk was followed by an era of events. The new barbarism of the twentieth century is the echo of words bandied about by brilliant speakers and writers in the second half of the nineteenth. HOFFER

A nation's preoccupation with history is not infrequently an effort to obtain a passport for the future. Often it is a forged passport. HOFFER

We all live in the past, because there is nothing else to live in. To live in the present is like proposing to sit on a pin. It is too minute, it is too slight a support, it is too uncomfortable a posture, and it is of necessity followed immediately by totally different experiences, analogous to those of jumping up with a yell. To live in the future is a contradiction in terms. The future is dead, in the perfectly definite sense that it is not alive. CHESTERTON

Our ignorance of history makes us vilify our own age.
                                                    FLAUBERT

It is the mission of history to make our fellow beings acceptable to us.   ORTEGA Y GASSET

Each generation criticizes the unconscious assumptions made by its parents. It may assent to them, but it brings them out into the open.   WHITEHEAD

Men resemble their contemporaries even more than their progenitors.   EMERSON

We are the children of our age, but children who can never know their mother.   L. P. SMITH

Suffering only becomes unbearable when, separated from the great silence in the world, it is merely a part of the noise of history, and then has to bear its burden alone.   PICARD

Perhaps war is becoming more and more violent and terrible today because it wants to be seen as what it really is, to be seen quite clearly as the terrible thing it really is, and not as a mere part of the noise of the radio.   PICARD

Chance is a mask, and it is precisely the historian's duty to lift it or tear it away.   GOURMONT

It is not true that contemporaries misjudge a man. Competent contemporaries judge him . . . much better than posterity, which is composed of critics no less egotistical, and obliged to rely exclusively on documents easily misinterpreted.
                                                    SANTAYANA

The reasonable man adapts himself to the world; the un-reasonable one persists in trying to adapt the world to himself. Therefore all progress depends on the unreasonable man.

SHAW

The obscurest epoch is today.   STEVENSON

Modern man no longer trusts his aunts and grandmothers; they, like old furniture, become the outfit of museums. He does trust textbooks.   ROSENSTOCK-HUESSY

We fret over improving things, that posterity may be happy; and posterity will say as usual: "In the past things were better, the present is worse than the past." CHEKHOV

A historian is a prophet in reverse. SCHLEGEL

By seeking after origins, one becomes a crab. The historian looks backward; eventually he also *believes* backward.

NIETZSCHE

The historian must have some conception of how men who are not historians behave. FORSTER

It requires an impartial man to make a good historian; but it is the partial and one-sided who hunt out the materials.

ACTON

The man who writes about himself and his own time is the only man who writes about all people and about all time.

SHAW

It is the province of the historian to find out, not what was, but what is. Where a battle has been fought, you will find nothing but the bones of men and beasts; where a battle is being fought, there are hearts beating. THOREAU

The first qualification for a historian is to have no ability to invent.   STENDHAL

All the historical books that contain no lies are extremely tedious.   FRANCE

The *historian*, essentially, wants more documents than he can really use; the *dramatist* only wants more liberties than he can really take.   HENRY JAMES

If a man could say nothing against a character but what he could prove, history could not be written.   DR. JOHNSON

The middle sort of historians . . . spoil all; they will chew our meat for us.   MONTAIGNE

Neither paganism nor Christianity ever produced a profound political historian whose mind was not turned to gloom by the contemplation of the affairs of men. It is almost a test to distinguish the great narrators from the great thinkers.

ACTON

It takes time to ruin a world, but time is all it takes.

FONTENELLE

The history of a soldier's wound beguiles the pain of it.

STERNE

Those who cannot remember the past are condemned to repeat it.   SANTAYANA

Life must be lived forwards, but can only be understood backwards.   KIERKEGAARD

Repetition is reality, and it is the seriousness of life.

KIERKEGAARD

Happy the people whose annals are boring to read.

MONTESQUIEU

You want to know how story go, wait till quarrel come.

NEGRO PROVERB

At the moment you are prophesying in the desert, the fine pollen of an oak is falling to the ground and, in a century, will grow up into a forest.

RICHTER

There is in all change something at once sordid and agreeable, smacking of infidelity and household removals.

BAUDELAIRE

Though a good deal is too strange to be believed, nothing is too strange to have happened.

HARDY

It is not obligatory for a generation to have great men.

ORTEGA Y GASSET

Whether a prophet is true or false does not depend upon the correctness of his predictions. It depends upon the purity and sincerity of his concern for the things threatened by human sin and divine anger. Indeed his predictions are the more likely to be correct, the less he is a true prophet and the more affinities he has within himself to the destructive tendencies of his age.

HELLER

"Necessity is the mother of invention" is a silly proverb. "Necessity is the mother of futile dodges" is much nearer the truth.

WHITEHEAD

ACTION

Action

Vice stirs up war; virtue fights.   VAUVENARGUES

To delight in war is a merit in the soldier, a dangerous quality
in the captain, and a positive crime in the statesman.
                                                  SANTAYANA

The martial character cannot prevail in a whole people but
by the diminution of all other virtues.   DR. JOHNSON

Loyalty implies loyalty in misfortune; and when a soldier
has accepted any nation's uniform he has already accepted
its defeat.   CHESTERTON

Three-quarters of a soldier's life is spent in aimlessly waiting
about.   ROSENSTOCK-HUESSY

Children play at being soldiers. That is sensible. But why
should soldiers play at being children?   KRAUS

To knock a thing down, especially if it is cocked at an
arrogant angle, is a deep delight to the blood. To fight for
a reason and in a calculating spirit is something your true
warrior despises.   SANTAYANA

I think Caesar was too old to find his amusement in conquering the world. Such a game was all right for Augustus or Alexander. They were still young and difficult to control. But Caesar ought to have been more mature.　　PASCAL

War appears to be as old as mankind, but peace is a modern invention.　　MAINE

The warrior provides for his grandfather and his grandson at the cost, if necessary, of his life. But his sacrifice only makes sense within a time span of at least three generations. There can be no genuine soldier or army unless there is a past to hand on to the future after a war is over.

ROSENSTOCK-HUESSY

War can protect; it cannot create.　　WHITEHEAD

I don't at all desire war, and I'd prevent it a thousand times over if it were in my power; but once this business is decided, I'd be delighted if it were waged and I was there. This is a case where it may nearly always be said, "You'll never see again what you've already seen," and I'm beginning to notice that this is the only thing that makes three-quarters of men and things bearable.　　STENDHAL

In peace, sons bury their fathers; in war, fathers bury their sons.　　HERODOTUS

This only makes a war lawful: that it is a struggle for law against force; for the life of a people as expressed in their laws, their language, their government, against any effort to impose on them a law, a language, a government which is not theirs.　　MAURICE

Wars may be caused, or empires fall, not necessarily through some extraordinary criminality in the first place, but from multitudinous cases of petty betrayal or individual neglect.

BUTTERFIELD

How good bad music and bad reasons sound when we march against an enemy.   NIETZSCHE

From noon until three o'clock, we had an excellent view of all that can be seen of a battle—i.e., nothing at all. The pleasure consists in being somewhat thrilled by the certainty that something is taking place before you that is known to be terrible. The majestic sound of the cannon fire is, in large measure, responsible for this effect. It is in complete harmony with the impression. If the cannon produced the shrill sound of a whistle, I don't believe it would arouse so much emotion. I realize quite well that the sound of a whistle would become terrible, but it would never be as fine a one as that of the cannon.   STENDHAL

A few conquer by fighting, but it is well to remember that more battles are won by submitting.   E. HUBBARD

The reward of the general is not a bigger tent, but command.

O. W. HOLMES, JR.

One bad general does better than two good ones.

NAPOLEON

Nothing except a battle lost can be half so melancholy as a battle won.   WELLINGTON

The third part of an army must be destroyed, before a good one can be made out of it.   HALIFAX

In order to have good soldiers a nation must be always at war.
NAPOLEON

The army is a school in which the niggardly become generous and the generous prodigal; if there are soldiers who are misers, like monsters they are very rarely seen.
CERVANTES

Generals cannot be entrusted with anything, not even with war.
CLEMENCEAU

Force and fraud are in war the two cardinal virtues.
HOBBES

In time of war the loudest patriots are the greatest profiteers.
BEBEL

War hath no fury like a noncombatant.   C. E. MONTAGUE

Soldiers who don't know what they're fighting for know, nevertheless, what they're not fighting for.
KRAUS

Liberty means responsibility. That is why most men dread it.
SHAW

Men that distrust their own subtlety are, in tumult and sedition, better disposed for victory than they that suppose themselves wise. For these love to consult; the other, fearing to be circumvented, to strike first.
HOBBES

The matter of seditions is of two kinds: much poverty and much discontentment. And if this poverty and broken estate in the better sort be joined with a want and necessity in the mean people, the danger is imminent and great. For the rebellions of the belly are the worst.
BACON

As a rule, insurrections—I mean even those which succeed—begin without a leader; but they always end by securing one.

TOCQUEVILLE

To reform means to shatter one form and to create another; but the two sides of this act are not always equally intended nor equally successful.

SANTAYANA

The purity of a revolution can last a fortnight.

COCTEAU

The men who lose their heads most easily, and who generally show themselves weakest on days of revolution, are the military; accustomed as they are to have an organized force facing them and an obedient force in their hands, they readily become confused before the tumultuous uproar of a crowd and in the presence of the hesitation and occasional connivance of their own men.

TOCQUEVILLE

In times of revolution, people boast almost as much about the imaginary crimes they propose to commit as, in normal times, they do of the good intentions they pretend to entertain.

TOCQUEVILLE

In revolution there is no *joy*. Nor ever will be.

ROZINOV

The secret of the demagogue is to make himself as stupid as his audience so that they believe they are as clever as he.

KRAUS

Heroes are created by popular demand, sometimes out of the scantiest materials . . . such as the apple that William Tell never shot, the ride that Paul Revere never finished, the flag that Barbara Frietchie never waved.

G. W. JOHNSON

It is absurd to speak of right and wrong *per se*. Injury, violation, exploitation, annihilation, cannot be wrong in themselves, for life essentially presupposes injury, violation, exploitation, and annihilation. NIETZSCHE

To be engaged in opposing wrong affords but a slender guarantee for being right. GLADSTONE

Force is not a remedy. BRIGHT

The only way to predict the future is to have power to shape the future. Those in possession of absolute power can not only prophesy and make their prophecies come true, but they can also lie and make their lies comes true. HOFFER

Let not thy will roar, when thy power can but whisper. DR. FULLER

It requires great abilities to have the *power* of being very wicked; but not to *be* very wicked. It requires great abilities to conquer an army, but none to massacre it after it is conquered. DR. JOHNSON

The more you are talked about, the less powerful you are. DISRAELI

The will to power, as the modern age from Hobbes to Nietzsche understood it, far from being a characteristic of the strong, is, like envy and greed, among the vices of the weak, and possibly even their most dangerous one. Power corrupts indeed when the weak band together in order to ruin the strong, but not before. HANNAH ARENDT

Power is not revealed by striking hard or often, but by striking true.   BALZAC

The tyrant dies and his rule is over; the martyr dies and his rule begins.   KIERKEGAARD

So much of an idealist about his ideals that he can be a ruthless realist in his methods.   CHESTERTON

Success has always been a great liar.   NIETZSCHE

Nothing arouses ambition so much . . . as the trumpet clang of another's fame.   GRACIAN

The man who can make others laugh secures more votes for a measure than the man who forces them to think.
                                                        CHAZAL

Success generally depends upon knowing how long it takes to succeed.   MONTESQUIEU

A man who could not seduce men cannot save them either.
                                                        KIERKEGAARD

For a man to achieve all that is demanded of him he must regard himself as greater than he is.   GOETHE

Great things are accomplished by those who do not feel the impotence of man. This insensibility is a precious gift; but it must be frankly admitted that, in this respect, criminals bear a certain resemblance to our heroes.   VALÉRY

It is best for great men to shoot over, and for lesser men to shoot short. **HALIFAX**

There may now exist great men for things that do not exist. **BURCKHARDT**

The great man is powerful, involuntarily and composedly powerful, but he is not avid for power. What he is avid for is the realization of what he has in mind, the incarnation of the spirit. So long as a man's power is bound to the goal, the work, the calling, it is, in itself, neither good nor evil, only a suitable or unsuitable instrument. But as soon as this bond with the goal is broken off or loosened, and the man ceases to think of power as the capacity to do something, but thinks of it as a possession, then his power, being cut off and self-satisfied, is evil and corrupts the history of the world. **BUBER**

> Great actions are not always true sons
> Of great and mighty resolutions.
> **SAMUEL BUTLER (I)**

For souls in growth, great quarrels are great emancipations. **L. P. SMITH**

The world will only, in the end, follow those who have despised as well as served it. **SAMUEL BUTLER (II)**

Great writers and artists should engage in politics only to the extent necessary to defend themselves against politics. Even without political considerations there are plenty of accusers, prosecutors, and policemen, and in any case the role of Paul suits them better than that of Saul. **CHEKHOV**

The initiator dies—or turns traitor. **HEINE**

The world is beholden to *generous mistakes* for the greatest part of the good that is done in it.　　HALIFAX

One should never wear one's best trousers to go out and battle for freedom and truth.　　IBSEN

No great man ever complains of want of opportunity.

EMERSON

To be a leader of men one must turn one's back on men.

ELLIS

Courage ought to have eyes as well as arms.

ENGLISH PROVERB

Except a person be part coward, it is not a compliment to say he is brave.　　MARK TWAIN

A great part of courage is the courage of having done the thing before.　　EMERSON

Some men have acted courage who had it not; but no man can act wit.　　HALIFAX

Courage is a quality so necessary for maintaining virtue that it is always respected, even when it is associated with vice.

DR. JOHNSON

It is better to wear out one's shoes than one's sheets.

GENOESE PROVERB

We work not only to produce but to give value to time.

DELACROIX

Living movements do not come of committees.   NEWMAN

In order to act wisely it is not enough to be wise.

DOSTOEVSKI

Beware of all enterprises that require new clothes.   THOREAU

I do not believe in a fate that falls on men however they act; but I do believe in a fate that falls on men unless they act.

CHESTERTON

A man who has to be convinced to act before he acts is *not* a man of action. . . . You must act as you breathe.

CLEMENCEAU

It is not given to the children of men to be philosophers without envy. Lookers-on can hardly bear the spectacle of the great world.   BAGEHOT

Action without a name, a "who" attached to it, is meaningless.

HANNAH ARENDT

There is no quicker way of getting the crowd to shout *Hosannah* than by riding into the city on the back of an ass.

NIETZSCHE

Our actions are like rhyme games: we fill out the rest of the lines with whatever motives for the actions we please.

LA ROCHEFOUCAULD

If a thing is worth doing, it is worth doing badly.

CHESTERTON

Men are much more apt to agree in what they do than in what they think.   GOETHE

It is intelligent to ask two questions: 1) Is it possible? 2) Can I do it? But it is unintelligent to ask these questions: 1) Is it real? 2) Has my neighbor Christopherson done it?

KIERKEGAARD

No sooner do men despair of living forever than they are disposed to act as though they were to exist for but a single day.

TOCQUEVILLE

It is the mark of a good action that it appears inevitable in restrospect.

STEVENSON

Pliny leaves mankind this only alternative: either of doing what deserves to be written, or of writing what deserves to be read.

CHESTERFIELD

The strength of a man's virtue should not be measured by his special exertions, but by his habitual acts.

PASCAL

In times when the passions are beginning to take charge of the conduct of human affairs, one should pay less attention to what men of experience and common sense are thinking than to what is preoccupying the imagination of dreamers.

TOCQUEVILLE

The most advantageous negotiations are those one conducts with human vanity, for one often obtains very substantial things from it while giving very little of substance in return. One never does so well when dealing with ambition or avarice.

TOCQUEVILLE

Next to knowing when to seize an opportunity, the most important thing in life is to know when to forgo an advantage.

DISRAELI

The secret of all victory lies in the organization of the non-obvious.   SPENGLER

There are exceptions to all rules, but it seldom answers to follow the advice of an opponent.   DISRAELI

In skating over thin ice, our safety is in our speed.

EMERSON

> Diplomacy is to do and say
> The nastiest thing in the nicest way.

GOLDBERG

It is unfortunate, considering that enthusiasm moves the world, that so few enthusiasts can be trusted to speak the truth.   BALFOUR

Vilify! Vilify! Some of it will always stick.   BEAUMARCHAIS

Every honest man is a prophet; he utters his opinion both of private and public matters. Thus, if you go on so, the result is so. He never says, such a thing shall happen let you do what you will. A prophet is a seer, not an arbitrary dictator.   BLAKE

A man may devote himself to death and destruction to save a nation; but no nation will devote itself to death and destruction to save mankind.   COLERIDGE

Bring out number, weight and measure in a year of dearth.

BLAKE

Romantic ruthlessness is no nearer to real politics than is romantic self-abnegation.   WHITEHEAD

When you say that you agree to a thing on principle, you mean that you have not the slightest intention of carrying it out in practice.   BISMARCK

A practical man is a man who practices the errors of his fore-fathers.   DISRAELI

Business is really more agreeable than pleasure; it interests the whole mind, the aggregate nature of man, more continuously, and more deeply. But it does not *look* as if it did.   BAGEHOT

Under certain circumstances, men who do not know how to speak produce a greater impression than the finest orator. They bring forward but a single idea, and somehow they lay it down on the rostrum like an inscription in capital letters, which everybody understands and in which each instantly recognizes his own particular thought.   TOCQUEVILLE

In contrast to revenge, which is the natural, automatic reaction to transgression and which, because of the irreversibility of the action process, can be expected and even calculated, the act of forgiving can never be predicted; it is the only reaction that acts in an unexpected way and thus retains, though being a reaction, something of the original character of action.

HANNAH ARENDT

If you wish to drown, do not torture yourself with shallow water.   BULGARIAN PROVERB

If some great catastrophe is not announced every morning, we feel a certain void. "Nothing in the paper today," we sigh.

VALÉRY

Exile immobilizes to some degree the minds of those who suffer it. It imprisons them forever within the circle of ideas which they had conceived or which were current when their exile began. For the exile, the new conditions which have been created in his native country and the new ways of thinking and behaving which have been established there do not exist.

TOCQUEVILLE

He that leaveth nothing to chance will do few things ill, but he will do very few things.　　　　　　HALIFAX

SCIENCE

Science

A fact, in science, is not a mere fact, but an instance.

RUSSELL

Put off your imagination, as you put off your overcoat, when you enter the laboratory. But put it on again, as you put on your overcoat, when you leave.

BERNARD

He is not a true man of science who does not bring some sympathy to his studies, and expect to learn something by behavior as well as by application. It is childish to rest in the discovery of mere coincidences, or of partial and extraneous laws. The study of geometry is a petty and idle exercise of the mind, if it is applied to no larger system than the starry one. Mathematics should be mixed not only with physics but with ethics; *that* is *mixed* mathematics. The fact which interests us most is the life of the naturalist. The purest science is still biographical.

THOREAU

If science tends to thicken the crust of ice on which, as it were, we are skating, it is all right. If it tries to find, or professes to have found, the solid ground at the bottom of the water, it is all wrong.

SAMUEL BUTLER (II)

Science increases our power in proportion as it lowers our pride.

BERNARD

The scientific method cannot lead mankind because it is based upon experiment, and every experiment postpones the present moment until one knows the result. We always come to each other and even to ourselves too late so soon as we wish to know in advance what to do.　　ROSENSTOCK-HUESSY

If physical science is dangerous, as I have said, it is dangerous because it necessarily ignores the idea of moral evil; but literature is open to the more grievous imputation of recognizing and understanding it too well.　　NEWMAN

The dangers threatening modern science cannot be averted by more experimenting, for our complicated experiments have no longer anything to do with nature in her own right, but with nature charged and transformed by our own cognitive activity.　　HEISENBERG

The great tragedy of science—the slaying of a beautiful hypothesis by an ugly fact.　　T. H. HUXLEY

There is no national science just as there is no national multiplication table; what is national is no longer science.

CHEKHOV

Many scientific theories have, for very long periods of time, stood the test of experience until they had to be discarded owing to man's decision, not merely to make other experiments, but to have different experiences.　　HELLER

Someone remarked to me once: "Physicians shouldn't say, I have cured this man, but, this man didn't die under my care." In physics too, instead of saying, I have explained such and such a phenomenon, one might say, I have determined causes for it the absurdity of which cannot be conclusively proved.　　LICHTENBERG

Astrology fosters astronomy. Mankind *plays* its way up.

LICHTENBERG

Science has promised us truth. . . . It has never promised us either peace or happiness.　　LE BON

The scientific view of the world, and the method of abstraction by which it is arrived at, is an autonomous and authentic manner of dealing with what is real in the world in which we live; it is not an instrument of merely practical utility, nor on the other hand a philosophy, much less the only true philosophy. It is not an art, it is not a religion, it is not history, it is not a philosophy; it is something different from all these, a special department and activity of the human spirit.

NEEDHAM

Bourgeois scientists make sure that their theories are not dangerous to God or to capital.　　PLEKHANOFF

The less anthropomorphic science believes itself to be, the more anthropomorphic it is. One by one it gets rid of the *separate* human traits in the nature-picture, only to find in the end that the supposed pure nature which it holds in its hand is—humanity pure and complete.　　SPENGLER

"One and one make two" assumes that the changes in the shift of circumstance are unimportant. But it is impossible for us to analyze this notion of unimportant change.

WHITEHEAD

A crystal lacks rhythm from excess of pattern, while a fog is unrhythmic in that it exhibits a patternless confusion of detail.

WHITEHEAD

Man cannot afford to be a naturalist, to look at nature directly, but only with the side of his eye. He must look through her and beyond her. To look at her is as fatal as to look at the head of Medusa. It turns the man of science to stone.

THOREAU

The mathematician may be compared to a designer of garments, who is utterly oblivious of the creatures whom his garments may fit. To be sure, his art originated in the necessity for clothing such creatures, but this was long ago; to this day a shape will occasionally appear which will fit into the garment as if the garment had been made for it. Then there is no end of surprise and delight.

DANTZIG

Mathematics is the only science where one never knows what one is talking about nor whether what is said is true.

RUSSELL

Algebra reverses the relative importance of the factors in ordinary language. It is essentially a written language, and it endeavors to exemplify in its written structures the patterns which it is its purpose to convey. The pattern of the marks on paper is a particular instance of the pattern to be conveyed to thought. The alegbraic method is our best approach to the expression of necessity, by reason of its reduction of accident to the ghostlike character of the real variable.

WHITEHEAD

I will not go so far as to say that to construct a history of thought without profound study of the mathematical ideas of successive epochs is like omitting Hamlet from the play which is named after him. That would be claiming too much. But it is certainly analogous to cutting out the part of Ophelia. This simile is singularly exact. For Ophelia is quite essential to the play, she is very charming—and a little mad.

WHITEHEAD

There can be mathematicians of the first order who cannot count.   NOVALIS

It is the stars as not known to science that I would know, the stars which the lonely traveler knows.   THOREAU

Although this may seem a paradox, all exact science is dominated by the idea of approximation.   RUSSELL

Science is spectrum analysis: art is photosynthesis.   KRAUS

THE ARTS

Theory and Practice

There is no patriotic art and no patriotic science.   GOETHE

Art is I; Science is We.   BERNARD

Art is Nature speeded up and God slowed down.   CHAZAL

The history of art is the history of revivals.
   SAMUEL BUTLER (II)

The beautiful remains so in ugly surroundings.   CHAZAL

Is it not strange that sheep's guts should hale souls out of their
bodies?   SHAKESPEARE

Mechanical excellence is the only vehicle of genius.   BLAKE

We have Art that we may not perish from Truth.
   NIETZSCHE

The best is the enemy of the good.   VOLTAIRE

The art of seeing nature is a thing almost as much to be acquired as the art of reading the Egyptian hieroglyphics.

CONSTABLE

The canons of art are merely the expression in specialized forms of the requirements for depth of experience.

WHITEHEAD

Art is a vice, a pastime which differs from some of the most pleasant vices and pastimes by consolidating and intensifying the organs which it exercises. SICKERT

Art may be said to be the individual quality of failure, or the individual coefficient of error, of each highly skilled and cultivated craftsman in his effort to attain to the expression of form.

SICKERT

Is it the essence of the artistic way of looking at things that it looks at the world with a happy eye? WITTGENSTEIN

The work of art is the object seen *sub specie aeternitatis*; and the good life is the world seen *sub specie aeternitatis*. This is the connection between art and ethics.

The usual way of looking at things sees objects as it were from the midst of them; the view *sub specie aeternitatis* from outside, in such a way that they have the whole world as background. WITTGENSTEIN

The whole of art is one long roll of revelation, and it is revealed only to those whose minds are to some extent what Horace, speaking of a woman whose heart is free, calls vacant. It is not for those whose minds are muddied with the dirt of politics, or heated with the vulgar chatter of society.

SICKERT

In a work of art the intellect asks questions; it does not answer them.   HEBBEL

Luck, that differs greatly from Art, creates many things that are like it.   ION OF CHIOS

Art, then, is that which gives a pure emotion . . . which invites to neither virtue nor patriotism, nor debauch, nor peace, nor war, nor laughter, nor tears, nor anything but art itself.
                                                                GOURMONT

You are not to consider that every new and personal beauty in art abrogates past achievement as an Act of Parliament does preceding ones, or that it is hostile to the past. You are to consider these beauties, these innovations, as enrichments, as variations, as additions to an existing family. How barbarous you would seem if you were unable to bestow your admiration and affection on a fascinating child in the nursery without at once finding yourselves compelled to rush downstairs and cut its mother's throat, and stifle its grandmother. These ladies may still have their uses.   SICKERT

There is no prejudice that the work of art does not finally overcome.   GIDE

The excellency of every art is its intensity, capable of making all disagreeables evaporate.   KEATS

"I'm hungry, I'm freezing, help me!": here is the stuff of a good deed, but not of a good work.   JOUBERT

There is no work of art that is without short cuts.   GIDE

One finds in art the means whereby he may rejoice in his nature, another the means whereby he may temporarily overcome and escape from his nature. In accordance with these two needs, there are two kinds of art and artist.   NIETZSCHE

The artist doesn't see things as they are, but as he is.

ANONYMOUS

It is useless . . . to urge the isolated individuality of the artist, apart from his attitude to his age. His attitude to his age is his individuality.   CHESTERTON

When I hear artists . . . making fun of businessmen I think of a regiment in which the band makes fun of the cooks.

ANONYMOUS

In order that a man may stop believing in some things, there must be germinating in him a confused faith in others. It is curious to note that almost always the dimension of life in which the new faith begins to establish itself is art.

ORTEGA Y GASSET

Imitation is criticism.   BLAKE

The artistic temperament is a disease that afflicts amateurs.

CHESTERTON

The luck of having talent is not enough; one must also have a talent for luck.   BERLIOZ

The artist who is not also a craftsman is no good; but, alas, most of our artists are nothing else.   GOETHE

He who does not know the mechanical side of a craft cánnot judge it.   GOETHE

Everyone has talent at twenty-five. The difficulty is to have it at fifty.   DEGAS

An artist chooses even when he confesses; perhaps above all when he confesses.   VALÉRY

Of the truly creative no one is ever master; it must be left to go its own way.   GOETHE

Will you refuse to recognize the divine because it is manifested in art and enjoyment and not just in conscience and action?   TAINE

In every work of genius we recognize our own rejected thoughts; they come back to us with a certain alienated majesty.   EMERSON

In periods of decadence only very independent geniuses have a chance to survive.   DELACROIX

I am afraid humility to genius is as an extinguisher to a candle.
                                                              SHENSTONE

To be a genius is to achieve complete possession of one's own experience, body, rhythm, and memories.   PAVESE

Genius is the instinct of self-preservation in a talent.
                                                    QUOTED BY SICKERT

What is the real reason why we want to be big, to be creative geniuses? For posterity? No. To be pointed out when we stroll in crowded places? No. To carry on with our daily toil under the conviction that whatever we do is worth the trouble, is something unique—for the day, not for eternity.　　PAVESE

Great geniuses have the shortest biographies: their cousins can tell you nothing about them.　　EMERSON

To represent vice and misery as the necessary accompaniments of genius is as mischievous as it is false, and the feeling is as unclassical as the language in which it is usually expressed.　　PEACOCK

A man who is a genius and doesn't know it probably isn't.　　LEC

The artist appeals to that part of our being which is not dependent on wisdom: to that in us which is a gift and not an acquisition—and, therefore, more permanently enduring.　　CONRAD

An artist is a dreamer consenting to dream of the actual world.　　SANTAYANA

Most artists are sincere and most art is bad, and some insincere art (sincerely insincere) can be quite good.　　STRAVINSKY

Every artist is a moralist, though he need not preach.　　SANTAYANA

When it seems that a new man or a new school has invented a new thing, it will only be found that the gifted among them have secured a firmer hold than usual of some old thing.　　SICKERT

The artist is like Sunday's child—he alone sees spirits. But, after he has told of their appearing to him, everybody sees them.   GOETHE

True perfection is achieved only by those who are prepared to destroy it. It is a by-product of greatness.   CLARK

The artists must be sacrificed to their art. Like the bees, they must put their lives into the sting they give.   EMERSON

I would have praised you more if you had praised me less.
          LOUIS XIV (to Boileau, on being praised in verse)

To justify our likes and dislikes, we generally say that the work we dislike is not serious.   SICKERT

Connoisseurs think the art is already done.   CONSTABLE

A good spectator also creates.   SWISS PROVERB

There is nothing more dreadful than imagination without taste.   GOETHE

A taste for simplicity cannot endure for long.   DELACROIX

Good taste, besides being inwardly clear, has to be outwardly fit.   SANTAYANA

It takes taste to account for taste.   SPANISH PROVERB

Devotion to the arts in France seems more concerned with connoisseurship than enjoyment.   JOUBERT

What is exhilarating in bad taste is the aristocratic pleasure of giving offense.   BAUDELAIRE

If it were not for the intellectual snobs who pay—in solid cash—the tribute which philistinism owes to culture, the arts would perish with their starving practitioners. Let us thank heaven for hypocrisy.   ALDOUS HUXLEY

Ladies who pursue Culture in bands, as though it were dangerous to meet it alone.   EDITH WHARTON

It is the grossness of the spectator that discovers nothing but grossness in the subject.   HAZLITT

To approve is more difficult than to admire.   HOFMANNSTHAL

What the public like best is fruit that is overripe.   COCTEAU

If a perfume manufacturer were to adopt the "naturalistic" aesthetic, what scents would he bottle?   VALÉRY

In the end physics will replace ethics just as metaphysics displaced theology. The modern statistical view of ethics contributes toward that.   KIERKEGAARD

Writers and Readers

A writer is someone who can make a riddle out of an answer.

KRAUS

There are two kinds of writers, those who are and those who aren't. With the first, content and form belong together like soul and body; with the second, they match each other like body and clothes.

KRAUS

A fluent writer always seems more talented than he is. To write well, one needs a natural facility and an acquired difficulty.

JOUBERT

There is not so poor a book in the world that would not be a prodigious effort were it wrought out entirely by a single mind, without the aid of prior investigators.

DR. JOHNSON

It is not so much what you say in a book that constitutes its value . . . [but] all you would like to say, which nourishes it secretly.

GIDE

If literature is to be made a study of human nature, you cannot have a Christian literature. It is a contradiction in terms to attempt a sinless literature of sinful man.

NEWMAN

It is the writer's business not to accuse and not to prosecute, but to champion the guilty, once they are condemned and suffer punishment.

CHEKHOV

Literature is the effort of man to indemnify himself for the wrongs of his condition.

EMERSON

The only reason people write is because they are not wonderful men. CARSON

It takes less time to learn how to write nobly than how to write lightly and straightforwardly. NIETZSCHE

The noblest deeds are well enough set forth in simple language; emphasis spoils them. LA BRUYÈRE

We all know how difficult it is, in drawing up the simplest communication, not to say the contrary of what we mean. SICKERT

> For all a rhetorician's rules
> Teach nothing but to name his tools.
> SAMUEL BUTLER (I)

Rhetoric is either very good or stark naught; there is no medium in rhetoric. If I am not fully persuaded I laugh at the orator. SELDEN

Literary egotism consists in playing the role of *self*, in making oneself a little more natural than nature, a little more oneself than one was a few minutes before. VALÉRY

He who has nothing to assert has no style and can have none. SHAW

Style is the physiognomy of the mind, and a safer index to character than the face. SCHOPENHAUER

Whether good or bad, style cannot be corrected. Style is inviolable. GOURMONT

Many intelligent people, when about to write books, force on their minds a certain notion about style, just as they screw up their faces when they sit for their portraits.　LICHTENBERG

When we encounter a natural style we are always surprised and delighted, for we thought to see an author and found a man.　PASCAL

To improve one's style means to improve one's thoughts and nothing else: he who does not admit this immediately will never be convinced of it.　NIETZSCHE

To write simply is as difficult as to be good.　MAUGHAM

It is neither the best nor the worst in a book which is untranslatable.　NIETZSCHE

The secret of authorship is in the tips of the fingers, and the secret of an orator is on the tip of the tongue.　ROZINOV

Originality does not consist in saying what no one has ever said before, but in saying exactly what you think yourself.

STEPHEN

How vain it is to sit down to write when you have not stood up to live.　THOREAU

To tell about a drunken muzhik's beating his wife is incomparably harder than to compose a whole tract about the "woman question."　TURGENEV

[277]

A little inaccuracy sometimes saves tons of explanation.

SAKI

The art of literature, vocal or written, is to adjust the language so that it embodies what it indicates.   WHITEHEAD

If immoral works of literature exist, they are works in which there is no plot.   PAVESE

It is the author's aim to say once and emphatically, "He said."

THOREAU

Posterity is always the author's favorite.   DR. JOHNSON

If you can speak what you will never hear, if you can write what you will never read, you have done rare things.

THOREAU

In lapidary inscriptions a man is not upon oath.

DR. JOHNSON

When one is polite in German, one lies.   GOETHE

Satire, being leveled at all, is never resented for an offense by any, since every individual person makes bold to understand it of others.   SWIFT

Satires which the censor can understand are justly forbidden.

KRAUS

The finest satire is that in which ridicule is combined with so little malice and so much conviction that it even rouses laughter in those who are hit.   LICHTENBERG

Prefaces are like speeches before the curtain; they make even the most self-forgetful performers self-conscious. NEILSON

'Tis very difficult to write like a madman, but 'tis a very easie matter to write like a fool. LEE

I wonder why murder is considered less immoral than fornication in literature. GEORGE MOORE

Cynicism in literary works usually signifies a certain element of disappointed ambition. When one no longer knows what to do in order to astonish and survive, one offers one's *pudenda* to the public gaze. Everyone knows perfectly well what he will see; but it is sufficient to make the gesture. VALÉRY

A successful author is equally in danger of the diminution of his fame whether he continues or ceases to write.

DR. JOHNSON

In a certain sense, printing proved a drawback to letters. It . . . cast contempt on books that failed to find a publisher.

GOURMONT

A book calls for pen, ink, and a writing desk; today the rule is that pen, ink, and a writing desk call for a book.

NIETZSCHE

Everything that is written merely to please the author is worthless. PASCAL

Diderot used to say that a writer may have a mistress who fashions books, but must have a wife who fashions shirts.

CHAMFORT

An author who speaks about his own books is almost as bad as a mother who talks about her own children   DISRAELI

The hardest thing is writing a recommendation for someone you know.   KIN HUBBARD

While an author is yet living we estimate his powers by his worst performance, and when he is dead we rate them by his best.   DR. JOHNSON

The author must keep his mouth shut when his work starts to speak.   NIETZSCHE

The conversation of authors is not so good as might be imagined; but, such as it is, . . . it is better than any other.   HAZLITT

Genuinely good remarks surprise their author as well as his audience.   JOUBERT

The reciprocal civility of authors is one of the most risible scenes in the farce of life.   DR. JOHNSON

The man who is asked by an author what he thinks of his work is put to the torture and is not obliged to speak the truth.   DR. JOHNSON

I never desire to converse with a man who has written more than he has read.   DR. JOHNSON

I will like and praise some things in a young writer which yet, if he continue in, I cannot but justly hate him for.   JONSON

No one ever told a story well standing up, or fasting.

BALZAC

The difference between journalism and literature is that journalism is unreadable and literature is not read.   WILDE

A journalist is stimulated by a deadline: he writes worse when he has time.   KRAUS

In a novel, the author gives the leading character intelligence and distinction. Fate goes to less trouble: mediocrities play a part in great events simply from happening to be there.

TALLEYRAND

The business of the novelist is not to chronicle great events but to make small ones interesting.   SCHOPENHAUER

In a good play, everyone is in the right.   HEBBEL

In merciless and rollicking comedy life is caught in the act.

SANTAYANA

Few tragedies die game.   COLERIDGE

What would be left of our tragedies if a literate insect were to present us his?   CIORAN

Fate in tragedy is the created form, the virtual future as an accomplished whole. It is not the expression of a belief at all. Macbeth's fate is the structure of his tragedy, not an instance of how things happen in the world.   SUSANNE LANGER

A poet puts the world into a nutshell; the orator, out of a nutshell, brings a world.   HURNAND

In the infancy of society every author is necessarily a poet.
                                                            SHELLEY

The art of life, of a poet's life, is, not having anything to do, to do something.   THOREAU

The fighting poets.
The literary vanguard.
This use of military metaphor reveals minds not militant but formed for discipline, that is, for compliance; minds born servile, Belgian minds, which can only think collectively.
                                                          BAUDELAIRE

Poetry is certainly something more than good sense, but it must be good sense . . . just as a palace is more than a house, but it must be a house.   COLERIDGE

I had toward the poetic art a quite peculiar relation which was only practical after I had cherished in my mind for a long time a subject which possessed me, a model which inspired me, a predecessor who attracted me, until at length, after I had molded it in silence for years, something resulted which might be regarded as a creation of my own; and finally, all at once, and almost instinctively, as if it had become ripe, I set it down on paper.   GOETHE

Poetry is not a turning loose of emotion, but an escape from emotion; it is not the expression of personality, but an escape from personality. But, of course, only those who have personality and emotions know what it means to want to escape from such things.   T. S. ELIOT

Reason no more makes a poem than salt makes a dish, but it is a constituent of a poem as salt is a constituent of a dish.
HEBBEL

Take a commonplace, clean and polish it, light it so that it produces the same effect of youth and freshness and spontaneity as it did originally, and you have done a poet's job.
COCTEAU

When writing poetry, it is not inspiration that produces a bright idea, but the bright idea that kindles the fire of inspiration.
PAVESE

A man is a poet if the difficulties inherent in his art provide him with ideas; he is not a poet if they deprive him of ideas.
VALÉRY

To write regular verses . . . destroys an infinite number of fine possibilities, but at the same time it suggests a multitude of distant and totally unexpected thoughts.
VALÉRY

In poetry everything which *must* be said is almost impossible to say well.
VALÉRY

Skilled verse is the art of a profound skeptic.
VALÉRY

The truest poetry is the most feigning.
SHAKESPEARE

A comic bard ought to look at life as a masked ball in which a prince isn't offended in the least when a wigmaker in domino crosses in front of him.
STENDHAL

Poetry is the language of a state of crisis.
MALLARMÉ

[283]

The Soil intended for *Pierian Seeds*
Must be well *purg'd*, from *rank Pedantick Weeds*.
Apollo starts, and all *Parnassus* shakes,
At the rude rumbling *Baralipton* makes.
For none have been with *Admiration* read,
But who (beside their *Learning*) were *Well-bred*.

ROSCOMMON

Beware *what Spirit* rages in your Breast;
For ten Inspir'd ten thousand are possest.
Thus make the *proper Use* of each *Extream*,
And *write* with *Fury*, but *correct* with *Phleam*.

ROSCOMMON

It is a great fault, in descriptive poetry, to describe everything.

POPE

How very unlike Ireland this whole place is. I only felt at home
once—when I came to a steep lane with a stream in the middle. The rest one noticed with a foreign eye, picking out the
stranger and not, as in one's own country, the familiar things
for interest—the fault, by the way, of all poetry about coun-
tries not the writer's own.

YEATS

Poetic fire sank low in me
When it was Good I sought to see,
But up it flamed, up to the sky,
When it was Evil I had to fly.

GOETHE

The crying of a nice child is ugly; so in bad verses you may
recognize that the author is a nice man.

CHEKHOV

The artist, depicting man disdainful of the storm and stress
of life, is no less reconciling and healing than the poet who,
while endowing Nature with Humanity, rejoices in its meas-
ureless superiority to human passions and human sorrows.

BERENSON

[284]

Children and lunatics cut the Gordian knot which the poet spends his life patiently trying to untie.　　　COCTEAU

Poets are the only people to whom love is not only a crucial, but an indispensable experience, which entitles them to mistake it for a universal one.　　　HANNAH ARENDT

Poetry avoids the last illusion of prose, which so gently sometimes and at others so passionately pretends that things are thus and thus. In poetry they are also thus and thus, but because the arrangement of the lines, the pattern within the whole, will have it so. Exquisitely leaning toward an implied untruth, prose persuades us that we can trust our natures to know things as they are; ostentatiously faithful to its own nature, poetry assures us that we cannot—we know only as we can.　　　WILLIAMS

Beauty lives by rhymes. Double a deformity is a beauty.
　　　THOREAU

It is unwise in a poet to goad the sleeping lion of laughter.
　　　CHESTERTON

Reputation is much oftener lost than gained by verse.
　　　DR. FULLER

You will find poetry nowhere unless you bring some of it with you.　　　JOUBERT

Every good poet includes a critic, but the reverse will not hold.
　　　SHENSTONE

Insects sting, not in malice, but because they want to live. It is the same with critics; they desire our blood, not our pain.
　　　NIETZSCHE

How much more flattering to see a critic turn disparaging from malice and spite than lenient from cliquishness. GIDE

The test of a good critic is whether he knows when and how to believe on insufficient evidence. SAMUEL BUTLER (II)

It is the proper province . . . of an inferior to criticize and advise. The best possible critic of the *Iliad* would be, *ipso facto*, and by virtue of that very character, incapable of being the author of it. FRANCIS

I regard reviews as a kind of infant's disease to which newborn books are subject. LICHTENBERG

There are books in which the footnotes, or the comments scrawled by some reader's hand in the margin, are more interesting than the text. The world is one of these books.

SANTAYANA

A book should contain pure discoveries, glimpses of terra firma, though by shipwrecked mariners, and not the art of navigation by those who have never been out of sight of land.

THOREAU

The test of a book (to a writer) is if it makes a space in which, quite naturally, you can say what you want to say.

VIRGINIA WOOLF

I have had more pleasure in reading the adventures of a novel than I ever had in my own. HAZLITT

People do not deserve to have good writing, they are so pleased with bad. EMERSON

The oldest books are still only just out to those who have not read them. SAMUEL BUTLER (II)

All good things are powerful stimulants to life, even every good book which is written against life. NIETZSCHE

Imaginary evil is romantic and varied; real evil is gloomy, monotonous, barren, boring. Imaginary good is boring; real good is always new, marvelous, intoxicating. "Imaginative literature," therefore, is either boring or immoral or a mixture of both. SIMONE WEIL

What one wrote playfully, another reads with tension and passion; what one wrote with tension and passion, another reads playfully. VALÉRY

Sperone-Speroni explains very well why a writer's form of expression may seem quite clear to him yet obscure to the reader: the reader is advancing from language to thought, the writer from thought to language. CHAMFORT

The only end of writing is to enable the readers better to enjoy life or better to endure it. DR. JOHNSON

> The bookful blockhead, ignorantly read,
> With loads of learned lumber in his head,
> With his own tongue still edifies his ears,
> And always list'ning to himself appears.
>
> POPE

Any book which is at all important should be reread immediately. SCHOPENHAUER

Sometimes I read a book with pleasure and detest the author.

SWIFT

One only reads well when one reads with some quite personal goal in mind. It may be to acquire some power. It can be out of hatred for the author. VALÉRY

Dictionaries are like watches: the worst is better than none, and the best cannot be expected to go quite right.

DR. JOHNSON

In the library of a young prince, the solemn folios are not much rumpled; books of a lighter digestion have the dog's ears. HALIFAX

A book is a mirror: if an ass peers into it, you can't expect an apostle to look out. LICHTENBERG

At least be sure that you go to the author to get at *his* meaning, not to find yours. RUSKIN

The reason why so few good books are written is that so few people who can write know anything. BAGEHOT

To pass judgment on people or on characters in a book is to make silhouettes of them. PAVESE

Sights and Sounds

Blowing is not playing the flute; you must make use of your fingers.   GOETHE

By concentrating on precision, one arrives at technique; but by concentrating on technique one does not arrive at precision.
                                                                                WALTER

Musical modes are nowhere altered without changes in the most important laws of the state.   DAMON OF ATHENS

Your ears will always lead you right, but you must know why.
                                                                                WEBERN

I am inclined to think that a hunt for folk songs is better than a manhunt of the heroes who are so highly extolled.
                                                                                BEETHOVEN

It takes no more energy to write *fortissimo* than to write *piano*, or *universe* than *garden*.   VALÉRY

Music has many resemblances to algebra.   NOVALIS

The composer opens the cage door for arithmetic, the draftsman gives geometry its freedom.   COCTEAU

Music is essentially useless, as life is.   SANTAYANA

Music is the brandy of the damned.   SHAW

In opera everything is based upon the not-true.

TCHAIKOVSKY

In opera the text must be the obedient daughter of the music.

MOZART

An actor is a sculptor who carves in snow.

ASCRIBED TO BOTH BARRETT AND BOOTH

The most difficult character in comedy is the fool, and he who plays the part must be no simpleton.   CERVANTES

As a painter, I become more lucid when confronted by nature.

CÉZANNE

Landscape painting is the obvious resource of misanthropy.

HAZLITT

Offensive objects, at a proper distance, acquire even a degree of beauty.   SHENSTONE

Query, whether beauty does not as much require an opposition of lines, as it does an harmony of colors?   SHENSTONE

We should talk less and draw more. Personally, I would like to renounce speech altogether and, like organic nature, communicate everything I have to say in sketches.

GOETHE

Painting is a science, and should be pursued as an inquiry into the laws of nature. Why, then, may not landscape painting be considered a branch of natural philosophy, of which pictures are but the experiments?   CONSTABLE

In painting you must give the idea of the true by means of the false. DEGAS

One line alone has no meaning; a second one is needed to give it expression. DELACROIX

There has never been a boy painter, nor can there be. The art requires a long apprenticeship, being *mechanical* as well as intellectual. CONSTABLE

The less an artifact interests our eye as imitation, the more it must delight our eye as a pattern, and an art of symbols always evolves a language of decoration. CLARK

Communication of all kinds is like painting—a compromise with impossibilities. SAMUEL BUTLER (II)

He who pretends to be either painter or engraver without being a master of drawing is an impostor. BLAKE

The artist who always paints the same scene pleases the public for the sole reason that it recognizes him with ease and thinks itself a connoisseur. STEVENS

I cannot judge my work while I am doing it. I have to do as painters do, stand back and view it from a distance, but not too great a distance. How great? Guess. PASCAL

The only good copies are those that reveal what is silly in the bad originals. LA ROCHEFOUCAULD

Servile copying is the great merit of copying.   BLAKE

Where the spirit does not work with the hand there is no art.
LEONARDO DA VINCI

The professional portrait painter is dragged by the nature
of his work along a diagonal resultant. If one side of his
triangle may be said to "pull painter," the other may be said
to "pull duchess." The hypotenuse is what we know.

SICKERT

One is never satisfied with the portrait of a person one knows.
GOETHE

If you may not treat pictorially the ways of men and women,
and their resultant babies, as one enchanted comedy or tragedy, human and *de moeurs*, then artists must needs draw
inanimate objects, picturesque, if possible. We must affect
to be thrilled by scaffolding or seduced by oranges.

SICKERT

Taste is the death of a painter. He has all his work cut out
for him, observing and recording. His poetry is the inter-
pretation of ready-made life. He has no business to have
time for preferences.   SICKERT

The plastic arts are gross arts, dealing joyously with gross
material facts. They call, in their servants, for a robust
stomach and a great power of endurance, and while they will
flourish in the scullery or on the dunghill, they fade at a
breath from the drawing room. Stay! I had forgot. We have
a use for the drawing room—to caricature it!   SICKERT

I have made a sketch of him so that, on the Day of Judgment,
he can the more easily find his body again.   LICHTENBERG

One always has to spoil a picture a little bit, in order to finish it.   DELACROIX

An artist may visit a museum, but only a pedant can live there.   SANTAYANA

We should comport ourselves with the masterpieces of art as with exalted personages—stand quietly before them and wait till they speak to us.   SCHOPENHAUER

A museum . . . oftenest induces the feeling that nothing could ever have been young.   PATER

That which, perhaps, hears more silly remarks than anything else in the world, is a picture in a museum.

THE BROTHERS GONCOURT

It is easier to understand a nation by listening to its music than by learning its language.   ANONYMOUS

STATES AND
GOVERNMENTS

Politics and Power

All governments are obscure and invisible.   BACON

A general idea is always a danger to the existing order.
                                                    WHITEHEAD

It is impossible to doubt the effect of any vigorous effort for the immediate abolition of the only social system that men know. It may be better that the heavens should fall, but it is folly to ignore the fact that they will fall.
                                                    WHITEHEAD

To commit violent and unjust acts, it is not enough for a government to have the will or even the power; the habits, ideas, and passions of the time must lend themselves to their committal.   TOCQUEVILLE

It is a bad witness to the goodness of a regime when people begin to praise it only after they have ceased to believe in the possibility of its restoration.   TOCQUEVILLE

I sit on a man's back, choking him and making him carry me, and yet assure myself and others that I am very sorry for him and wish to lighten his load by all possible means— except by getting off his back.   TOLSTOI

It is one of the dangerous characteristics of the sort of information supplied by secret agents that it becomes rarer and less explicit as the peril increases and the need for information becomes greater. Doubting the duration of the government which employs them, and already afraid of its successor, such agents either scarcely speak at all or keep absolute silence.   TOCQUEVILLE

Harsh is the law, but it is certain.   VICO

Decision by majorities is as much an expedient as lighting by gas.   GLADSTONE

Dullness is decent in the Church and State.   DRYDEN

The world is ruled by force, not by opinion; but opinion uses force.   PASCAL

The combination of a repressive political order with a permissive moral order is not unheard of in human history.

RIEFF

Bad laws are the worst sort of tyranny.   E. BURKE

Tyranny is the wish to have in one way what can only be had in another.   PASCAL

The worst form of tyranny the world has ever known: the tyranny of the weak over the strong. It is the only tyranny that lasts.   WILDE

States decree the most illustrious rewards, not to him who catches a thief, but to him who kills a tyrant.   ARISTOTLE

Tyrants are always assassinated too late; that is their great excuse.   CIORAN

Tyranny over a man is not tyranny: it is rebellion, for man is royal.   CHESTERTON

It is far easier to act under conditions of tyranny than to think.   HANNAH ARENDT

Unanimity is almost always an indication of servitude.

RÉMUSAT

Being unable to make what is just strong, we have made what is strong just.   PASCAL

Despotism tempered by assassination—there is our Magna Charta.   ANONYMOUS RUSSIAN

The magistrate has a right to enforce what he thinks; and he who is conscious of the truth has the right to suffer. I am afraid there is no other way of ascertaining the truth, but by persecution on the one hand, and enduring it on the other.   DR. JOHNSON

I know no method to secure the repeal of bad or obnoxious laws so effective as their stringent execution.   GRANT

Any class is all right if it will only let others be so.

SAMUEL BUTLER (II)

All the cities of the earth should rise up against the man who
ruins one.   LANDOR

The mode of government is incomparably more important
for a nation than the form of state.   KANT

It is a certain sign of a wise government and proceeding that
it can hold men's hearts by hopes when it cannot by satisfaction.   BACON

No matter how noble the objectives of a government, if it
blurs decency and kindness, cheapens human life, and breeds
ill will and suspicion—it is an evil government.   HOFFER

It is muddleheaded to say, I am in favor of this kind of
political regime rather than that: what one really means is,
I prefer this kind of police.   CIORAN

Foreign policy demands scarcely any of those qualities which
are peculiar to a democracy; on the contrary it calls for the
perfect use of almost all those qualities in which a democracy
is deficient. Democracy is favorable to the increase of the
internal resources of a state, it diffuses wealth and comfort,
and fortifies the respect for law in all classes of society, but
it can only with great difficulty regulate the details of an
important undertaking, persevere in a fixed design, and work
out its execution in spite of serious obstacles. It cannot
combine its measures with secrecy or await their consequences with patience. These are qualities which are more
characteristic of an individual or an aristocracy.

TOCQUEVILLE

Power does not corrupt men; fools, however, if they get into a position of power, corrupt power.   SHAW

It is always observable that the physical and exact sciences are the last to suffer under despotisms.   DANA

In general, despite all the talk about freedom, peoples and governments demand unlimited state power internally.   BURCKHARDT

Lawgivers or revolutionaries who promise equality and liberty at the same time are either utopian dreamers or charlatans.   GOETHE

No government can be long secure without a formidable opposition.   DISRAELI

Power is so apt to be insolent, and liberty to be saucy, that they are very seldom upon good terms.   HALIFAX

In the tumult of civil discord the laws of society lose their force, and their place is seldom supplied by those of humanity.   GIBBON

Wretches hang that jurymen may dine.   POPE

In France we threaten the man who rings the alarm bell and leave him in peace who starts the fire.   CHAMFORT

The triumph of demagogies is short-lived. But the ruins are eternal.   PÉGUY

If the private rights of an individual are violated in a period when the human mind is fully impressed with the importance and sanctity of such rights, the injury done is confined to the individual whose rights are infringed; but to violate such rights at the present day is deeply to corrupt the manners of the nation and to put the whole community in jeopardy, because the very notion of this kind of right among us tends constantly to be impaired and lost.　　　TOCQUEVILLE

Burning stakes do not lighten the darkness.　　　LEC

Those who give the first shock to a state are the first over-whelmed in its ruin.　　　MONTAIGNE

Republics come to an end through luxury; monarchies through poverty.　　　MONTESQUIEU

Who shall stand guard to the guards themselves?　　　JUVENAL

　　The accursed power which stands on Priviledge
　　And goes with Women and Champagne and Bridge,
　　Broke, and Democracy resumed her reign
　　Which goes with Bridge and Women and Champagne.
　　　　　　BELLOC

Dinners have become a means of government, and the fates of nations are decided at a banquet.　　　BRILLAT-SAVARIN

The notion of a farseeing and despotic statesman, who can lay down plans for ages yet unborn, is a fancy generated by the pride of the human intellect to which facts give no support.　　　BAGEHOT

Many even of those who desire to form aristocratical governments make a mistake, not only in giving too much power
to the rich, but in attempting to overreach the people. There
comes a time when out of a false good there arises a true
evil, since the encroachments of the rich are more destructive
to the constitution than those of the people.   ARISTOTLE

> A dog starved at his master's gate
> Predicts the ruin of the State.
>
> BLAKE

Despotism or unlimited sovereignty is the same in a majority
of a popular assembly, an aristocratical council, an oligarchical
junta, and a single emperor.   J. Q. ADAMS

Every man seeks peace by waging war, but no man seeks
war by making peace. For even they who intentionally interrupt the peace in which they are living have not hatred of
peace, but only wish it changed into a peace that suits them
better. And in the case of sedition, when men have separated
themselves from the community, they do not effect what
they wish, unless they maintain some kind of peace with
their fellow conspirators.   SAINT AUGUSTINE

If you cry "Forward!" you must without fail make plain in
what direction to go. Don't you see that if, without doing
so, you call out the word to both a monk and a revolutionary,
they will go in directions precisely opposite?   CHEKHOV

Terrorism is essentially the rage of literati in its last stage.
    BURCKHARDT

Military glory pure and simple withers in time into mere
recognition by specialists and military historians.
    BURCKHARDT

A state in which the law is powerless to punish a thief, or in which society is unable to restrict the action of the government, are equally opposed to the notion of polity.　ACTON

There is only one way of speaking well from the tribune, and that is to be fully persuaded as you get into it that you are the most intelligent man in the world.　ANONYMOUS

No state at war with another state should engage in hostilities of such a kind as to render mutual confidence impossible when peace will have been made.　KANT

Though men, nations, and causes are so aggressive, in the long run everybody at least wants to see everybody else subjected to the rules of a civilized world.　BUTTERFIELD

There is a holy mistaken zeal in politics as well as in religion. By persuading others, we convince ourselves.　JUNIUS

Practical politics consists in ignoring facts.　HENRY ADAMS

The world of politics is always twenty years behind the world of thought.　CHAPMAN

Whenever a man has cast a longing eye on offices, a rottenness begins in his conduct.　JEFFERSON

Combinations of wickedness would overwhelm the world did not those who have long practiced perfidy grow faithless to each other.　DR. JOHNSON

Injustice cannot reign if the community does not furnish a due supply of unjust agents.   SPENCER

Complete publicity makes it absolutely impossible to govern. No one has understood that better than the daily press; for no power has watched more carefully over the secret of its whole organization, who its contributors are, and its real aims, etc., as the daily press, which then continually cries out that the *government* should be quite public. Quite right; the intention of the press was to do away with government —and then itself govern, and that is why it safeguarded the secrecy which is necessary in order to be able to—*govern*.

                                              KIERKEGAARD

Our politicians are like the Greek reciprocals (*alleloin*) which are wanting in the nominative singular and all subjective cases. They can only be thought of in the plural and possessive cases.   KIERKEGAARD

He was a power politically fer years, but he never got prominent enough t' have his speeches garbled.   KIN HUBBARD

State business is a cruel trade; good-nature is a bungler in it.
                                                 HALIFAX

Tyranny is always better organized than freedom.   PÉGUY

The dappled deer is said to see the wind; your statesman only sees which way it blows.   HURNAND

At Court, people embrace without acquaintance, serve one another without friendship, and injure one another without hatred.   CHESTERFIELD

Politicians neither love nor hate. Interest, not sentiment, governs them.   CHESTERFIELD

The art of taxation consists in so plucking the goose as to get the most feathers with the least hissing.
                                    ASCRIBED TO COLBERT

There is a demand today for men who can make wrong appear right.   TERENCE

The dispensing of injustice is always in the right hands.
                                    LEC

Of what matter whether Titus or Tiberius occupy the throne, when every minister is a Sejanus?   CHAMFORT

There is a certain satisfaction in coming down to the lowest ground of politics, for we get rid of cant and hypocrisy.
                                    EMERSON

Nothing doth more hurt in a state than that cunning men pass for wise.   BACON

One constantly sees a political party exaggerating its feelings in order to embarrass its opponents, and the latter, in order to avoid the trap, pretending to sentiments which they do not feel.   TOCQUEVILLE

The last thing a political party gives up is its vocabulary. This is because, in party politics as in other matters, it is the crowd who dictates the language, and the crowd relinquishes the ideas it has been given more readily than the words it has learned.   TOCQUEVILLE

[306]

Political parties never know each other: they approach, touch, seize, but never *see* each other.   TOCQUEVILLE

Political parties are constantly deceived because they always only think of the pleasure they themselves derive from the speech of their great orator, and never of the dangerous excitement he arouses in their opponents.   TOCQUEVILLE

All parties, without exception, when they seek for power are varieties of absolutism.   PRUDHON

Cease being the slave of a party and you become its deserter.   SIMON

The party system is arranged on the same principle as a three-legged race: the principle that union is not always strength and is never activity.   CHESTERTON

A party which is not afraid of letting culture, business, and welfare go to ruin completely can be omnipotent for a while.   BURCKHARDT

The state has learned from the merchants and industrialists how to exploit credit; it defies the nation ever to let it go into bankruptcy. Alongside all swindlers the state now stands there as swindler-in-chief.   BURCKHARDT

The dismay and fury of the men who depend for their living on the dwindling horse traffic in a town is natural, and excites sympathy and pity. But these are unfortunately not the men whom it would be useful to elect on a traffic board for the consideration of the future lines on which an electrical system should be laid down and linked up.   SICKERT

In politics a community of hatred is almost always the foundation of friendships.   TOCQUEVILLE

Democracy becomes a government of bullies tempered by editors.   EMERSON

For those who govern, the first thing required is indifference to newspapers.   THIERS

The real object is to vote for the good politician, not for the kind-hearted or agreeable man: the mischief is just the same to the country whether I am smiled into a corrupt choice or frowned into a corrupt choice.   SYDNEY SMITH

Democracy substitutes election by the incompetent many for appointment by the corrupt few.   SHAW

Three systems of colonization: the English, colonies with colonials; the French, colonies without colonials; the German, colonials without colonies.   ANONYMOUS

A nation cannot be an object of charity. But a country can be one—as an environment bearing traditions which are eternal. Every country can be that.   SIMONE WEIL

The real science of political economy, which has yet to be distinguished from the bastard science, as medicine from witchcraft, and astronomy from astrology, is that which teaches nations to desire and labor for the things that lead to life.   RUSKIN

In every party there is someone who, by his over-devout expression of party principles, provokes the rest to defect.

NIETZSCHE

Whatever the human law may be, neither an individual nor a nation can ever *deliberately* commit the least act of injustice without having to pay the penalty for it.   THOREAU

Next to its cultural habits, the thing which a nation is least apt to change is its civil legislation.   TOCQUEVILLE

Liberty and Union

It is useless to close the gates against ideas; they overleap them.   METTERNICH

Liberty is to faction what air is to fire, an element without which it instantly expires. But it could not be a less folly to abolish liberty, which is essential to political life, because it nourishes faction than it would be to wish the annihilation of air, which is essential to animal life, because it imparts to fire its destructive agency.   MADISON

There is no generalized idea of liberty, and it is hard to form one, since the liberty of a particular man is exercised only at the expense of other people's. Formerly liberty was called privilege; all things considered, that is perhaps its true name.

GOURMONT

We should not let ourselves be burned for our opinions themselves, since we can never be quite sure of them; but perhaps we might for the right to hold and alter them.   NIETZSCHE

The scrupulous and the just, the noble, humane and devoted natures, the unselfish and the intelligent, may begin a movement—but it passes away from them. They are not the leaders of a revolution. They are its victims.   CONRAD

A disposition to preserve, and an ability to improve, taken together, would be my standard of a statesman.   T. BURKE

Democratic contrivances are quarantine measures against that ancient plague, the lust for power: as such, they are very necessary and very boring.   NIETZSCHE

Great is the good fortune of a state in which the citizens have a moderate and sufficient property.   ARISTOTLE

A constitutional statesman is in general a man of common opinions and uncommon abilities.   BAGEHOT

Constitutional statesmen are obliged, not only to employ arguments which they do not think conclusive, but likewise to defend opinions which they do not believe to be true.
BAGEHOT

He is not the best statesman who is the greatest doer, but he who sets others doing with the greatest success.
ANONYMOUS

In the contest between ease and liberty, the first hath generally prevailed.   HALIFAX

If none were to have liberty but those who understand what it is, there would not be many freed men in the world.

HALIFAX

There is always a certain meanness in the argument of conservatism, joined with a certain superiority in its fact.

EMERSON

It is not by sitting still at a grand distance and calling the human race *larvae* that men are to be helped.   EMERSON

Every reform is only a mask under cover of which a more terrible reform, which dares not yet name itself, advances.

EMERSON

It is essential to the triumph of reform that it shall never succeed.   HAZLITT

The anarchist . . . is disappointed with the future as well as with the past.   CHESTERTON

A respectable vague liberalism, though it often disappears with the first gray hair, marriage, and professional success, does nevertheless raise a man's character.   HERZEN

The traces of national origin are a matter of expression even more than of feature.   HENRY JAMES

A nation is a detour of nature to arrive at six or seven great men—and then get around them.   NIETZSCHE

No nation can last which has made a mob of itself, however generous at heart.   RUSKIN

The nations which have put mankind most in their debt have been small states—Israel, Athens, Florence, Elizabethan England.   DEAN INGE

Unhappy the Juvenal whom Rome greets with amusement; unhappier still, the Rome that can be amused by a Juvenal.
                                                                                   FATHER KNOX

Only the history of free peoples merits our attention; that of men under despotisms is simply a collection of anecdotes.
                                                                                   CHAMFORT

Aristocracies often commit very tyrannical and inhuman actions, but they rarely entertain groveling thoughts; and they show a kind of haughty contempt for petty pleasures, even when they indulge in them.   TOCQUEVILLE

By nature, aristocracies are too liable to narrow the scope of human perfectability, democracies to expand it beyond reason.   TOCQUEVILLE

Forms become more necessary as the government becomes more active and powerful, and private persons become more indolent and feeble. By their nature, democratic nations stand more in need of forms than other nations, and respect them less.   TOCQUEVILLE

They that are discontented under monarchy call it tyrany, and they that are displeased with aristocracy call it oligarchy; so also, they which find themselves grieved under a democracy call it anarchy.   HOBBES

As a rule, democracies have very confused or erroneous ideas on external affairs, and generally solve outside questions only for internal reasons.   TOCQUEVILLE

It should never be forgotten by leaders of democratic nations that nothing except the love and habit of freedom can maintain an advantageous contest with the love and habit of physical well-being. I can conceive of nothing better prepared for subjection in case of defeat than a democratic people without free institutions.   TOCQUEVILLE

I think that democratic communities have a natural taste for freedom; left to themselves, they will seek it, cherish it, and view any privation of it with regret. But for equality their passion is ardent, insatiable, incessant, invincible; they call for equality in freedom; and if they cannot obtain that, they will call for equality in slavery. They will endure poverty, servitude, barbarism, but they will not endure aristocracy.   TOCQUEVILLE

A fanatical belief in democracy makes democratic institutions impossible.   RUSSELL

In times of peace, the well-being of small nations is undoubtedly more general and complete; but they are apt to suffer more acutely from the calamities of war than great empires. If none but small nations existed, I do not doubt that mankind would be more happy and more free; but the existence of great nations is unavoidable. It profits a state but little to be affluent and free if it is perpetually exposed to be pillaged or subjected.   TOCQUEVILLE

The patriotism of antiquity becomes in most modern societies a caricature. In antiquity, it developed naturally from the whole condition of a people, its youth, its situation, its culture—with us it is an awkward imitation. Our life demands, not separation from other nations, but constant intercourse; our city life is not that of the ancient city-state.
                   GOETHE

The reluctant obedience of distant provinces generally costs more than it is worth.   MACAULAY

What scoundrels we would be if we did for ourselves what we stand ready to do for Italy.   CAVOUR

You'll never have a quiet world till you knock the patriotism out of the human race.   SHAW

Patriotism is the last refuge of a scoundrel.   DR. JOHNSON

Liberty is generally established with difficulty in the midst of storms; it is perfected by civil discord; and its benefits cannot be appreciated until it is already old.   TOCQUEVILLE

People and Princes

Let the people think they govern, and they will be governed.
PENN

If you ask me, "Why should not the people make their own laws?" I need only ask you, "Why should not the people write their own plays?" They cannot. It is much easier to write a good play than to make a good law. And there are not a hundred men in the world who can write a play good enough to stand the daily wear and tear as long as a law must.
SHAW

The masses of men are very difficult to excite on bare grounds of self-interest; most easy if a bold orator tells them confidently they are wronged.   BAGEHOT

To succeed in chaining the crowd you must seem to wear the same fetters.   VOLTAIRE

The most essential mental quality for a free people, whose liberty is to be progressive, permanent, and on a large scale, is much stupidity.   BAGEHOT

The people are to be taken in very small doses.   EMERSON

While the natural instincts of democracy induce the people to reject distinguished citizens as their rulers, an instinct no less strong induces able men to retire from the political arena, in which it is difficult to retain their independence, or to advance without becoming servile.   TOCQUEVILLE

The people are that part of the state that does not know what it wants.   HEGEL

When the people contend for their liberty, they seldom get anything by their victory but new masters.   HALIFAX

The liberty of writing, like all other liberties, is most formidable when it is a novelty. A people who have never been accustomed to hearing state affairs discussed in front of them place implicit confidence in the first tribune who presents himself.   TOCQUEVILLE

The people cannot see, but they can feel.   HARRINGTON

The people are deceived by names, but not by things.

HARRINGTON

The people will ever suspect the remedies for the diseases of the state where they are wholly excluded from seeing how they are prepared.

HALIFAX

I do not think a single people can be cited, since human society began, that has, of its own free will and by its own exertions, created an aristocracy within its bosom.

TOCQUEVILLE

A decent provision for the poor is the true test of civilization.

DR. JOHNSON

Until its decline in the twentieth century, the territory of the nation-state offered all classes a substitute for the privately owned home of which the class of the poor had been deprived.

HANNAH ARENDT

When there is no middle class, and the poor greatly exceed in number, troubles arise, and the state soon comes to an end.

ARISTOTLE

The public good requires us to betray, and to lie, and to massacre: let us resign this commission to those who are more pliable, and more obedient.

MONTAIGNE

The tumultuous love of the populace must be seized and enjoyed in its first transports . . . ; it will not keep.

CHESTERFIELD

Democracy is Lovelace and the people is Clarissa.

JOHN ADAMS

The nobility, say its members, is the intermediary between the King and the People. . . . Quite; just as the hounds are the intermediary between the men and the hares.

CHAMFORT

How small, of all that human hearts endure,
That part which kings or laws can cause or cure.

DR. JOHNSON

Vulgarity in a king flatters the majority of the nation.

SHAW

In absolute monarchies the king often has great virtues, but the courtiers are invariably servile. TOCQUEVILLE

Had he never been emperor, no one would have doubted his ability to reign. TACITUS

Princes had need, in tender matters and ticklish times, to beware what they say; especially in those short speeches which fly abroad like darts, and are thought to be shot out of their secret intentions. For as to large discourses, they are flat things and not much noted. I have remarked that some witty and sharp speeches, which have fallen from princes, have given fire to seditions. BACON

A prince who will not undergo the difficulty of understanding must undergo the danger of trusting. HALIFAX

Men are so unwilling to displease a prince that it is as dangerous to inform him right as to serve him wrong. HALIFAX

Power always has most to apprehend from its own illusions. Monarchs have incurred more hazards from the follies of their own that have grown up under the adulation of parasites, than from the machinations of their enemies. COOPER

It is safer for a prince to judge of men by what they do to one another than what they do to him.　　HALIFAX

They say princes learn no art truly, but the art of horsemanship. The reason is, the brave beast is no flatterer. He will throw a prince as soon as his groom.　　JONSON

Princes have this remaining of humanity, that they think themselves obliged not to make war without a reason. Their reasons are, indeed, not always very satisfactory.

DR. JOHNSON

What makes a nation great is not primarily its great men, but the stature of its innumerable mediocre ones.

ORTEGA Y GASSET

Kings will be tyrants from policy when subjects are rebels from principle.　　E. BURKE

Children and subjects . . . are much seldomer in the wrong than parents and kings.　　CHESTERFIELD

THE LIFE OF THE MIND

Truth and Error

A thing is not truth till it is so strongly believed in that the believer is convinced that its existence does not depend upon him.   CHAPMAN

On the mountains of truth you can never climb in vain: either you will reach a point higher up today, or you will be training your powers so that you will be able to climb higher tomorrow.   NIETZSCHE

He who does not know truth at sight is unworthy of her notice.   BLAKE

Convictions are more dangerous foes of truth than lies.
                                                        NIETZSCHE

Truth can never be told so as to be understood, and not be believed.   BLAKE

The honest man must be a perpetual renegade, the life of an honest man a perpetual infidelity. For the man who wishes to remain faithful to truth must make himself perpetually unfaithful to all the continual, successive, indefatigable, renascent errors.   PÉGUY

[321]

On a huge hill,
Cragged and steep, Truth stands, and hee that will
Reach her, about must, and about must goe;
And what the hills suddennes resists, winne so.

DONNE

It is the customary fate of new truths to begin as heresies
and to end as superstititions.   T. H. HUXLEY

Apart from blunt truth, our lives sink decadently amid the
perfume of hints and suggestions.   WHITEHEAD

There is nothing more likely to drive a man mad than . . .
an obstinate, constitutional preference of the true to the
agreeable.   HAZLITT

Truth generally is kindness, but where the two diverge and
collide, kindness should override truth.

SAMUEL BUTLER (II)

Truth does less good in the world than its appearances do
harm.   LA ROCHEFOUCAULD

The opinion which is *fated* to be ultimately agreed to by
all who investigate it is what we mean by the truth, and the
object represented in this opinion is the real.   PEIRCE

Two elements are needed to form a truth—a fact and an
abstraction.   COURMONT

There is no such source of error as the pursuit of absolute
truth.   SAMUEL BUTLER (II)

A system-grinder hates the truth.   EMERSON

Truths turn into dogmas the moment they are disputed.
                                                              CHESTERTON

When you have eliminated the impossible, whatever remains,
however improbable, must be the truth.   CONAN DOYLE

It is good to express a matter in two ways simultaneously so
as to give it both a right foot and a left. Truth can stand on
one leg, to be sure; but with two it can walk and get about.
                                                              NIETZSCHE

It requires as much caution to tell the truth as to conceal it.
                                                                GRACIAN

Belief in truth begins with doubting all that has hitherto
been believed to be true.   NIETZSCHE

To get to know a truth properly, one must polemicize it.
                                                                NOVALIS

We have to change truth a little in order to remember it.
                                                              SANTAYANA

I have an instinct for loving the truth; but only an instinct.
                                                                VOLTAIRE

Truth is such a fly-away, such a sly-boots, so untranslatable
and unbarrelable a commodity, that it is as bad to catch as
light.   EMERSON

Truth is a clumsy scullery maid who breaks the dishes as
she washes them up.   KRAUS

[323]

There is no philosopher in the world so great but he believes a million things on the faith of other people and accepts a great many more truths than he demonstrates.

TOCQUEVILLE

All perception of truth is a perception of an analogy; we reason from our hands to our heads.   THOREAU

One may sometimes tell a lie, but the grimace with which one accompanies it tells the truth.   NIETZSCHE

It is more important that a proposition be interesting than that it be true. This statement is almost a tautology. For the energy of operation of a proposition in an occasion of experience is its interest and is its importance. But of course a true proposition is more apt to be interesting than a false one.   WHITEHEAD

There is no worse lie than a truth misunderstood by those who hear it.   WILLIAM JAMES

Contradiction is not a sign of falsity, nor the lack of contradiction a sign of truth.   PASCAL

We have become so democratic in our habits of thought that we are convinced that truth is determined through a plebiscite of facts.   HELLER

Truth is a river that is always splitting up into arms that reunite. Islanded between the arms, the inhabitants argue for a lifetime as to which is the main river.   CONNOLLY

[324]

The comprehension of truth calls for higher powers than the defense of error. GOETHE

Truth must necessarily be stranger than fiction; for fiction is the creation of the human mind and therefore congenial to it. CHESTERTON

The loss of certainty of truth has ended in a new, entirely unprecedented zeal for truthfulness—as though man could afford to be a liar only so long as he was certain of the unchallengeable existence of truth and objective reality, which surely would survive and defeat all his lies.

HANNAH ARENDT

Truth is beautiful. Without doubt; and so are lies.

EMERSON

Remember: one lie does not cost you one truth but the truth. HEBBEL

To disavow an error is to invent retroactively. GOETHE

We never fully grasp the import of any true statement until we have a clear notion of what the opposite untrue statement would be. WILLIAM JAMES

All err the more dangerously because each follows a truth. Their mistake lies not in following a falsehood but in not following another truth. PASCAL

Error of opinion may be tolerated where reason is left free to combat it. JEFFERSON

Experience does not err; it is only your judgment that errs in expecting from her what is not in her power.

LEONARDO DA VINCI

Error itself may be happy chance.   WHITEHEAD

The honest liar is the man who tells the truth about his old lies; who says on Wednesday, "I told a magnificent lie on Monday."   CHESTERTON

The visionary lies to himself, the liar only to others.

NIETZSCHE

Some of the most frantic lies on the face of life are told with modesty and restraint; for the simple reason that only modesty and restraint will save them.   CHESTERTON

The quack is a man whose sentiment is not satisfied until he discovers something that is not there. If he should find a true thing, it would coalesce with the rest of truth and somewhat defeat his ambition; he would never be satisfied with it.

CHAPMAN

There are visual errors in time as well as in space.   PROUST

When we return from error, it is through knowing that we return.   SAINT AUGUSTINE

Error has turned beasts into men. Will truth be able to turn men back into beasts?   NIETZSCHE

They who are engrossed in the rapid realization of an extravagant hope tend to view facts as something base and unclean. Facts are counterrevolutionary.   HOFFER

Opinions and Beliefs

A hatred of mediocrity ill becomes a philosopher. . . .
Exactly because he is the exception, he must protect the rule.

NIETZSCHE

The philosopher has to be the bad conscience of his age.

NIETZSCHE

Every great philosophy is . . . a species of involuntary and
unconscious autobiography.

NIETZSCHE

It takes a great deal of elevation of thought to produce a very
little elevation of life.

EMERSON

The intelligent man finds almost everything ridiculous, the
sensible man hardly anything.

GOETHE

The wise man does at once what the fool does finally.

GRACIAN

There is somebody wiser than any of us, and that is everybody.

NAPOLEON

Only when we know little do we know anything; doubt grows
with knowledge.

GOETHE

To have doubted one's own first principles is the mark of a
civilized man.

O. W. HOLMES, JR.

Men may be convinced, but they cannot be pleased, against
their will.

DR. JOHNSON

We are not won by arguments that we can analyze but by tone and temper, by the manner which is the man himself.

SAMUEL BUTLER (II)

It is always easy to be on the negative side. If a man were not to deny that there is salt on the table, you could not reduce him to an absurdity.

DR. JOHNSON

The majority of those who flatter themselves on their knowledge of the human heart do not separate their boasted insight from their unfavorable feeling about humanity. . . . Nothing indeed imparts a *psychological* air so much as an habitual attitude of depreciation.

VALÉRY

To deny A is to put A behind bars.

VALÉRY

Joyous distrust is a sign of health. Everything absolute belongs to pathology.

NIETZSCHE

The mind of a bigot is like the pupil of the eye; the more light you pour upon it, the more it will contract.

O. W. HOLMES, JR.

Unmitigated seriousness is always out of place in human affairs. Let not the unwary reader think me flippant for saying so; it was Plato, in his solemn old age, who said it.

SANTAYANA

People talk fundamentals and superlatives and then make some changes of detail.

O. W. HOLMES, JR.

The idealist is incorrigible—if he is turned out of his heaven, he makes an ideal of his hell.

NIETZSCHE

I'll not listen to reason. . . . Reason always means what someone else has got to say.   MRS. GASKELL

It seemed so simple when one was young and new ideas were mentioned not to grow red in the face and gobble.

L. P. SMITH

He swallowed a lot of wisdom, but it seemed as if all of it had gone down the wrong way.   LICHTENBERG

We are ungrateful to the intellects of the past; or rather, like children we take it for granted that somebody must supply us with our supper and our ideas.   CHAPMAN

There are boxes in the mind with labels on them: To study on a favorable occasion; Never to be thought about; Useless to go into further; Contents unexamined; Pointless business; Urgent; Dangerous; Delicate; Impossible; Abandoned; Reserved; For others; My forte; etc.   VALÉRY

Some minds are as little logical or argumentative as nature; they can offer no reason or "guess," but they exhibit the solemn and incontrovertible fact. If a historical question arises, they cause the tombs to be opened.   THOREAU

Experience, as a *desire* for experience, does not come off. We must not study ourselves while having an experience.

NIETZSCHE

We suffer less from having had to renounce our desires when we have trained our imagination to see the past as ugly.

NIETZSCHE

We often refuse to accept an idea merely because the tone of voice in which it has been expressed is unsympathetic to us.   NIETZSCHE

Many things are not believed because their current explanation is not believed.   NIETZSCHE

When we are tired, we are attacked by ideas we conquered long ago.   NIETZSCHE

By nature's kindly disposition, most questions which it is beyond a man's power to answer do not occur to him at all.   SANTAYANA

If the greatest philosopher in the world find himself upon a plank wider than actually necessary, but hanging over a precipice, his imagination will prevail, though his reason convince him of his safety.   PASCAL

Everybody calls "clear" those ideas which have the same degree of confusion as his own.   PROUST

Every man takes the limits of his own field of vision for the limits of the world.   SCHOPENHAUER

The more unintelligent a man is, the less mysterious existence seems to him.   SCHOPENHAUER

Science commits suicide when it adopts a creed.
                                                                T. H. HUXLEY

Every great advance in natural knowledge has involved the absolute rejection of authority.　　　　T. H. HUXLEY

Tolerance meant, at worst, sullenly putting up with what one could not alter; at best, willingly accepting what one could not alter. It was a little limited by the fact that "to tolerate" was always considered as an active and hardly ever as a passive verb. The idea that others had, so to speak, to "put up with" oneself was rarely practiced deeply and consistently.　　　　WILLIAMS

We do not need the learned man to teach us the important things. We all know the important things, though we all violate and neglect them. Gigantic industry, abysmal knowledge, are needed for the discovery of the tiny things—the things that seem hardly worth the trouble.　　　　CHESTERTON

Human learning has often been an instrument, not a source, of hostility to religion.　　　　ACTON

In a war of ideas it is people who get killed.　　　　LEC

The felicity of princes and great persons had long since turned to rudeness and barbarism, if the poverty of learning had not kept up civility and honor of life.　　　　BACON

Crafty men contemn studies; simple men admire them; and wise men use them.　　　　BACON

As it asketh some knowledge to demand a question not impertinent, so it requireth some sense to make a wish not absurd.　　　　BACON

Most ignorance is vincible ignorance. We don't know because we don't want to know.　　ALDOUS HUXLEY

Seeking to know is only too often learning to doubt.
　　ANTOINETTE DESHOULIÈRES

A man in the wrong may more easily be convinced than one half right.　　EMERSON

Curiosity is almost, almost, the definition of frivolity.
　　ORTEGA Y GASSET

Perhaps we never hate any opinion or can do until we have impersonated it.　　COLERIDGE

It is a golden rule not to judge men by their opinions but rather by what their opinions make of them.
　　LICHTENBERG

People are usually more firmly convinced that their opinions are precious than that they are true.　　SANTAYANA

Some men plant opinions they seem to pull up.
　　ENGLISH PROVERB

To change his opinions is for one nature an expression of purity of mind, like somebody who changes his clothing; but for another nature it is only an expression of his vanity.
　　NIETZSCHE

Both sides of a question do not belong to the poor old question at all, but to the opposing views which bedevil it.
　　HASKINS

To prejudge other men's notions before we have looked into them is not to show their darkness but to put out our own eyes.   LOCKE

Man is what he believes.   CHEKHOV

Man adapts himself to everything, to the best and the worst. To one thing only does he not adapt himself: to being not clear in his own mind what he believes about things.
                                              ORTEGA Y GASSET

A thing "is" whatever it gives us least trouble to think it is. There is no other "is" than this.   SAMUEL BUTLER (II)

There are some statements that no one ever thinks of believing, however often they are made.   CHESTERTON

The history of Christendom would have been far happier if we all had remembered one rule of intelligence—not to believe a thing more strongly at the end of a bitter argument than at the beginning, not to believe it with the energy of the opposition rather than one's own.   WILLIAMS

"In my heart I have determined on it." And one is even inclined to point to one's breast as one says it. Psychologically this way of speaking should be taken seriously. Why should it be taken less seriously than the assertion that belief is a state of mind?   WITTGENSTEIN

If there were a verb meaning "to believe falsely," it would not have any significant first person, present indicative.
                                                 WITTGENSTEIN

There might actually occur a case where we should say, "This man believes he is pretending."   WITTGENSTEIN

There can never be any reason for rejecting one instinctive belief except that it clashes with others. It is of course *possible* that all or any of our beliefs may be mistaken, and therefore all ought to be held with at least some element of doubt. But we cannot have *reason* to reject a belief except on the ground of some other belief.   RUSSELL

A fool hath no dialogue within himself, the first thought carrieth him without the reply of a second.   HALIFAX

Some like to understand what they believe in. Others like to believe in what they understand.   LEC

The brute necessity of believing something so long as life lasts does not justify any belief in particular.   SANTAYANA

No man does anything from a single motive.   COLERIDGE

The chief phenomenon in our days is the sense of the provisional.   BURCKHARDT

He who thinks much and to some purpose easily forgets his own experiences but not the thoughts which each experience provoked.   NIETZSCHE

Everything seems possible when we are absolutely helpless or absolutely powerful—and both states stimulate our credulity.   HOFFER

One mood is the natural critic of another. When possessed with a strong feeling on any subject foreign to the one I may be writing on, I know very well what of good and what of bad I have written on the latter.　　　THOREAU

The "silly" question is the first intimation of some totally new development.　　　WHITEHEAD

It is not true that X never thinks. On the contrary, he is always thinking—about something else.　　　BRADLEY

The people who are most bigoted are the people who have no convictions at all.　　　CHESTERTON

There is no skeptic who does not feel that men have doubted before, but no man who is in love thinks that anyone has been in love before.　　　CHESTERTON

We fear something before we hate it; a child who fears noises becomes a man who hates noise.　　　CONNOLLY

Bodily offspring I do not leave, but mental offspring I do. Well, my books do not have to be sent to school and college and then insist on going into the Church or take to drinking or marry their mother's maid.　　　SAMUEL BUTLER (II)

Mere financial dishonesty is of very little importance in the history of civilization. Who cares whether Caesar stole or Caesar Borgia cheated? . . . The real evil that follows . . . a commercial dishonesty so general as ours is the intellectual dishonesty it generates.　　　CHAPMAN

To make our idea of morality center on forbidden acts is to defile the imagination and to introduce into our judgments of our fellow men a secret element of gusto.   STEVENSON

A philosophical fashion catches on like a gastronomical fashion: one can no more refute an idea than a sauce.   CIORAN

Tell me to what you pay attention and I will tell you who you are.   ORTEGA Y GASSET

Reporting facts is the refuge of those who have no imagination.   VAUVENARGUES

I do not mind lying, but I hate inaccuracy.
SAMUEL BUTLER (II)

No one would be angry with a man for unintentionally making a mistake about a matter of fact; but if he perversely insists on spoiling your story in the telling of it, you want to kick him; and this is the reason why every philosopher and theologian is justly vexed with every other.   SANTAYANA

Games give pleasure but bear no fruit, and only that which bears fruit is real. All games and all thoughts seek to exclude the necessity of death, suffering, injustice, downfall. The thinker turns the pangs of birth into causes, death into evolution.   ROSENSTOCK-HUESSY

We play gladly and think gladly because in these activities we feel ourselves masters of the situation: the space of play and the space of thought are the two theaters of freedom.
ROSENSTOCK-HUESSY

Nothing is more hopeless than a scheme of merriment.

DR. JOHNSON

Hope is itself a species of happiness, and perhaps the chief happiness which this world affords. DR. JOHNSON

Pessimists as a rule live to a ripe old age. It is questionable if a despairing view of the universe even impairs the digestion as much as a single slice of new bread. LYND

At certain moments a single almost insignificant sorrow may, by association, bring together all the little relicts of pain and discomfort, bodily and mental, that we have endured even from infancy. COLERIDGE

Life is not long, and too much of it must not pass in idle deliberation how it shall be spent. DR. JOHNSON

In wonder all philosophy began: in wonder it ends. . . . But the first wonder is the offspring of ignorance: the last is the parent of adoration. COLERIDGE

Very unlike a divine man would he be, who is unable to count one, two, three, or to distinguish odd and even numbers.

PLATO

Materialists unwilling to admit the mysterious element of our nature make it all mysterious. COLERIDGE

Our quaint metaphysical opinions, in an hour of anguish, are like playthings by the bedside of a child deathly sick.

COLERIDGE

Be careful how you interpret the world: it *is* like that.

HELLER

Compromise is odious to passionate natures because it seems a surrender; and to intellectual natures because it seems a confusion.

SANTAYANA

I do not greatly care whether I have been right or wrong on any point, but I care a good deal about knowing which of the two I have been.

SAMUEL BUTLER (II)

Nothing requires a rarer intellectual heroism than willingness to see one's equation written out.

SANTAYANA

Perhaps the only true dignity of man is his capacity to despise himself.

SANTAYANA

In all institutions from which the cold wind of open criticism is excluded, an innocent corruption begins to grow like a mushroom—for example, in senates and learned societies.

NIETZSCHE

To understand oneself is the classic form of consolation; to elude oneself is the romantic.

SANTAYANA

Reason and Thought

Life is judged with all the blindness of life itself.

SANTAYANA

To know the world, one must construct it.   PAVESE

Give me matter and I will build a world from it; that is, give me matter and I will show you how a world developed from it.   KANT

He who would rightly comprehend the world must be, now Democritus, and now Heraclitus.   SILESIUS

Man was not born to solve the problems of the universe, but to put his finger on the problem and then to keep within the limits of the comprehensible.   GOETHE

Existence should be met on its own terms: we may dance a round with it, and perhaps steal a kiss; but it tempts us only to flout us, not being dedicated to any constant love.

SANTAYANA

Logic is like the sword—those who appeal to it shall perish by it. Faith is appealing to the living God, and one may perish by that too, but somehow one would rather perish that way than the other, and one has got to perish sooner or later.   SAMUEL BUTLER (II)

You must see the infinite, i.e., the universal, in your particular, or it is only gossip.   O. W. HOLMES, JR.

No question is so difficult to answer as that to which the answer is obvious. SHAW

The struggle for existence holds as much in the intellectual as in the physical world. A theory is a species of thinking, and its right to exist is coextensive with its power of resisting extinction by its rivals. T. H. HUXLEY

Eternity is in love with the productions of time. BLAKE

While we talk logic, we are unanswerable; but then, on the other hand, the universal living scene of things is after all as little a logical world as it is a poetical; and as it cannot without violence be exalted into poetical perfection, neither can it be attenuated into a logical formula. NEWMAN

A *gloss on Descartes:* Sometimes I think: and sometimes I am. VALÉRY

What is now proved was once only imagined. BLAKE

If the cultivation of the understanding consists in one thing more than in another, it is surely in learning the grounds of one's own opinions. MILL

The man who sees the consistency in things is a wit. . . . The man who sees the inconsistency in things is a humorist. CHESTERTON

Analysis makes for *unity*, but not necessarily for *goodness*. FREUD

The natural flights of the human mind are not from pleasure to pleasure, but from hope to hope.   DR. JOHNSON

On proportion the classic whole depends. That whole has a place for the romantic beginning; it puts the romantic into its place certainly, and firmly keeps it there. But the anti-classic has no place for any image at all—either of the beginning or of the end, only for a makeshift.   WILLIAMS

The value of a principle is the number of things it will explain.
                                                        EMERSON

Principles always become a matter of vehement discussion when practice is at ebb.   GISSING

The man who listens to reason is lost: reason enslaves all whose minds are not strong enough to master her.   SHAW

In an unreasonable age, a man's reason let loose would undo him.   HALIFAX

Synthetical reasoning, setting up as its goal some unattainable abstraction, like an imaginary quantity in algebra, and commencing its course with taking for granted some two assertions which cannot be proved, from the union of these two assumed truths produces a third assumption, and so on in an infinite series, to the unspeakable benefit of the human intellect. The beauty of this process is, that at every step it strikes out into two branches, in a compound ratio of ramification; so that you are perfectly sure of losing your way, and keeping your mind in perfect health, by the perpetual exercise of an interminable quest.   PEACOCK

All reasoning ends in an appeal to self-evidence. PATMORE

The world of reason is poor compared to the world of the senses—until *or, but, because, when, if, and, unless* populate it with endless possibilities. KAUFMANN

Man's rational life consists in those moments in which reflection not only occurs but proves efficacious. SANTAYANA

Reason is God's gift; but so are the passions: reason is as guilty as passion. NEWMAN

Reason can ascertain the profound difficulties of our condition; it cannot remove them. NEWMAN

Imagination cannot make fools wise; but she can make them happy, to the envy of reason, who can only make her friends miserable. PASCAL

It is the triumph of reason to get on well with those who possess none. VOLTAIRE

Nothing hath an uglier look to us than reason, when it is not of our side. HALIFAX

Most people reason dramatically, not quantitatively.
O. W. HOLMES, JR.

The method which begins by doubting in order to philosophize is just as suited to its purpose as making a soldier lie down in a heap in order to teach him to stand upright.
KIERKEGAARD

If I carried all the thoughts of the world in my hand, I would take care not to open it.   FONTENELLE

The thinker philosophizes as the lover loves. Even were the consequences not only useless but harmful, he must obey his impulse.   WILLIAM JAMES

Philosophy destroys itself when it indulges in brilliant feats of explaining away. It is then trespassing with the wrong equipment upon the field of particular sciences. Its ultimate appeal is to the general consciousness of what in practice we experience.   WHITEHEAD

If an angel were to tell us something of his philosophy, I do believe some of his propositions would sound like $2 \times 2 = 13$.   LICHTENBERG

There are no sects in geometry.   VOLTAIRE

If there is any good in philosophy it is this: it never inspects pedigrees.   SENECA

The fruits of philosophy [are the important thing], not the philosophy itself. When we ask the time, we don't want to know how watches are constructed.   LICHTENBERG

If we lacked curiosity, we should do less for the good of our neighbor. But, under the name of duty or pity, curiosity steals into the home of the unhappy and the needy. Perhaps even in the famous mother-love there is a good deal of curiosity.   NIETZSCHE

Wonder is what the philosopher endures most; for there is no other beginning of philosophy than this.   PLATO

[343]

Philosophy contemplates reason, whence comes knowledge of the true; philology observes that of which human choice is the author, whence comes consciousness of the certain.

VICO

A great philosophy is not one which is never defeated. But a petty philosophy is always one which will not fight. A great philosophy is not a philosophy without reproach; it is a philosophy without fear.

PÉGUY

Philosophy is not the concern of those who pass through Divinity and Greats, but of those who pass through birth and death. If the ordinary man may not discuss existence, why should he be asked to conduct it?

CHESTERTON

There may be some branches of human study—mechanics perhaps—where the personal spirit of the investigator does not affect the result; but philosophy is not one of them.

CHAPMAN

Religion is a man using a divining rod. Philosophy is a man using a pick and shovel.

ANONYMOUS

The value of philosophy is to be sought largely in its very uncertainty. He who has no tincture of philosophy goes through life imprisoned in the prejudices derived from common sense, from the habitual beliefs of his age or his nation, and from convictions which have grown up in his mind without the cooperation or consent of his deliberate reason. As soon as we begin to philosophize, on the contrary, we find that even the most everyday things lead to problems to which only very incomplete answers can be given. Philosophy, though unable to tell us with certainty what is the true answer to the doubts which it raises, is able to suggest many possibilities which enlarge our thoughts and free them from the tyranny of custom.

RUSSELL

There was never yet philosopher that could endure the tooth-
ache patiently.   SHAKESPEARE

> Who can hold a fire in his hand
> While thinking on the frosty Caucasus?
>   SHAKESPEARE

My body is that part of the world which my thoughts can
alter. Even imaginary illnesses can become real ones. In the
rest of the world my hypotheses cannot disturb the order of
things.   LICHTENBERG

Perfect accuracy of thought is unattainable, *theoretically unattainable*, and undue striving for it is worse than time wasted:
it positively renders thought unclear.   PEIRCE

Every abstract thinker tears love and time asunder.
                                        ROSENSTOCK-HUESSY

It is a profoundly erroneous truism, repeated by all copy
books and by eminent people when they are making speeches,
that we should cultivate the habit of thinking what we are
doing. The precise opposite is the case. Civilization advances
by extending the number of important operations which we
can perform without thinking about them.   WHITEHEAD

Daring ideas are like chessmen moved forward; they may be
beaten, but they may start a winning game.   GOETHE

A man is infinitely more complicated than his thoughts.
                                                      VALÉRY

The world overcomes us, not merely by appealing to our
reason, or by exciting our passions, but by imposing on our
imagination.   NEWMAN

The history of thought can be summarized in these words: It is absurd by what it seeks, great by what it finds.

VALÉRY

The proper, unique, and perpetual object of thought: that which does not exist, that which is not before me, that which was, that which will be, that which is possible, that which is impossible.

VALÉRY

One gives birth to a thought, a second assists at its baptism, a third produces children with it, a fourth visits it on its death bed, and the fifth buries it.

LICHTENBERG

The wise only possess ideas; the greater part of mankind are possessed by them.

COLERIDGE

In the study of ideas, it is necessary to remember that insistence on hardheaded clarity issues from sentimental feeling, as it were a mist, cloaking the perplexities of fact. Insistence on clarity at all costs is based on sheer superstition as to the mode in which human intelligence functions.

WHITEHEAD

Whenever I hear people talking about "liberal" ideas, I am always astounded that men should so love to fool themselves with empty sounds. An idea should never be liberal: it must be vigorous, positive, and without loose ends so that it may fulfill its divine mission and be productive. The proper place for liberality is in the realm of the emotions.

GOETHE

Fundamental progress has to do with the reinterpretation of basic ideas.

WHITEHEAD

Ideas, as distinguished from events, are never unprecedented.

HANNAH ARENDT

We can never get rid of mouse ideas completely; they keep turning up again and again, and nibble, nibble—no matter how often we drive them off. The best way to keep them down is to have a few good strong cat ideas which will embrace them and ensure their not reappearing till they do so in another shape.   SAMUEL BUTLER (II)

The mind's direction is more important than its progress.
                                                        JOUBERT

When he was expected to use his mind, he felt like a right-handed person who has to do something with his left.
                                                        LICHTENBERG

Any mental activity is easy if it need not take reality into account.   PROUST

Perfect clarity would profit the intellect but damage the will.
                                                        PASCAL

In the field of observation, chance favors only the prepared minds.   PASTEUR

Our minds want clothes as much as our bodies.
                                          SAMUEL BUTLER (II)

The mind of the Renaissance was not a pilgrim mind, but a sedentary city mind, like that of the ancients.
                                                        SANTAYANA

The mind must have some worldly objects to excite its attention, otherwise it will stagnate in indolence, sink into melancholy, or rise into visions and enthusiasm.
                                                        CHESTERFIELD

Good sense is the concierge of the mind: its business is not to let suspicious-looking ideas enter or leave.   STERN

For a thing to be problematic it is necessary that we be not altogether convinced of its opposite being true.

ORTEGA Y GASSET

In the establishment of any true axiom, the negative instance is the more forcible of the two.   BACON

Think of a white cloud as being holy, you cannot love it; but think of a holy man within the cloud, love springs up in your thoughts, for to think of holiness distinct from man is impossible to the affections. Thought alone can make monsters, but the affections cannot.   BLAKE

The unexamined life is not worth living.   SOCRATES

The primary questions for an adult are not *why* or *how*, but *when* and *where*.   ROSENSTOCK-HUESSY

The concept of number is the obvious distinction between the beast and man. Thanks to number, the cry becomes song, noise acquires rhythm, the spring is transformed into a dance, force becomes dynamic, and outlines figures.   MAISTRE

Neither in the subjective nor in the objective world can we find a criterion for the reality of the number-concept, because the first contains no such concept, and the second contains nothing that is free from the concept. How then can we arrive at a criterion? Not by evidence, for the dice of evidence are loaded. Not by logic, for logic has no existence independent of mathematics: it is only one phase of this multiplied necessity that we call mathematics.

How then shall mathematical concepts be judged? *They shall not be judged.* Mathematics is the supreme arbiter. From its decisions there is no appeal.

We cannot change the rules of the game, we cannot ascertain whether the game is fair. We can only study the player at his game; not, however, with the detached attitude of a bystander, for we are watching our own minds at play.

DANTZIG

In mathematical analysis we call x the undetermined part of line *a*; the rest we don't call *y*, as we do in common life, but *a-x*. Hence mathematical language has great advantages over the common language.

LICHTENBERG

I have often noticed that when people come to understand a mathematical proposition in some other way than that of the ordinary demonstration, they promptly say, "Oh, I see. That's how it must be." This is a sign that they explain it to themselves from within their own system.

LICHTENBERG

With most people unbelief in one thing is founded upon blind belief in another.

LICHTENBERG

Comparison is the expedient of those who cannot reach the heart of the things compared.

SANTAYANA

Look everywhere with your eyes; but with your soul never look at many things, but at *one*.

ROZINOV

A clash of doctrines is not a disaster—it is an opportunity.

WHITEHEAD

We need a categorical imperative in the natural sciences just as much as we need one in ethics.   GOETHE

In science the credit goes to the man who convinces the world, not to the man to whom the idea first occurs.

OSLER

There are some men who are counted great because they represent the actuality of their own age. . . . Such a one was Voltaire. There are other men who attain greatness because they embody the potentiality of their own day . . . they express the thoughts which will be everybody's two or three centuries after them. Such a one was Descartes.

T. H. HUXLEY

Consciousness, which is the principle of liberty, is not the principle of art. We listen badly to a symphony when we know we are listening. We think badly when we know we are thinking. Consciousness of thinking is not thought.

GOURMONT

There are not many examples, in any literature, of new ideas expressed in a new form. The most captious mind must generally be satisfied with one pleasure or the other.

GOURMONT

The mere observing of a thing is no use whatsoever. Observing turns into beholding, beholding into thinking, thinking into establishing connections, so that one may say that every attentive glance we cast on the world is an act of theorizing. However, this ought to be done consciously, with self-criticism, with freedom, and, to use a daring word, with irony.

GOETHE

Thinking is more interesting than knowing, but less interesting than looking.   GOETHE

Consciousness reigns but doesn't govern. VALÉRY

There is a great difference between *still* believing something and believing it *again*. LICHTENBERG

To study the abnormal is the best way of understanding the normal. WILLIAM JAMES

Egoism puts the feelings in Indian file. CHAZAL

The man who cannot believe his senses, and the man who cannot believe anything else, are both insane. CHESTERTON

With God thoughts are colors, with us they are pigments— even the most abstract one may be accompanied by physical pain. LICHTENBERG

Our most important thoughts are those which contradict our emotions. VALÉRY

Those who are accustomed to judge by feeling do not understand the process of reasoning, because they want to comprehend at a glance and are not used to seeking for first principles. Those, on the other hand, who are accustomed to reason from first principles do not understand matters of feeling at all, because they look for first principles and are unable to comprehend at a glance. PASCAL

Madness is to think of too many things in succession too fast, or of one thing too exclusively. VOLTAIRE

An emotion ceases to be a passion as soon as we form a clear
and distinct idea of it.   SPINOZA

We hear and apprehend only what we already half know.
                                                          THOREAU

Once a rigid idea of duty has got inside a narrow mind, it
can never again get out.   JOUBERT

Any system which is without its paradoxes is by the same
token as suspicious as an exact correspondence of several
witnesses in a trial at the Old Bailey.   PALMER

In relation to their systems most systemizers are like a man
who builds an enormous castle and lives in a shack nearby;
they do not live in their own enormous systematic buildings.
                                                       KIERKEGAARD

Dogma does not mean the absence of thought, but the end
of thought.   CHESTERTON

A man may dwell so long upon a thought that it may take
him prisoner.   HALIFAX

Every great idea exerts, on first appearing, a tyrannical influence: hence the advantages it brings are turned all too soon
into disadvantages.   GOETHE

The best human intelligence is still decidedly barbarous; it
fights in heavy armor and keeps a fool at court.   SANTAYANA

Opinions have vested interests just as men have.
                                              SAMUEL BUTLER (II)

Intellectual blemishes, like facial ones, grow more prominent with age.　　　　　　　　　　　　　　LA ROCHEFOUCAULD

New ideas are for the most part like bad sixpences, and we spend our lives trying to pass them off on one another.
　　　　　　　　　　　　　　SAMUEL BUTLER (II)

We should treat our minds as innocent and ingenuous children whose guardians we are—be careful what objects and what subjects we thrust on their attention.　　　THOREAU

The public buys its opinions as it buys its milk, on the principle that it is cheaper to do this than keep a cow. So it is, but the milk is more likely to be watered.
　　　　　　　　　　　　　　SAMUEL BUTLER (II)

Let us settle about the facts first and fight about the moral tendencies afterward.　　　　　　　SAMUEL BUTLER (II)

　　　　Wisdom is ofttimes nearer when we stoop
　　　　Than when we soar.
　　　　　　　　　　　　　　WORDSWORTH

The highest and deepest thoughts do not "voluntary move harmonious numbers," but run rather to grotesque epigram and doggerel.　　　　　　　　　　PATMORE

It is not in the power of the most exalted wit or enlarged understanding . . . to invent or frame one simple new idea.
　　　　　　　　　　　　　　LOCKE

Serious things cannot be understood without laughable things, nor opposites at all without opposites.　　　PLATO

Skepticism is the chastity of the intellect.   SANTAYANA

To deny, to believe, and to doubt well are to a man as the race is to a horse.   PASCAL

The liker anything is to wisdom, if it be not plainly the thing itself, the more directly it becomes its opposite.

   SHAFTESBURY

Ultimate insights have a tendency to undermine the orthodox approaches by which they have been reached.   SANTAYANA

To give a reason for anything is to breed a doubt of it.

   HAZLITT

Intellectuals cannot tolerate the chance event, the unintelligible; they have a nostalgia for the absolute, for a universally comprehensive scheme.   ARON

A man cannot ask another a question without at the same time answering it himself. This is "physiological." If it were not so, my answer would always satisfy him.   VALÉRY

One can live in this world on soothsaying but not on truth-saying.   LICHTENBERG

An open mind is all very well in its way, but it ought not to be so open that there is no keeping anything in or out of it. It should be capable of shutting its doors sometimes, or it may be found a little drafty.   SAMUEL BUTLER (II)

Seek simplicity and distrust it.   WHITEHEAD

Logic and consistency are luxuries for the gods and the lower animals. SAMUEL BUTLER (II)

Having precise ideas often leads to a man doing nothing. VALÉRY

Thou hast commanded that an ill-regulated mind should be its own punishment. SAINT AUGUSTINE

Our minds are lazier than our bodies. LA ROCHEFOUCAULD

Mind is rather a little bourgeois, yet you can't dispense with the *tiers état*. ROZINOV

That life is worth living is the most necessary of assumptions and, were it not assumed, the most impossible of conclusions. SANTAYANA

Culture is on the horns of this dilemma: if profound and noble it must remain rare, if common it must become mean. SANTAYANA

For an idea ever to be fashionable is ominous, since it must afterward be always old-fashioned. SANTAYANA

A man doubtful of his dinner, or trembling at a creditor, is not much disposed to abstracted meditation, or remote inquiries. DR. JOHNSON

Language and Ideas

If language had been the creation, not of poetry, but of
logic, we should only have one.   HEBBEL

If there were only one language, then language would be in
a much too triumphant position in regard to silence. Language
would seem too much like territory conquered from silence,
and silence too much subject to the will of language.
                                                    PICARD

Grammar and logic free language from being at the mercy
of the tone of voice. Grammar protects us against misunderstanding the sound of an uttered name; logic protects us
against what we say having a double meaning.
                                        ROSENSTOCK-HUESSY

The French language is a pianoforte without a pedal.
                                                      GIDE

I have drawn from the well of language many a thought
which I do not have and which I could not put into words.
                                               LICHTENBERG

It is as if our languages were confounded: when we want
a thought, they bring us a word; when we ask for a word,
they give us a dash; and when we expect a dash, there comes
a piece of bawdy.   LICHTENBERG

Every individual or national degeneration is immediately revealed by a directly proportional degradation in language.
                                                   MAISTRE

My language is the universal whore whom I have to make
into a virgin.   KRAUS

[356]

Words, like eyeglasses, blur everything that they do not make more clear.   JOUBERT

To say "this combination of words make no sense" excludes it from the sphere of language and thereby bounds the domain of language. But when one draws a boundary, it may be for various kinds of reason. If I surround an area with a fence or a line or otherwise, the purpose may be to prevent someone from getting in or out; but it may also be a part of a game and the players be supposed, say, to jump over the boundary; or it may show where the property of one man ends and that of another begins. So, if I draw a boundary line, that is not yet to say what I am drawing it for.

                                                    WITTGENSTEIN

In regard to language, democratic nations prefer obscurity to labor.   TOCQUEVILLE

The public doesn't understand German; and in journalese I can't tell them so.   KRAUS

Words differently arranged have a different meaning, and meanings differently arranged have a different effect.

                                                    PASCAL

Words do not change their meanings so drastically in the course of centuries as, in our minds, names do in the course of a year or two.   PROUST

It seems to me that the soul, when alone with itself and speaking to itself, uses only a small number of words, none of them extraordinary. This is how one recognizes that there *is* a soul at that moment, if at the same time one experiences the sensation that everything else—everything that would require a larger vocabulary—is mere possibility.   VALÉRY

Most men make little use of their speech than to give evidence against their own understanding.   HALIFAX

There is no such way to gain admittance, or give defense, to strange and absurd doctrines, as to guard them round about with legions of obscure, doubtful, and undefined words: which yet make these retreats more like the dens of robbers, or holes of foxes, than fortresses of fair warriors.   LOCKE

Words signify man's refusal to accept the world as it is.
          KAUFMANN

What makes men of genius, or rather, what they make, is not new ideas; it is the idea by which they are obsessed that what has been said has still not been said enough.
          DELACROIX

How can I tell what I think till I see what I say?   FORSTER

With a knowledge of the name comes a distincter recognition and knowledge of the thing.   THOREAU

Speech is the mother, not the handmaid, of thought.
          KRAUS

"Virtually" is apt to cover more intellectual sins than "charity" does moral delicts.   T. H. HUXLEY

In all pointed sentences, some degree of accuracy must be sacrificed to conciseness.   DR. JOHNSON

Look wise, say nothing, and grunt. Speech was given to conceal thought.   OSLER

People do not think about the events of life as differently as they speak about them.   LICHTENBERG

One often makes a remark and only later sees *how* true it is.
                                        WITTGENSTEIN

The one who loves and understands a thing best will incline to use the personal pronouns in speaking of it. To him there is no *neuter* gender.   THOREAU

Women are the simple, and poets the superior, artisans of language. . . . The intervention of grammarians is almost always bad.   GOURMONT

If you can describe clearly without a diagram the proper way of making this or that knot, then you are a master of the English tongue.   BELLOC

It is almost impossible to state what one in fact believes, because it is almost impossible to hold a belief and to define it at the same time.   WILLIAMS

I had rather feel compunction than understand the definition of it.   THOMAS A KEMPIS

A definition is the enclosing a wilderness of idea within a wall of words.   SAMUEL BUTLER (II)

Similarities are not as susceptible of definition as differences.
                                        HALLE

What a deal of talking there would be in the world if we desired at all costs to change the names of things into definitions.   LICHTENBERG

Superfluity of lecturing causes ischial bursitis.   OSLER

Memories and Dreams

Some people do not become thinkers simply because their memories are too good.   NIETZSCHE

Some men's memory is like a box, where a man should mingle his jewels with his old shoes.   HALIFAX

Our memories are card indexes consulted, and then put back in disorder by authorities whom we do not control.

CONNOLLY

What recalls another to us most vividly is precisely that which we had forgotten because it was unimportant: it has remained as it was, unaltered by our thought.   PROUST

Some memories are like friends in common; they can effect reconciliations.   PROUST

It's very difficult to describe from memory what has been natural for you; the factitious, the shammed, is described more easily because the effort that's been made to sham it has engraved it on the memory.   STENDHAL

We don't remember pure (unalloyed) sensations.

STENDHAL

When we have understood, we hear in retrospect.   PROUST

A very great memory often forgetteth how much time is lost by repeating things of no use.   HALIFAX

The existence of forgetting has never been proved: we only know that some things do not come to our mind when we want them to.   NIETZSCHE

To want to forget something is to think of it.

FRENCH PROVERB

Then the band would play a march, amnesty would be declared, the Pope would agree to retire from Rome to Brazil: then there would be a ball for the whole of Italy at the Villa Borghese on the shores of Lake Como (the Lake of Como being for that purpose transferred to the neighborhood of Rome); there would come a scene in the bushes, and so on, and so on.   DOSTOEVSKI

Sensations are rapid dreams.   SANTAYANA

Here we are all by day; by night w'are hurled
By dreams, each one into a sev'rall world.

HERRICK

[361]

The civil wilderness of sleep. HERRICK

If people would recount their dreams truthfully, one might divine character more correctly from dreams than from faces.
LICHTENBERG

In dreams I do not recollect that state of feeling so common when awake, of thinking on one subject and looking at another. COLERIDGE

Authentic symbolism is present when something specific represents something more universal, not as a dream or a shadow, but as a living momentary revelation of what is inscrutable. GOETHE

What is beneath the earth is quite as natural as what is above ground, and he who cannot summon spirits in the daytime under the open sky will not evoke them at midnight in a vault. GOETHE

I am so unhappy at the present time that in my dreams I am indescribably happy. KIERKEGAARD

Dreaming permits each and every one of us to be quietly and safely insane every night of our lives. FISHER

The inquiry into a dream is another dream. HALIFAX

LIFE'S MINOR PLEASURES AND TRIALS

Life's Minor Pleasures and Trials

Home is the only place where you can go out and in. There are places you can go into, and places you can go out of, but the one place, if you do but find it, where you may go out and in both, is home.

MACDONALD

Home is the place where, when you have to go there,
They have to take you in.
                              I should have called it
Something you somehow haven't to deserve.

FROST

One does not love a place the less for having suffered in it.

JANE AUSTEN

But Islands of the Blessèd, bless you son,
I never came upon a blessèd one.

FROST

Hearts may fail, and Strength outwear, and Purpose turn
    to Loathing,
But the everyday affair of business, meals, and clothing,
Builds a bulkhead 'twixt Despair and the Edge of
    Nothing.

KIPLING

No man is a hypocrite in his pleasures.   DR. JOHNSON

[365]

Take care to get what you like or you will be forced to like what you get. Where there is no ventilation, fresh air is declared unwholesome.   SHAW

Life would be tolerable were it not for its amusements.
                                                        G. C. LEWIS

A variety of nothing is superior to a monotony of something.
                                                        RICHTER

Amusement is the happiness of those that cannot think.
                                                        POPE

Nothing is more hopeless than a scheme of merriment.
                                                        DR. JOHNSON

Simple pleasures . . . are the last refuge of the complex.
                                                        WILDE

Where one's work is concerned, one should be an epicure.
                                                        DELACROIX

You never find people laboring to convince you that you may live very happily upon a plentiful fortune.
                                                        DR. JOHNSON

Money is the most important thing in the world. It represents health, strength, honor, generosity, and beauty as conspicuously as the want of it represents illness, weakness, disgrace, meanness, and ugliness. Not the least of its virtues is that it destroys base people as certainly as it fortifies and dignifies noble people.   SHAW

The value of money is that with it we can tell any man to go to the devil. It is the sixth sense which enables you to enjoy the other five.   MAUGHAM

The gods are those who either have money or do not want it.
SAMUEL BUTLER (II)

Money is human happiness in the abstract: he, then, who is
no longer capable of enjoying human happiness in the con-
crete devotes himself utterly to money.   SCHOPENHAUER

They may talk as they please about what they call pelf,
And how one ought never to think of oneself,
How pleasures of thought surpass eating and drinking,—
My pleasure of thought is the pleasure of thinking
  How pleasant it is to have money, heigh-ho!
  How pleasant it is to have money.

CLOUGH

When I lack money, I'm bashful wherever I go. I must absolutely get over this. The best way would be to carry a
hundred gold louis in my pocket every day for a year. The
constant weight of the gold would destroy the root of the evil.
STENDHAL

Rich people would not enjoy their little meannesses if they
knew how much their friends enjoy them.   L. P. SMITH

After buying into the Consols . . . I read Seneca "On the
Contempt of Wealth." What intolerable nonsense!
SYDNEY SMITH

There are few sorrows, however poignant, in which a good
income is of no avail.   L. P. SMITH

Poverty does not produce unhappiness: it produces degradation.   SHAW

There are several ways in which to apportion the family income, all of them unsatisfactory.   BENCHLEY

Small rooms discipline the mind; large ones distract it.
                                         LEONARDO DA VINCI

He who wants to eat cannot sleep.   BRILLAT-SAVARIN

Is sleep a mating with oneself?   NOVALIS

Sleep faster, we need the pillows.   YIDDISH PROVERB

The happiest part of a man's life is what he passes lying awake in bed in the morning.   DR. JOHNSON

Cleanliness does not presage civilization. It results from it.
                                         DUMAS

> I test my bath before I sit,
> And I'm always moved to wonderment
> That what chills the finger not a bit
> Is so frigid upon the fundament.
>
>   NASH

I look upon it, that he who does not mind his belly will hardly mind anything else.   DR. JOHNSON

Grub first, then ethics.   BRECHT

Any of us would kill a cow rather than not have beef.
                                         DR. JOHNSON

Gastronomy rules all life: the newborn baby's tears demand the nurse's breast, and the dying man receives, with some pleasure, the last cooling drink. BRILLAT-SAVARIN

What is patriotism but the love of the good things we ate in our childhood? LIN YUTANG

The discovery of a new dish does more for human happiness than the discovery of a new star. BRILLAT-SAVARIN

You first parents of the human race . . . who ruined yourself for an apple, what might you not have done for a truffled turkey? BRILLAT-SAVARIN

Soup and fish explain half the emotions of life.
SYDNEY SMITH

Few among those who go to restaurants realize that the man who first opened one must have been a man of genius and a profound observer. BRILLAT-SAVARIN

Plain cooking cannot be entrusted to plain cooks.
COUNTESS MORPHY

There is more simplicity in the man who eats caviar on impulse than in the man who eats grapenuts on principle.
CHESTERTON

This was a good dinner enough, to be sure, but it was not a dinner to ask a man to. DR. JOHNSON

To make good soup, the pot must only simmer or "smile."
FRENCH PROVERB

There is no such thing as a pretty good omelet.

FRENCH PROVERB

Fish, to taste right, must swim three times—in water, in butter, and in wine.   POLISH PROVERB

The truffle is not an outright aphrodisiac, but it may in certain circumstances make women more affectionate and men more amiable.   BRILLAT-SAVARIN

The salad—for which, like everybody else I ever met, he had a special receipt of his own.   DU MAURIER

Some [foods] should be eaten before fully ripe, such as capers, asparagus, sucking-pigs, and pigeons . . . ; others, at the moment of perfection, such as melons, most fruit, mutton, and beef . . . ; others, when they start to decompose, such as medlars, woodcocks, and especially pheasants; others, finally, after the methods of art have removed their deleterious qualities, such as the potato and the cassava root.

BRILLAT-SAVARIN

Frying gives cooks numerous ways of concealing what appeared the day before, and in a pinch facilitates sudden demands, for it takes little more time to fry a four-pound carp than to boil an egg.   BRILLAT-SAVARIN

Salt is the policeman of taste: it keeps the various flavors of a dish in order and restrains the stronger from tyrannizing over the weaker.   CHAZAL

Let the salad-maker be a spendthrift for oil, a miser for vinegar, a statesman for salt, and a madman for mixing.

SPANISH PROVERB

Of wine the middle, of oil the top, and of honey the bottom is best.   ENGLISH PROVERB

Vodka is the aunt of wine.   RUSSIAN PROVERB

Coffee from the top of the cup, chocolate from the bottom.
                                                       VENETIAN PROVERB

For unknown foods, the nose acts always as a sentinel and cries, "Who goes there?"   BRILLAT-SAVARIN

If we eat while holding our nose, we . . . taste in an obscure, imperfect manner. By this means the most disgusting medicines are swallowed almost without being tasted.
                                                       BRILLAT-SAVARIN

How much depends upon the way things are presented in this world can be seen from the very fact that coffee drunk out of wineglasses is really miserable stuff, as is meat cut at the table with a pair of scissors. Worst of all, as I once actually saw, is butter spread on a piece of bread with an old though very clean razor.   LICHTENBERG

Eating alone fosters egotism, encourages one to care only for oneself, isolates one from one's surroundings, dissuades one from paying little polite attentions. . . . It is easy, in society, to observe those guests who ordinarily eat in restaurants.   BRILLAT-SAVARIN

A man is in general better pleased when he has a good dinner upon his table than when his wife talks Greek.
                                                        DR. JOHNSON

[371]

Dinnertime is the most wonderful period of the day and perhaps its goal—the blossoming of the day. Breakfast is the bud. The dinner itself is, like life, a curve: it starts off with the lightest courses, then rises to the heavier, and concludes with light courses again.   NOVALIS

And now with some pleasure I find that it's seven; and must cook dinner. Haddock and sausage meat. I think it is true that one gains a certain hold on sausage and haddock by writing them down.   VIRGINIA WOOLF

Let me smile with the wise, and feed with the rich.
                                        DR. JOHNSON

Crowd not your table: let your number be
Not more than seven, and never less than three.
                                        KING

Let the number of guests not exceed twelve . . . so chosen that their occupations are varied, their tastes similar . . . ; the dining room brilliantly lighted, the cloth pure white, the temperature between 60° and 68°; the men witty and not pedantic, the women amiable and not too coquettish; the dishes exquisite but few, the wines vintage . . . ; the eating unhurried, dinner being the final business of the day . . . ; the coffee hot . . . ; the drawing room large enough to give those who must have it a game of cards while leaving plenty of room for after-dinner talk . . . ; the tea not too strong, the toast artistically buttered . . . ; the signal to leave not before eleven, and everyone in bed at midnight.
                                        BRILLAT-SAVARIN

Gastronomical perfection can be reached in these combinations: one person dining alone, usually upon a couch or a hillside; two persons, of no matter what sex or age, dining in a good restaurant; six people, of no matter what sex or age, dining in a good home. The six should be capable of decent social behavior: that is, no two of them should be so much in love as to bore the others, nor, at the opposite extreme, should they be carrying on any sexual or professional feud which could put poison in the plates all must eat from. A good combination would be one married couple, for warm composure; one less firmly established, to add a note of investigation to the talk; and two strangers of either sex, upon whom the better-acquainted could sharpen their questioning wits. Hunger and fair-to-good health are basic requirements, for no man stayed by a heavy midafternoon snack or gnawed by a gastric ulcer can add much to the general well-being.

M. F. K. FISHER

A host is like a general: it takes a mishap to reveal his genius.

HORACE

There is only one proper way to wear a beautiful dress: to forget you are wearing it.   MME. DE GIRARDIN

Hearts that are delicate and kind and tongues that are neither —these make the finest company in the world.   L. P. SMITH

The men and women who make the best boon companions seem to have given up hope of doing something else. They have, perhaps, tried to be poets and painters; they have tried to be actors, scientists, and musicians. But some defect of talent or opportunity has cut them off from their pet ambition and has thus left them with leisure to take an interest in the lives of others. Your ambitious man is selfish. No matter how secret his ambition may be, it makes him keep his thoughts at home. But the heartbroken people—if I may use the word in a mild benevolent sense—the people whose wills are subdued to fate, give us consolation, recognition, and welcome.   CHAPMAN

[373]

It is difficult to speak out a sentiment that your table companions disapprove of. CHAPMAN

One of a hostess's duties is to serve as a procuress. PROUST

A prohibitionist is the sort of man one wouldn't care to drink with—even if he drank. MENCKEN

The dipsomaniac and the abstainer are not only both mistaken, but they both make the same mistake. They both regard wine as a drug and not as a drink. CHESTERTON

There are no opium cults. Opium is profane and quantitative like money. BURROUGHS

Junk is the ultimate merchandise. The junk merchant does not sell his product to the consumer, he sells the consumer to the product. He does not improve and simplify his merchandise, he degrades and simplifies the client. BURROUGHS

The roulette table pays nobody except him that keeps it. Nevertheless, a passion for gambling is common, though a passion for keeping roulette tables is unknown. SHAW

Gambling promises the poor what property performs for the rich: that is why the bishops dare not denounce it fundamentally. SHAW

If the Prince of Monaco has a roulette table, surely convicts may play cards. CHEKHOV

Everything seems flat and tasteless when you come from a place where the seasoning is high—that's one of the causes of the boredom experienced in the provinces by a man of the world.   STENDHAL

Silence is the only phenomenon today that is "useless": it cannot be exploited.   PICARD

The most sensible and intelligent nation in Europe lays down, as the Eleventh Commandment, the rule *Never interrupt*. Noise is the most impertinent of all forms of interruption.   SCHOPENHAUER

Noise: a stench in the ear. The chief product and authenticating sign of civilization.   BIERCE

Noise is manufactured in the city, just as goods are manufactured. The city is the place where noise is kept in stock, completely detached from the object from which it came.
                                                              PICARD

Radio sets are like continuously-firing automatic pistols shooting at silence.   PICARD

I hate war: it ruins conversation.   FONTENELLE

Visits always give pleasure—if not the arrival, the departure.
                                                   PORTUGUESE PROVERB

Every parting gives a foretaste of death; every remeeting a foretaste of the resurrection. That is why even people who are indifferent to each other rejoice so much if they meet again after twenty or thirty years of separation.
                                                              SCHOPENHAUER

We read often with as much talent as we write.   EMERSON

When I stop drinking tea and eating bread and butter I say, "I've had enough." But when I stop reading poems or novels I say, "No more of that, no more of that."   CHEKHOV

Nine-tenths of the letters in which people speak unreservedly of their inmost feelings are written after ten at night.

HARDY

There is a theater public that is never so much amused as when it cries.   SILVESTRE

The great pleasure of a dog is that you may make a fool of yourself with him and not only will he not scold you, but he will make a fool of himself too.   SAMUEL BUTLER (II)

When I play with my cat, who knows but that she regards me more as a plaything than I do her?   MONTAIGNE

When ages grow to civility and elegancy men come to build stately sooner than to garden finely; as if gardening were the greater perfection.   BACON

The most significant element in the Western garden art is the *point-de-vue* of the great rococo park, upon which all its avenues and clipped hedge walks open and from which vision may travel out to lose itself in the distances. A feeling for the faraway is at the same time one for history. At a distance, space becomes time and the horizon signifies the future. The baroque park is the park of the Late season, of the approaching end, of the falling leaf. A Renaissance park brings us a vision of a midsummer noon. It is timeless, and nothing in its form-language reminds us of mortality.   SPENGLER

In things to be seen at once, much variety makes confusion, another vice of beauty. In things that are not seen at once, and have no respect one to another, great variety is commendable, provided this variety transgress not the rules of optics and geometry. WREN

I believe it is no wrong observation that persons of genius, and those who are most capable of art, are always most fond of nature. On the contrary, people of the common level of understanding are principally delighted with the little niceties and fantastical operations of art, and constantly think that finest which is least natural. A citizen is no sooner proprietor of a couple of yews, but he entertains thoughts of erecting them into giants, like those of Guildhall. POPE

It must be at least confessed, that to embellish the form of nature is an innocent amusement; and some praise will be allowed, by the most supercilious observer, to him who does best what such multitudes are contending to do well.

DR. JOHNSON

In natural objects we feel ourselves, or think of ourselves, only by *likenesses*—among men too often by *differences*. Hence the soothing love-kindling effect of rural nature and the bad passions of human societies. COLERIDGE

I would give up part of my lifetime for the sake of knowing what is the average barometer reading in Paradise.

LICHTENBERG

There are people who go look at gardens and fountains while empires are being overthrown. CHATEAUBRIAND

Scenery seems to wear in one's consciousness better than any other element in life. WILLIAM JAMES

No man, I suspect, ever lived long in the country without being bitten by . . . meteorological ambitions. He likes to be hotter and colder, to have been more deeply snowed up, to have more trees and larger blown down than his neighbors.

LOWELL

Worth seeing? Yes; but not worth going to see.

DR. JOHNSON

Travel makes a wise man better but a fool worse.

THOMAS FULLER

Being in a ship is being in a jail, with the chance of being drowned.   DR. JOHNSON

Nothing makes a man or woman look so saintly as seasickness.

SAMUEL BUTLER (II)

The whole object of travel is not to set foot on foreign land; it is at last to set foot on one's own country as foreign land.

CHESTERTON

To know a foreign country at all well you must not only have lived in it and in your own, but also lived in at least one other one.   MAUGHAM

What is it sacrilege to destroy? The *metaxu*. No human being should be deprived of his *metaxu*, that is to say, of those relative and mixed blessings (home, country, traditions, culture, etc.) which warm and nourish the soul and without which, short of sainthood, a *human* life is impossible.

SIMONE WEIL

My life's amusements have been just the same
Before and after standing armies came.

POPE

It is an odd thing about patriotism, the true love of one's country. A man can love his native land and never know that he loves it, though he live to be eighty—but then he must have stayed at home.   HEINE

If you want to discover your true opinion of anybody, observe the impression made on you by the first sight of a letter from him.   SCHOPENHAUER

Human nature is so well disposed toward those in interesting situations, that a young person who either marries or dies, is sure to be kindly spoken of.   JANE AUSTEN

I would live all my life in nonchalance and insouciance
Were it not for making a living, which is rather a nouciance.
                                                                      NASH

A good cigar is as great a comfort to a man as a good cry is to a woman.   BULWER-LYTTON

Every man has a lurking wish to appear considerable in his native place.   DR. JOHNSON

Honest bread is very well—it's the butter that makes the temptation.   JERROLD

AGES OF MAN

Ages of Man

Except during the nine months before he draws his first breath, no man manages his affairs as well as a tree does.

SHAW

An infant of two or three months will smile at even half a painted dummy face, if that half of the face is fully represented and has at least two clearly defined points or circles for eyes; more the infant does not need, but he will not smile for less. The infant's instinctive smile seems to have exactly that purpose which is its crowning effect, namely, that the adult feels recognized, and in return expresses recognition in the form of loving and providing.

ERIKSON

Gradually I came to know where I was, and I tried to express my wants to those who could gratify them, yet could not, because my wants were inside me, and they were outside, nor had they any power of getting into my soul. And so I made movements and sounds, signs like my wants, the few I could, the best I could; for they were not really like my meaning. And when I was not obeyed, because people did not understand me, or because they would not do me harm, I was angry, because elders did not submit to me, because freemen would not slave for me, and I avenged myself on them by tears.

SAINT AUGUSTINE

Babies do not want to hear about babies; they like to be told of giants and castles.

DR. JOHNSON

The gestures of an adult are those of a carpenter, the gestures of an infant those of a mason. CHAZAL

The serious side of life is the toy of the adult. Only it is not to be compared with the sensible things that fill a nursery. KRAUS

The earlier in life the first fright occurs, the more dangerous it is. RICHTER

If a child tells a lie, tell him that he has told a lie, but don't call him a liar. If you define him as a liar, you break down his confidence in his own character. RICHTER

The child sees everything which has to be experienced and learned as a doorway. So does the adult. But what to the child is an entrance is to the adult only a passage. NIETZSCHE

No one ever keeps a secret so well as a child. HUGO

In every man there lies hidden a child between five and eight years old, the age at which naïveté comes to an end. It is this child whom one must detect in that intimidating man with his long beard, bristling eyebrows, heavy mustache, and weighty look—a captain. Even he conceals, and not at all deep down, the youngster, the booby, the little rascal, out of whom age has made this powerful monster. VALÉRY

In the child, happiness dances; in the man, at most it smiles or weeps. When a man dances, he can only express the beauty of the art, not himself or his feelings. RICHTER

Children find it difficult to distinguish between human arti-
facts and natural objects.   GOETHE

If you strike a child, take care that you strike it in anger,
even at the risk of maiming it for life. A blow in cold blood
neither can nor should be forgiven.   SHAW

The child does not know that men are not only bad from
good motives, but also often good from bad motives. Therefore the child has a hearty, healthy, unspoiled, and insatiable
appetite for mere morality, for the mere difference between
a good little girl and a bad little girl.   CHESTERTON

> Children aren't happy with nothing to ignore,
> And that's what parents were created for.
>
>   NASH

It is not that the child lives in a world of imagination, but
that the child within us survives and starts into life only
at rare moments of recollection, which makes us believe, and
it is not true, that, as children, we were imaginative.

                                                PAVESE

It is to be noted that children's plays are not sports, and
should be regarded as their most serious actions.

                                                MONTAIGNE

Unlike grownups, children have little need to deceive themselves.   GOETHE

The language of the child is silence transformed into sound:
the language of the adult is sound that seeks for silence.

                                                PICARD

Childhood is not only the childhood we really had but also
the impressions we formed of it in our adolescence and ma-
turity. That is why childhood seems so long. Probably every
period of life is multiplied by our reflections upon it in the
next. The shortest is old age because we shall never to be
able to think back on it.   PAVESE

Credulity is the man's weakness but the child's strength.
                                                              LAMB

Women make us poets, children make us philosophers.
                                                             CHAZAL

> From infancy through childhood's giddy maze,
> Froward at school and fretful in his plays,
> The puny tyrant burns to subjugate
> The free republic of the whip-gig state.
> If one, his equal in athletic frame,
> Or, more provoking still, of nobler name,
> Dare step across his arbitrary views,
> An Iliad, only not in verse, ensues:
> The little Greeks look trembling at the scales,
> Till the best tongue, or heaviest hand prevails.
>
>   COWPER

Of all the intellectual faculties, judgment is the last to mature.
   A child under the age of fifteen should confine its attention
either to subjects like mathematics, in which errors of judgment are impossible, or to subjects in which they are not very
dangerous, like languages, natural science, history, etc.

                                                      SCHOPENHAUER

A girl of fifteen generally has a greater number of secrets
than an old man, and a woman of thirty more arcana than
a chief of state.   ORTEGA Y GASSET

The bookish flavor of the language of adolescence is natural to this age which knows theory and is ignorant of practice.

HERZEN

Hope is the last gift given to man, and the only gift not given to youth. Youth is pre-eminently the period in which a man can be lyric, fanatical, poetic; but youth is the period in which a man can be hopeless. The end of every episode is the end of the world. But the power of hoping through everything, the knowledge that the soul survives its adventures, that great inspiration comes to the middle-aged.   CHESTERTON

What is more enchanting than the voices of young people when you can't hear what they say?   L. P. SMITH

The young man is deliberately odd and prides himself on it; the old man is unintentionally so, and it mortifies him.

RICHTER

The spirit of a young man ripens from strength to beauty as his body ripens from beauty to strength.   RICHTER

Don't let young people confide in you their aspirations; when they drop them, they will drop you.   L. P. SMITH

Youth, which is forgiven everything, forgives itself nothing: age, which forgives itself everything, is forgiven nothing.

SHAW

The younger we are, the more each individual object represents for us the whole class to which it belongs.

SCHOPENHAUER

Sensuality is the vice of young men and of old nations.

LECKY

Young people are always more given to admiring what is gigantic than what is reasonable. DELACROIX

The young man plays at busying himself with problems of the collective type, and at times with such passion and such heroism that anyone ignorant of the secrets of human life would be led to believe that his preoccupation was genuine. But, in truth, all this is a pretext for concerning himself with himself, and so that he may be occupied with self.

ORTEGA Y GASSET

In his youth, everybody believes that the world began to exist only when he was born, and that everything really exists only for his sake. GOETHE

All that is good in man lies in youthful feeling and mature thought. JOUBERT

Young men are fitter to invent than to judge, fitter for execution than for counsel, and fitter for new projects than for settled business. BACON

During the first period of a man's life the greatest danger is: not to take the risk. When once the risk has really been taken, then the greatest danger is to risk too much. By not risking at first one turns aside and serves trivialities; in the second case, by risking too much, one turns aside to the fantastic, and perhaps to presumption. KIERKEGAARD

Youth ends when we perceive that no one wants our gay abandon. And the end may come in two ways: the realization that other people dislike it, or that we ourselves cannot continue with it. Weak men grow older in the first way, strong men in the second. PAVESE

Every man over thirty identifies his youth with the worst fault he thinks he has discovered in himself.   PAVESE

From thirty to forty-five runs the stage in which a man normally finds all his ideas, the first principles, at least, of that ideology which he is to make his own. After forty-five he devotes himself to the full development of the inspirations he has had between thirty and forty-five.   ORTEGA Y GASSET

Whoever is not a misanthrope at forty can never have loved mankind.   CHAMFORT

The first forty years of life give us the text: the next thirty supply the commentary.   SCHOPENHAUER

I know not whether increasing years do not cause us to esteem fewer people and to bear with more.   SHENSTONE

When young we are faithful to individuals; when older we grow more loyal to situations and to types. When we meet such specimens, we seem to know all about them in an instant (which is true), and thus in spite of our decreasing charms we sweep them off their feet, for young people do not understand themselves and, fortunately for us, can still be hypnotized by those who do   CONNOLLY

There is more felicity on the far side of baldness than young men can possibly imagine.   L. P. SMITH

After a certain age, the more one becomes oneself, the more obvious one's family traits become.   PROUST

No wise man ever wished to be younger.　　　SWIFT

Every generation is a secret society and has incommunicable enthusiasms, tastes, and interests which are a mystery both to its predecessors and to posterity.　　　CHAPMAN

When a man takes to his bed, nearly all his friends have a secret desire to see him die; some to prove that his health is inferior to their own, others in the disinterested hope of being able to study a death agony.　　　BAUDELAIRE

There are people whose watch stops at a certain hour and who remain permanently at that age.　　　SAINTE-BEUVE

Perhaps no one can be really a good appreciating pagan who has not once been a bad puritan.　　　BOURNE

The course of a river is almost always disapproved of by its source.　　　COCTEAU

Youth is a blunder; manhood a struggle; old age a regret.
　　　DISRAELI

The man who is too old to learn was probably always too old to learn.　　　HASKINS

Senescence begins
And middle age ends
The day your descendants
Outnumber your friends.

　　　NASH

A man of fifty is responsible for his face.   STANTON

Our life resembles the Sibylline Books: the less there is left
of it, the more precious it becomes.   GOETHE

Old age lives minutes slowly, hours quickly; childhood chews
hours and swallows minutes.   CHAZAL

The character we exhibit in the latter half of our life need not
necessarily be, though it often is, our original character, developed further, dried up, exaggerated, or diminished: it can
be its exact opposite, like a suit worn inside out.   PROUST

There is no cure for birth and death save to enjoy the interval.
          SANTAYANA

A person is always startled when he hears himself seriously
called an old man for the first time.   O. W. HOLMES, SR.

> The Child's Toys & the Old Man's Reasons
> Are the Fruits of the Two seasons.
>
>   BLAKE

There is a wicked inclination in most people to suppose an
old man decayed in his intellects. If a young or middle-aged
man, when leaving a company, does not recollect where he
laid his hat, it is nothing; but if the same inattention is discovered in an old man, people will shrug up their shoulders
and say, "His memory is going."   DR. JOHNSON

An old man concludeth from his knowing mankind that
they know him too, and that maketh him very wary.
          HALIFAX

An old man forfeits one of the greatest of human rights: no longer is he judged by his peers.　　　GOETHE

Old men have in some degree their reprisals upon younger, by making nicer observations upon them, by virtue of their experience.　　　HALIFAX

> No memory of having starred
> Atones for later disregard,
> Nor keeps the end from being hard.
>
> Better to go down dignified
> With boughten friendship at your side
> Than none at all. Provide, provide!
>
> 　　　FROST

To deprive elderly people of their bogeys is as brutal as snatching from babies their big stuffed bears.　　　L. P. SMITH

When men grow virtuous in their old age, they only make a sacrifice to God of the devil's leavings.　　　POPE

Old men and comets have been reverenced for the same reason: their long beards and pretenses to foretell events.

　　　SWIFT

Animals are born and bred in litters. Solitude grows blessed and peaceful only in old age.　　　SANTAYANA

Old men love to give advice to console themselves for not being able to set a bad example.　　　LA ROCHEFOUCAULD

An evil name—a drawback at first—sheds luster on old age.

L. P. SMITH

After the age of eighty, all contemporaries are friends.

MME. DE DINO

Since Penelope Noakes of Duppas Hill is gone, there is no one who will ever call me Nellie again.   AN OLD LADY

Nothing is more beautiful than cheerfulness in an old face.

RICHTER

Next to the very young, I suppose the very old are the most selfish.   THACKERAY

Few envy the consideration enjoyed by the eldest inhabitant.

EMERSON

To honor with hymns and panegyrics those who are still alive is not safe; a man should run his course and make a fair ending, and then we will praise him; and let praise be given equally to women as well as men who have been distinguished in virtue.   PLATO

One of the two things that men who have lasted for a hundred years always say: either that they have drunk whisky and smoked all their lives, or that neither tobacco nor spirits ever made the faintest appeal to them.   LUCAS

I've never known a person to live to 110 or more, and then die, to be remarkable for anything else.   BILLINGS

Everyone is born a king, and most people die in exile.

WILDE

Men execute nothing so faithfully as the wills of the dead, to the last codicil and letter. *They* rule this world, and the living are but their executors.   THOREAU

Death is that after which nothing is of interest.   ROZINOV

We shall lose the advantage of a man's dying if we are to have a statue of him forthwith. It is very offensive to my imagination to see the dying stiffen into statues at this rate. We should wait till their bones begin to crumble—and then avoid too near a likeness to the living.   THOREAU

It is death, and not what comes after death, that men are generally afraid of.   SAMUEL BUTLER (II)

All men are born truthful, and die liars.   VAUVENARGUES

Often I have wished myself dead, but well under my blanket, so that neither death nor man could hear me.   LICHTENBERG

Death destroys a man, but the idea of death saves him.

FORSTER

What really belongs to a man except what he has already lived? What has a man to live for except what he is not yet living?   PAVESE

Who must die must die in the dark, even though he sells candles.   COLOMBIAN PROVERB

Make sure to send a lazy man for the Angel of Death.
                                        YIDDISH PROVERB

All I desire for my own burial is not to be buried alive.
                                        CHESTERFIELD

Nowhere probably is there more true feeling, and nowhere worse taste, than in a churchyard.   JOWETT

Index of Authors

About, Edmond, 192
Acton, Lord (John Dalberg-Acton), 74, 82, 238, 239, 304, 331
Adams, Henry, 60, 61, 304
Adams, John, 316
Adams, John Quincy, 303
Addison, Joseph, 169
Ade, George, 191
Æ (George William Russell), 209
Alcott, Bronson, 110, 221
Amiel, Henri Frédéric, 70
Andrewes, Lancelot, 90
Anonymous, 14 (Irish), 17 (Anglo-Saxon), 33, 35, 50, 51, 54, 68, 77, 87, 99, 126 (Irish), 130, 135, 145, 155, 162, 170, 200, 217, 270, 293, 299 (Russian), 304, 308, 310, 344, 393 (An Old Lady)
Aquinas, Saint Thomas, 48
Archilocus, 156
Arendt, Hannah, 16–17, 17, 106, 137, 143, 182, 230, 248, 252, 255, 285, 299, 316, 325, 346
Aristotle, 49, 149, 209, 299, 303, 310, 316
Arnold, Thomas, 230
Arnold, W. E., Jr., 232
Aron, Raymond, 354
Augustine, Saint, 5, 9, 10, 41, 82, 88, 97, 114, 200, 303, 326, 355, 383
Ausonius, 169
Austen, Jane, 17, 365, 379
Author of Nero, 187

Bacon, Sir Francis, 8, 46, 53, 55, 56, 59, 67, 92, 105, 111, 136, 148, 151, 155, 157, 158, 159, 161, 183, 184, 194, 199, 208, 209, 213, 230, 246, 297, 300, 306, 317, 331, 348, 376, 388
Bagehot, Walter, 9, 43, 49, 82, 110, 125, 154, 163, 167, 232,

252, 255, 288, 302, 310, 315
Balfour, Earl of (Arthur James Balfour), 254
Balzac Honoré de, 169, 170, 184, 187, 193, 249, 281
Barbey d'Aurevilly, Jules, 170, 174
Barrett, Lawrence, 290
Barth, Karl, 75
Baudelaire, Charles, 47, 53, 93, 144, 159, 161, 188, 218, 223, 240, 274, 282, 390
Beaumarchais, Pierre Augustin Caron de, 254
Bebel, August, 246
Beerbohm, Sir Max, 47, 111, 132, 170
Beethoven, Ludwig von, 289
Belloc, Hilaire, 302, 359
Benchley, Robert, 63, 368
Béranger, Pierre Jean de, 64
Berenson, Bernard, 284
Berkeley, George, 73
Berlioz, Hector, 270
Bernard, Claude, 111, 222, 259, 267
Bibesco, Elizabeth, 134
Bierce, Ambrose, 375
Billings, Josh, 84, 150, 162, 393
Birrell, Augustine, 220
Bismarck, Prince Otto von, 160, 255
Blake, William, 7, 20, 27, 28, 29, 33, 44, 53, 62, 69, 78, 81, 90, 92, 97, 100, 101, 102, 103, 104, 111, 114, 126, 149, 153, 156, 193, 210, 212, 254, 267, 270, 291, 292, 303, 321, 340, 348, 391
Bloy, Léon, 90
Bolingbroke, Viscount (Henry St. John), 235
Bonaparte, Napoleon, 145, 245, 246, 327
Booth, Edwin, 290
Bourne, Randolph, 123, 145, 390

Bradley, Francis Herbert, 35, 65, 97, 114, 193, 195, 200, 335
Braun, Wernher von, 222
Brecht, Bertolt, 368
Bright, John, 248
Brillat-Savarin, Anthelme, 302, 368, 369, 370, 371, 372
Broad, C. D., 34
Browne, Sir Thomas, 104, 156
Bryce, James, 216
Buber, Martin, 39, 50, 91, 106, 250
Bulwer-Lytton, *see* Lytton
Burbank, Luther, 103
Burckhardt, Jakob, 227, 228, 231, 232, 234, 250, 301, 303, 307, 334
Burke, Edmund, 27, 58, 159, 298, 318
Burke, Thomas, 310
Burroughs, William, 374
Burton, Robert, 109
Butler, Joseph, 146
Butler, Samuel (I), 151, 157, 250, 276
Butler, Samuel (II), 9, 10, 31, 32, 33, 42, 48, 57, 61, 65, 102, 104, 106, 120, 124, 133, 144, 153, 154, 156, 160, 191, 201, 207, 250, 259, 267, 286, 287, 291, 299, 322, 328, 333, 335, 336, 338, 339, 347, 352, 353, 354, 355, 359, 367, 376, 378, 394
Butterfield, Henry, 144, 245, 304
Byron, Lord (George Gordon), 68

Carlyle, Thomas, 18, 34
Carson, Anthony, 276
Casanova, Giovanni Jacopo, 62
Cavour, Conte Camillo Benso di, 314
Cervantes, Miguel de, 196, 246, 290
Cézanne, Paul, 290
Chamfort, Sébastien Roch Nicolas, 8, 18, 26, 65, 119, 120, 121, 127, 140, 148, 156, 163, 185, 189, 190, 201, 203, 207, 216, 218, 220, 231, 279, 287, 301, 306, 312, 317, 389
Chapman, John Jay, 26, 34, 58, 65, 80, 82, 110, 111, 120, 140, 221, 227, 304, 321, 326, 329, 335, 344, 373, 374, 390
Chardonne, Jacques, 198

Chateaubriand, Vicomte François René de, 377
Chazal, Malcolm de, 5, 9, 12, 13, 14, 15, 24, 39, 82, 86, 100, 101, 103, 104, 138, 167, 171, 173, 190, 249, 267, 351, 370, 384, 386, 391
Chekhov, Anton, 3, 19, 20, 60, 80, 113, 124, 142, 146, 147, 155, 180, 190, 193, 197, 199, 216, 220, 238, 250, 260, 275, 284, 303, 333, 374, 376
Chesterfield, Earl of (Philip Dormer Stanhope), 26, 30, 40, 46, 121, 123, 124, 125, 126, 130, 139, 147, 149, 153, 155, 158, 171, 202, 217, 221, 253, 305, 306, 316, 318, 347, 395
Chesterton, Gilbert Keith, 3, 14, 40, 50, 56, 57, 60, 62, 63, 65, 68, 70, 74, 78, 120, 129, 133, 139, 148, 149, 163, 167, 169, 173, 186, 195, 207, 217, 221, 231, 235, 236, 243, 249, 252, 270, 285, 299, 307, 311, 323, 325, 326, 331, 333, 335, 340, 344, 351, 352, 369, 374, 378, 385, 387
Cioran, E. Michel, 153, 188, 230, 281, 299, 300, 336
Clark, Sir Kenneth, 4, 273, 291
Clemenceau, Georges, 246, 252
Clough, Arthur Hugh, 158, 161, 367
Cobbett, William, 163
Cocteau, Jean, 51, 247, 274, 283, 285, 289, 390
Colbert, Jean Baptiste, 306
Coleridge, Samuel Taylor, 19, 24, 34, 36, 45, 58, 69, 81, 104, 115, 176, 140, 174, 175, 194, 201, 254, 281, 282, 332, 334, 337, 346, 362, 377
Collins, John Churton, 32, 41, 59, 123, 187, 218
Colton, Charles Caleb, 48, 187
Conan Doyle, *see* Doyle
Connolly, Cyril, 6, 9, 19, 61, 139, 187, 188, 189, 194, 324, 335, 360, 389
Conrad, Joseph, 40, 203, 272, 310
Constable, John, 268, 273, 290, 291
Cooper, James Fenimore, 317
Cowley, Abraham, 155

Cowper, William, 35, 386
Creighton, Bishop Mandell, 129
Cullen, William, 213

Damon of Athens, 289
Dana, Richard Henry, 301
Dante, Alighieri, 83
Dantzig, Tobias, 262, 348–49
Darling, C. J., 211
Daudet, Alphonse, 129
De Casseres, Benjamin, 170
Defoe, Daniel, 208
Degas, Edgar, 271, 291
Delacroix, Eugène, 10, 99, 251,
    271, 273, 291, 293, 358, 366,
    388
Democritus of Abdera, 181
Dépret, Louis, 219
De Roberto, Frederico, 25
Deshoulières, Antoinette, 332
Dickens, Charles, 143, 211, 215
Diderot, Denis, 105
Dino, Mme. de, 393
Disraeli, Benjamin, 10, 60, 150,
    185, 248, 253, 254, 255, 280,
    301, 390
Dix, George, 227
Donne, John, 88, 99, 322
Dostoevski, Fëdor, 4, 5, 252, 361
Douglas, Norman, 122, 198, 223
Doyle, Sir Arthur Conan, 208,
    323
Dryden, John, 298
Du Bois, Henri, 189
Dumas, Alexandre, 171, 194,
    368
Du Maurier, George, 370

Eliot, George, 66, 113, 135, 137,
    162, 174, 187
Eliot, T. S., 231, 282
Ellis, Havelock, 100, 221, 251
Emerson, Ralph Waldo, 18, 22,
    24, 36, 37, 43, 52, 61, 65, 86,
    89, 100, 119, 122, 124, 128,
    129, 133, 140, 147, 154, 171,
    196, 199, 220, 227, 231, 237,
    251, 254, 271, 272, 273, 275,
    286, 306, 308, 311, 315, 323,
    325, 327, 332, 341, 376, 393
Epicurus, 52
Epimenides of Crete, 98
Erikson, Eric, 383

Faber, William, 90
Farquhar, George, 113

Feather, William, 132, 146, 169,
    195
Fénelon, François, 87
Fielding, Henry, 180
Firbank, Ronald, 88
Fisher, Charles, 362
Fisher, M. F. K., 372–73
Fitzgerald, F. Scott, 222
Flaubert, Gustave, 237
Fontenelle, Bernard de, 219,
    239, 343, 375
Forster, Edward Morgan, 129,
    238, 358, 394
France, Anatole, 112, 208, 239
Francis, Sir Philip, 286
Fraser, Sir James, 199
Freeman, Edward Augustus, 230
Freud, Sigmund, 56, 105, 168,
    182, 216, 217, 340
Frost, Robert, 54, 76, 134, 150,
    365, 392
Froude, James Anthony, 76
Fuller, Margaret, 57
Fuller, Dr. Thomas, 51, 123,
    125, 128, 132, 192, 203, 248,
    285
Fuller, Thomas, 19, 39, 44, 51,
    147, 150, 200, 211, 219, 221,
    222, 378

Galen, 212
Galsworthy, John, 13
Garnett, Richard, 179
Gaskell, Mrs. Elizabeth Cleg-
    horn, 329
Gibbon, Edward, 79, 301
Gide, André, 57, 269, 275, 286,
    356
Girardin, Mme. Delphine de,
    373
Gissing, George, 236, 341
Gladstone, William Ewart, 248,
    298
Goethe, Johann Wolfgang von,
    6, 21, 29, 34, 38, 44, 46, 48,
    50, 52, 52–53, 54, 55, 57, 58,
    74, 76, 98, 101, 102, 105, 106,
    115, 122, 124, 125, 137, 149,
    162, 169, 170, 173, 180, 182,
    191, 192, 203, 249, 252, 267,
    270, 271, 273, 278, 282, 284,
    289, 290, 292, 301, 313, 325,
    327, 339, 345, 346, 350, 352,
    362, 385, 388, 391, 392
Goldberg, Isaac, 254
Goldsmith, Oliver, 43
Goncharov, I. A., 159

Goncourt, the Brothers, 293
Gourmont, Remy de, 89, 100,
    111, 112, 113, 168, 171, 237,
    269, 276, 279, 309, 322, 350,
    359
Gracian, 53, 55, 112, 122, 133,
    140, 147, 171, 249, 323, 327
Grahame, Kenneth, 104
Grant, General Ulysses S., 299
Groddeck, Georg, 36
Gypsy curse, 210

Hales, Sir James, 137
Halifax, Marquis of (George
    Savile), 8, 16, 22, 30, 32, 33,
    35, 44, 45, 50, 53, 55, 60, 69,
    79, 80, 81, 123, 130, 131, 134,
    138, 139, 148, 151, 152, 154,
    155, 157, 190, 194, 198, 200,
    203, 208, 222, 229, 245, 250,
    251, 256, 288, 301, 305, 310,
    311, 315, 316, 317, 318, 334,
    341, 342, 352, 358, 360, 361,
    362, 391, 392
Halle, Louis J., 359
Hardy, Thomas, 240, 376
Harrington, James, 315, 316
Harvey, Gabriel, 130
Haskins, Henry S., 22, 33, 35,
    50, 142, 168, 213, 332, 390
Hazlitt, William, 4, 5, 31, 33,
    38, 42, 46, 47, 49, 54, 81, 113,
    121, 125, 126, 133, 147, 219,
    222, 274, 280, 286, 290, 311,
    322, 354
Hebbel, Friedrich, 11, 22, 28, 31,
    64, 141, 159, 228, 229, 269,
    281, 283, 325, 356
Hegel, Georg Wilhelm Friedrich,
    229, 315
Heine, Heinrich, 192, 234, 235,
    250, 379
Heisenberg, Werner, 260
Heller, Erich, 240, 260, 324, 338
Heraclitus, 13, 73, 98, 211, 212
Herbert, George, 87, 89, 219
Herodotus, 244
Herrick, Dr., and Tyson, 213
Herrick, Robert, 361, 362
Herzen, Aleksander I., 74, 109,
    109–110, 232, 233, 311, 387
Hippocrates, 213
Hitopadesa, The, 218
Hobbes, Thomas, 149, 150, 160,
    246, 312
Hodgson, Ralph, 15, 87, 227
Hoffer, Eric, 11, 22, 26, 28, 59,

    112, 154, 158, 159, 163, 191,
    211, 233, 236, 248, 300, 326,
    334
Hofmannsthal, Hugo von, 15, 21,
    144, 200, 201, 228, 274
Holmes, Oliver Wendell, Jr., 55,
    110, 139, 142, 208, 231, 234,
    245, 327, 328, 339, 342
Holmes, Oliver Wendell, Sr., 391
Hooton, Earnest, 8
Hope, Anthony (Anthony Hope
    Hawkins), 119
Hopkins, Gerard Manley, 101
Horace, 373
Howell, James, 130
Hubbard, Elbert G., 18, 56, 59,
    61, 67, 83, 109, 110, 113, 146,
    193, 245
Hubbard, Frank McKinney
    (Kin), 18, 48, 151, 280, 305
Hugo, Victor, 45, 384
Hume, David, 73
Huntington, Collis P., 222
Hurnand, James, 282, 305
Huxley, Aldous, 54, 208, 274,
    332
Huxley, Thomas Henry, 11, 16,
    139, 219, 222, 260, 322, 330,
    331, 340, 350, 358

Ibsen, Henrik, 251
Ignatius, Saint, 89
Inge, Dean William Ralph, 84,
    312
Ingersoll, Robert, 99
Ion of Chios, 269
Irving, Washington, 119

Jacobs, Jane, 136–37
James, Henry, 16, 122, 239, 311
James, William, 4, 12, 128, 200,
    324, 325, 343, 351, 377
Janin, Jules, 168
Jefferson, Thomas, 31, 82, 304,
    325
Jenkins, Elizabeth, 172
Jerrold, Douglas, 379
Johnson, Gerald W., 247
Johnson, Dr. Samuel, 17, 19, 20,
    23, 34, 35, 38, 39, 43, 46, 48,
    50, 59, 67, 90, 113, 115, 123,
    127, 128, 131, 132, 133, 135,
    138, 141, 146, 154, 172, 174,
    182, 192, 193, 195, 196, 202,
    203, 213, 217, 219, 220, 229,
    239, 243, 248, 251, 275, 278,
    279, 280, 287, 288, 299, 304,

314, 316, 317, 318, 327, 328, 337, 341, 355, 358, 365, 366, 368, 369, 371, 372, 377, 378, 379, 383, 391
Jonson, Ben, 85, 160, 172, 221, 280, 318
Joubert, Joseph, 8, 20, 30, 52, 54, 76, 109, 112, 145, 153, 160, 269, 274, 275, 280, 285, 347, 352, 357, 388
Jowett, Benjamin, 395
Juan Manuel, Don, 41
Junius, 304
Juvenal, 146, 302

Kafka, Franz, 74, 75, 83, 84, 85, 88, 89, 90, 92
Kant, Immanuel, 3, 129, 139, 300, 304, 339
Kassner, Rudolf, 13
Kaufmann, Walter, 342, 358
Keats, John, 172, 269
Kepler, Johannes, 98
Kerr, Alphonse, 187
Kierkegaard, Sören, 8, 11, 62, 63, 67, 77, 80, 83, 84, 85, 87, 91, 115, 115–16, 138, 141, 183, 191, 193, 223, 228, 239, 240, 249, 252, 253, 274, 305, 342, 352, 362, 388
King, William, 372
Kipling, Rudyard, 58, 365
Knox, Father Ronald A., 62, 222, 312
Kraus, Karl, 35, 63, 64, 105, 109, 135, 169, 171, 180, 215, 223, 236, 243, 246, 247, 263, 275, 278, 281, 323, 356, 357, 358, 384

La Bruyère, Jean de, 20, 45, 51, 52, 59, 61, 121, 123, 136, 138, 149, 154, 157, 159, 173, 175, 184, 185, 186, 187, 188, 189, 202, 276
Lacordaire, Jean, 90
La Fontaine, Jean de, 31
Lamb, Charles, 132, 207, 386
Landor, Walter Savage, 82, 300
Langer, Susanne, 281
La Rochefoucauld, François, Duc de, 8, 15, 20, 22, 23, 28, 34, 37, 38, 39, 40, 41, 42, 43, 51, 52, 61, 70, 119, 124, 132, 149, 150, 152, 153, 182, 183, 184, 185, 189, 202, 213, 252, 291, 322, 353, 355, 392

Lavater, Johann Kaspar, 131, 140, 152
Lawrence, David Herbert, 30
Le Bon, Gustave, 261
Lec, Stanislaus J., 32, 33, 45, 76, 86, 101, 103, 155, 229, 230, 272, 302, 306, 331, 334
Lecky, William Edward Hartpole, 387
Lee, Nathaniel, 279
Leonardo da Vinci, 56, 98, 99, 292, 326, 368
Leverson, Ada, 171, 172
Lewes, George Henry, 196
Lewis, C. S., 85
Lewis, George Cornewall, 366
Lichtenberg, Georg Christoph, 23, 25, 30, 39, 42, 79, 105, 106, 112, 119, 133, 135, 140, 146, 147, 152, 157, 174, 181, 208, 228, 260, 261, 277, 278, 286, 288, 292, 329, 332, 343, 345, 346, 347, 349, 351, 354, 356, 359, 360, 362, 371, 377, 394
Lin Yutang, 369
Locke, John, 333, 353, 358
Lorenz, Konrad Z., 6
Louis XIV, 273
Lowell, James Russell, 378
Lucan, 32
Lucas, Edward Verrall, 393
Lyly, John, 194
Lynd, Robert, 337
Lytton, Edward Bulwer-, 62, 112, 124, 152, 169, 379

Macaulay, Thomas Babington, 79, 111, 314
Macdonald, George, 27, 90, 365
Machiavelli, Niccolò, 145, 153
Madison, James, 309
Maine, Sir Henry, 244
Mairet, Paul, 143
Maistre, Joseph Marie de, 99, 109, 348, 356
Maitland, Frederic W., 227
Mallarmé, Stéphane, 25, 283
Marbeau, Emmanuel, 152
Marcus Aurelius, 44
Marquis, Don, 172
Martineau, Harriet, 52
Marvell, Andrew, 5, 7
Marx, Karl, 18, 139
Mascall, Eric L., 195
Maugham, Somerset, 60, 277, 366, 378

Maurice, Frederick Denison, 244
McLaughlin, Mignon, 203
Melancthon, 75
Melbourne, Viscount (William Lamb), 68; 69
Menander, 198
Mencken, Henry Louis, 32, 140, 172, 374
Meredith, George, 11, 49
Metternich, Prince Klemens von, 163, 309
Michelet, Jules, 114
Mill, John Stuart, 168, 340
Molière (Jean Baptiste Poquelin), 49, 190, 201
Mondeville, Henri de, 213
Montagu, Lady Mary Wortley, 12
Montague, Charles Edward, 246
Montaigne, Michel Eyquem de, 31, 33, 51, 59, 63, 66, 75, 87, 98, 112, 155, 239, 302, 316, 376, 385
Montesquieu, Baron de La Brède et de (Charles de Secondat), 19, 20, 81, 143, 156, 240, 249, 302
Monti, Vincenzo, 68
Moore, George, 135, 181, 279
Moore, Marianne, 3, 36, 191
Morley, John, 68, 82
Morphy, Countess, 369
Morton, J. D., 36
Mozart, Wolfgang Amadeus, 290
Muir, Edwin, 11, 42
Mumford, Lewis, 135
Musset, Alfred de, 37

Napoleon, *see* Bonaparte
Nash, Ogden, 35, 168, 189, 198, 216, 368, 379, 385, 390
Necker, Mme. Suzanne, 54
Needham, Joseph, 261
Neilson, William Allen, 279
Newman, Cardinal John Henry, 75, 82, 136, 213, 252, 260, 275, 340, 342, 345
Nietzsche, Friedrich Wilhelm, 5, 9, 10, 16, 19, 20, 21, 25, 28, 29, 30, 31, 33, 37, 38, 39, 41, 43, 45, 46, 49, 54, 55, 57, 58, 60, 62, 65, 66, 67, 79, 81, 93, 104, 110, 112, 114, 115, 131, 132, 133, 145, 148, 152, 156, 162, 168, 172, 175, 191,

196, 199, 201, 211, 235, 236, 238, 245, 248, 249, 252, 267, 270, 276, 277, 279, 280, 285, 287, 309, 310, 311, 321, 323, 324, 326, 327, 328, 329, 330, 332, 334, 338, 343, 360, 361, 384
Novalis (Baron Friedrich von Hardenberg), 8, 24, 102, 103, 190, 195, 196, 215, 234, 263, 289, 323, 368, 372

Ortega y Gasset, José, 3, 14, 64, 144, 169, 174, 181, 186, 208, 210, 229, 230, 231, 234, 237, 240, 270, 318, 332, 333, 336, 348, 386, 388, 389
Osler, Sir William, 4, 15, 105, 212, 214, 215, 216, 217, 350, 358, 360

Palmer, Samuel, 352
Pascal, Blaise, 12, 18, 23, 25, 26, 31, 38, 40, 58, 63, 75, 77, 81, 88, 89, 103, 130, 133, 135, 158, 161, 199, 201, 244, 253, 277, 279, 291, 298, 299, 324, 325, 330, 342, 347, 351, 354, 357
Pasteur, Louis, 347
Pater, Walter, 293
Patmore, Coventry, 27, 69, 81, 88, 93, 342, 353
Pavese, Cesare, 9, 11, 20, 26, 27, 35, 40, 44, 53, 54, 55, 58, 73, 83, 121, 156, 170, 173, 181, 271, 272, 278, 283, 288, 339, 385, 386, 388, 389, 394
Peacock, Thomas Love, 141, 272, 341
Péguy, Charles Pierre, 160, 162, 163, 197, 214, 301, 305, 321, 344
Peirce, Charles S., 322, 345
Penn, William, 314
Picard, Max, 12, 15, 85, 104, 237, 356, 375, 385
Pieper, Josef, 47, 48, 132, 141
Plato, 179–80, 214, 337, 343, 353, 393
Plekhanoff, Georgi V., 261
Poitiers, Diane de, 152, 170, 201
Pope, Alexander, 30, 39, 42, 43, 44, 113, 121, 127, 188, 202, 284, 287, 301, 366, 377, 378, 392
Proust, Marcel, 6, 13, 21, 27, 28,

29, 30, 61, 66, 121, 139, 149,
182, 183, 184, 185, 186, 187,
188, 189, 216, 326, 330, 347,
357, 360, 361, 374, 389, 391
Proverbs
American, 218
Bosnian, 69, 124
Bulgarian, 175, 255
Colombian, 395
Continental, 32
Dutch, 197
English, 51, 173, 174, 251,
332, 371
Flemish, 67, 219
French, 127, 148, 159, 184,
361, 369, 370
Genoese, 101, 173, 251
German, 202, 203
Icelandic, 37
Irish, 32, 138, 162, 212
Italian, 138
Maltese, 69
Negro, 31, 240
New England, 150
Polish, 128, 132, 137, 142,
218, 370
Portuguese, 61, 375
Russian, 371
Savoyard, 48
Scottish, 84
Slovenian, 126
Spanish, 126, 172, 198, 273,
370
Swedish, 87, 100
Swiss, 6, 125, 155, 192, 221,
273
Venetian, 217, 371
Yiddish, 47, 49, 68, 69, 76, 79,
83, 88, 111, 123, 147, 151,
157, 162, 193, 197, 198,
199, 214, 221, 368, 395
Prudhon, Pierre-Paul, 307
Publilius Syrus, 141

Rabelais, François, 150
Ray, John, 102
Rémusat, Charles de, 299
Richter, Jean Paul, 8, 18, 27, 40,
44, 48, 49, 63, 70, 86, 115,
131, 145, 163, 168, 172, 182,
197, 240, 366, 384, 387, 393
Rieff, Philip, 298
Riehl, Wilhelm Heinrich von,
144
Rilke, Rainer Maria, 4
Rivarol, Antoine de, 103

Rochester, Earl of (John Wil-
mot), 190
Rogers, Samuel, 192
Roscommon, Earl of (Went-
worth Dillon), 284
Rosenstock-Huessy, Eugen, 74,
75, 77–78, 99, 128, 134–35,
144, 181, 185, 233, 238, 243,
244, 260, 336, 345, 348, 356
Rousseau, Jean Jacques, 40
Rozinov, V. V., 34, 65, 81, 143,
147, 148, 185, 235, 247, 277,
349, 355, 394
Ruskin, John, 65, 142, 288, 308,
311
Russell, Bertrand, 20, 97, 137,
141, 259, 262, 263, 313, 334,
344

Sainte-Beuve, Charles Augustin,
390
Saint-Exupéry, Antoine de, 186
Saki (H. H. Munro), 148, 278
Santayana, George, 9, 16, 22, 26,
38, 48, 50, 52, 73, 76, 97, 99,
111, 122, 138, 139, 144, 145,
153, 191, 199, 218, 237, 239,
243, 247, 272, 273, 281, 286,
289, 293, 323, 328, 330, 332,
334, 336, 338, 339, 342, 347,
349, 352, 354, 355, 361, 391,
392
Schiller, Friedrich von, 4, 11, 18,
44, 188, 200, 210
Schlegel, Friedrich, 238
Schopenhauer, Arthur, 6, 10, 19,
23, 36, 48, 60, 64, 73, 104,
121, 130, 132, 134, 136, 159,
170, 201, 212, 236, 276, 281,
287, 293, 330, 367, 375, 379,
386, 387, 389
Selden, John, 120, 276
Seneca, 99, 133, 343
Shaftesbury, Earl of (Anthony
Ashley Cooper), 148, 354
Shakespeare, William, 10, 24,
31, 34, 74, 126, 167, 179, 180,
185, 194, 223, 267, 283, 345
Shaw, George Bernard, 29, 38,
41, 57, 64, 122, 124, 125, 126,
128, 139, 140, 152, 170, 192,
195, 196, 197, 209, 210, 212,
219, 223, 238, 246, 276, 289,
301, 308, 314, 317, 340, 341,
366, 367, 374, 383, 385, 387
Shelley, Percy Bysshe, 282

Shenstone, William, 44, 122, 146, 148, 155, 271, 285, 290, 389

Sickert, Walter, 131, 140, 141, 150, 156, 268, 269, 271, 272, 273, 276, 292, 307

Silesius, Angelus, 339

Silvestre, Paul Armand, 376

Simon, Jules, 307

Smith, A. B., 211

Smith, Logan Pearsall, 25, 35, 68, 125, 129, 161, 190, 202, 203, 223, 237, 250, 329, 367, 373, 387, 389, 392, 393

Smith, Sydney, 87, 129, 131, 151, 196, 308, 367, 369

Socrates, 348

Spencer, Herbert, 153, 305

Spengler, Oswald, 254, 261, 376

Spinoza, Baruch, 66, 86, 352

Staël, Mme. Germaine Necker de, 181, 233

Stanislaus, King of Poland, 66

Stanton, Edwin M., 391

Stendhal (Henri Beyle), 15, 62, 131, 138, 179, 183, 184, 188, 239, 244, 245, 283, 361, 367, 375

Stephen, James, 277

Stern, Daniel, 348

Sterne, Laurence, 239

Stevens, Alfred, 291

Stevenson, Robert Louis, 59, 124, 131, 203, 238, 253, 336

Stravinsky, Igor, 272

Surtees, Robert Smith, 42

Swift, Jonathan, 40, 53, 80, 113, 119, 152, 228, 278, 288, 390, 392

Tacitus, 317

Taine, Hippolyte Adolphe, 271

Talleyrand-Périgord, Charles Maurice de, 202, 281

Talmud, The, 196

Taylor, Jeremy, 190

Taylor, Sir Henry, 33, 67, 127, 130, 146, 196

Tchaikovsky, Pëtr Ilich, 290

Terence, 306

Thackeray, William Makepeace, 168, 393

Theresa, Saint, 91

Thiers, Louis Adolphe, 308

Thomas a Kempis, 26, 359

Thoreau, Henry David, 21, 24, 30, 36, 50, 51, 55, 66, 67, 104, 157, 200, 202, 211, 212, 216, 238, 252, 259, 262, 263, 277, 278, 282, 285, 286, 309, 324, 329, 335, 352, 353, 358, 359, 394

Tocqueville, Alexis de, 22, 29, 47, 53, 56, 76, 142, 161, 196, 209, 210, 211, 212, 218, 223, 228, 233, 247, 253, 255, 256, 297, 298, 300, 302, 306, 307, 308, 309, 312, 313, 314, 315, 316, 317, 324, 357

Tolstoi, Leo, 80, 234, 297

Topsell, Edward, 114

Trollope, Anthony, 60, 192

Turgenev, Ivan, 277

Twain, Mark (Samuel Clemens), 38, 61, 125, 140, 251

Tyson, see Herrick, Dr.

Valéry, Paul, 5, 7, 21, 22, 23, 56, 57, 64, 67, 70, 98, 110, 130, 147, 218, 227, 228, 249, 255, 271, 274, 276, 279, 283, 287, 288, 289, 328, 329, 340, 345, 346, 351, 354, 355, 357, 384

Van Gogh, Vincent, 86

Vapereau, Gustave, 36, 147

Vauvenargues, Marquis de (Luc de Clapiers), 11, 22, 27, 53, 57, 126, 144, 183, 243, 336, 394

Vico, Giovanni Battista, 228, 229, 298, 344

Voltaire (François Marie Arouet), 66, 99, 124, 160, 192, 267, 315, 323, 342, 343, 351

Walpole, Horace, 43

Walsh, Howel, 221

Walter, Bruno, 289

Webern, Anton von, 289

Webster, Daniel, 67

Weil, Simone, 17, 18, 45, 50, 83, 86, 88, 89, 90, 91, 92, 143, 150, 160, 183, 235, 287, 308, 378

Wellington, Duke of (Arthur Wellesley), 245

Wharton, Edith, 274

Whitehead, Alfred North, 30, 73, 77, 98, 99, 102, 104, 105, 128, 230, 237, 240, 244, 254, 261, 268, 278, 297, 322, 324, 326, 335, 343, 345, 346, 349, 354

Wilde, Oscar, 5, 21, 31, 35, 37, 47, 54, 56, 87, 122, 123, 127, 129, 131, 146, 150, 151, 175, 194, 197, 210, 281, 298, 366, 394

Williams, Charles, 7, 75, 76, 77, 78, 83, 84, 91, 127, 181, 183, 184, 229, 285, 331, 333, 341, 359

Wilson, Bishop Thomas, 79, 85, 183

Wittgenstein, Ludwig, 10, 83, 268, 333, 334, 357, 359

Woolf, Virginia, 175, 198, 286, 372

Wordsworth, William, 353

Wren, Sir Christopher, 377

Xenophanes of Colophon, 79

Yeats, William Butler, 284

Young, Edward, 60

LOVE, MARRIAGE, AND FRIENDSHIP

Love, Marriage, and Friendship

The lover thinks oftener of reaching his mistress than does the husband of guarding his wife; the prisoner thinks oftener of escaping than does the jailer of shutting the door.

STENDHAL

Love is immanent in nature, but not incarnate. GARNETT

Hail Sovereign Queen of secrets, that hast power
To call the fiercest Tyrant from his rage;
And weep unto a girl; that hast the might
Even with an eye-glance, to cloak Mars's Drum
And turn th'allarm to whispers, that canst make
A Cripple flourish with his Crutch, and cure him
Before Apollo; that may'st force the King
To be his subjects' vassal, and induce
Stale gravity to daunce.

SHAKESPEARE

EROS: As his parentage is, so also are his fortunes. In the first place he is always poor, and anything but tender and fair, as the many imagine him; and he is rough and squalid, and has no shoes, nor a house to dwell in; on the bare earth exposed he lies under the open heaven, in the streets, or at the doors of houses, taking his rest; and like his mother (*Poverty*) he is always in distress. Like his father (*Plenty*)

[179]

too, whom he also partly resembles, he is always plotting against the fair and good; he is bold, enterprising, strong, a mighty hunter, always weaving some intrigue or other, keen in the pursuit of wisdom, fertile in resources; a philosopher at all times, terrible as an enchanter, sorcerer, sophist. He is by nature neither mortal nor immortal, but alive and flourishing at one moment when he is in plenty, and dead at another moment, and again alive by reason of his father's nature.

PLATO

Cupid: his disgrace is to be called boy; but his glory is to subdue men.   SHAKESPEARE

For the butterfly, mating and propagation involve the sacrifice of life; for the human being, the sacrifice of beauty.

GOETHE

Love is either the shrinking remnant of something which was once enormous; or else it is part of something which will grow in the future into something enormous. But in the present it does not satisfy. It gives much less than one expects.

CHEKHOV

LOVE: A word properly applied to our delight in particular kinds of food; sometimes metaphorically spoken of the favorite objects of all our appetites.   FIELDING

Love is merely a madness; and, I tell you, deserves a dark house and a whip as madmen do: and the reason why they are not so punished and cured is that the lunacy is so ordinary that the whippers are in love too.   SHAKESPEARE

Love between the sexes is a sin in theology, a forbidden intercourse in jurisprudence, a mechanical insult in medicine, and a subject philosophy has no time for.   KRAUS